Social Reproduction and the City

Social Reproduction and the City

WELFARE REFORM, CHILD CARE, AND RESISTANCE IN NEOLIBERAL NEW YORK

SIMON BLACK

THE UNIVERSITY OF GEORGIA PRESS
Athens

© 2020 by the University of Georgia Press
Athens, Georgia 30602
www.ugapress.org
All rights reserved
Set in 10.25/13.5 Minion 3 by Kaelin Chappell Broaddus

Most University of Georgia Press titles are
available from popular e-book vendors.

Printed digitally

Library of Congress Cataloging-in-Publication Data

Names: Black, Simon (assistant professor), author.
Title: Social reproduction and the city : welfare reform, child care, and resistance in
    neoliberal New York / Simon Black.
Description: Athens : The University of Georgia Press, [2020] | Series: Geographies
    of justice and social transformation ; volume 49 | Includes bibliographical
    references and index.
Identifiers: LCCN 2020006575 | ISBN 9780820357546 (hardback) | ISBN
    9780820357553 (paperback) | ISBN 9780820357539 (ebook)
Subjects: LCSH: Public welfare—New York (State)—New York. | Public welfare
    administration—New York (State)—New York. | Child care—New York (State)—
    New York. | New York (N.Y.)—Social conditions.
Classification: LCC HV99.N59 B59 2020 | DDC 362.7/25680974710904—dc23
LC record available at https://lccn.loc.gov/2020006575

CONTENTS

ACKNOWLEDGMENTS

The writing of this book would not have been possible without the support, guidance, and labors of family, friends, and colleagues.

The roots of the project are to be found in the social movements and struggles that have been the focus of my activism. It was in the streets with comrades in the Ontario Coalition Against Poverty and Peel Poverty Action Group that the idea for this project first took shape. Much of the research was conducted in the midst of the global economic crisis, the bulk of the writing done in years of neoliberal austerity, and the study was extended and transformed into book form as the populist right rose to power in the United States and elsewhere. Through these years, I have been fortunate to find myself in communities of committed activists, and also in communities of critical social scientists who believe the point of their work is not simply to interpret the world but to change it.

I wish to thank Leah Vosko, who was an exceptional supervisor throughout my doctoral studies and has remained a supportive mentor. Leah pushed me (gently, as only a good supervisor can) to sharpen my theoretical insights and refine my arguments and analysis. I am also deeply grateful to Frances Fox Piven, who welcomed me at the Graduate Center at the City University of New York. Frances was a generous host, sharing institutional resources and community connections that set me on my research path in the city and providing words of encouragement during each step of the way. Barbara Cameron and Kate Bezanson offered incisive and helpful feedback on early versions of the manuscript. Conversations with Meg Luxton and Susan Braedley have deepened my appreciation of the feminist political economy tradition and feminist conceptualizations of social reproduction.

In the early stages of the research, Betty Holcomb, Director of Policy at the Center for Children's Initiatives, provided invaluable assistance in navigating the complex child care landscape in New York City. Veteran community organizer Fran Streich did likewise when it came to the myriad community-based organizations and advocacy groups contesting New York City's workfare regime. The good folks at Families United for Racial and Economic Equality in Brooklyn inspired me with their activism and were generous with their time. My friend Howard Grandison opened his home to me on more than one research trip to the city.

Roger Keil and Linda Peake, past and present directors of the City Institute at York University, provided me with an intellectual home while finishing the research for this book and informed my thinking about urban neoliberalism and its counter-politics. Financial support from the Social Sciences and Humanities Research Council of Canada, the Canada–U.S. Fulbright Program, the Faculty of Graduate Studies at York University, and the Canadian Union of Public Employees Local 3903 made this research possible.

My colleagues in the Department of Labour Studies at Brock University, Larry Savage and Kendra Coulter, offered helpful advice as this project was transformed from dissertation to book. Along with Larry and Kendra, Alison Braley-Rattai and Paul Gray help make Brock Labour Studies a collegial and enjoyable place to work. I also am grateful for the work of our department's administrative assistant, Elizabeth Wasylowich.

I would like to offer my special thanks to the team at the University of Georgia Press, especially executive editor Mick Gusinde-Duffy, who guided me through the publishing process; acquisitions coordinator Beth Snead; ever-so-patient production editor Thomas Roche; and three anonymous reviewers who shared thoughtful feedback on previous drafts. Thanks also to freelance copy editor extraordinaire Chris Dodge in Montana, and to Jane Springer and Asam Ahmad in Toronto for editing assistance on early versions of the manuscript.

Before submitting a formal proposal to the press, I pitched the project to Nik Heynen, founding editor of the Geographies of Justice and Social Transformation series. Nik's warm response encouraged this non-geographer to push on with a proposal. I wish to thank Nik, the current series editors, Mathew Coleman and Sapana Doshi, and the editorial advisory board for believing in this project and for creating the space for interdisciplinary urban scholarship with a critical edge.

Finally, I would like to thank my family. Maxine and Ken Black instilled in me a passion for learning and their unwavering love has nurtured and sustained me. At a young age, my socialist-feminist mother taught me to value the work of care, and to see it as work. My sister Samantha, along with the rest of the Campo family, is a source of love and laughter. This book would not have been written without the love and support of Joanna Newton: the irony is not lost on me that in the latter stages of this project, while I was parked in front of the computer writing about child care, you took on more than your fair share of social reproductive labor in our household; for this I am deeply grateful. Joanna's own work as an educator committed to building a better world inspires me daily. It is to Joanna and our daughter Coretta, a source of such joy in our lives, that I dedicate this book.

LIST OF ABBREVIATIONS

ACD   Agency for Child Development
ACORN   Association of Community Organizations for Reform Now
ACS   Administration for Children's Services
AFDC   Aid to Families with Dependent Children
AFSCME   American Federation of State, County, and Municipal
            Employees
BEGIN   Begin Employment Gain Independence Now
CBC   Citizens Budget Commission
CCCDC   Committee for Community Controlled Day Care
CCDBG   Child Care and Development Block Grant
CCDF   Child Care and Development Fund
CCI   Child Care Inc.
CUNY   City University of New York
CWE   Consortium for Worker Education
DC 1707   District Council 1707 of American Federation of State,
            County, and Municipal Employees
DCC   Day Care Council of New York
EFCB   Emergency Financial Control Board
FPE   feminist political economy
FSA   Family Support Act
FUREE   Families United for Racial and Economic Equality
HRA   Human Resources Administration
IBO   Independent Budget Office
NOW-LDEF   National Organization for Women Legal Defense and
            Education Fund
NYC-WAY   New York City–Work, Accountability, and You program
OBRA   Omnibus Budget Reconciliation Act

PRWORA	Personal Responsibility and Work Opportunity Reconciliation Act
SBLS	South Brooklyn Legal Services
SEIU	Service Employees International Union
SSA	Social Security Act
TANF	Temporary Assistance for Needy Families
TCC	transitional child care
TTF	temporary task force on child care funding (New York City)
UFT	United Federation of Teachers
UPA	United Parents' Association
WEP	Work Experience Program
WIN	Work Incentive Program
WWT	WEP Workers Together

Social Reproduction and the City

In a City of Workers, Who Cares for the Children?

> One of the greatest things I have done in New York City, and one of the things
> I will be remembered for years from now, is workfare—putting people back to
> work! . . . When students read history books twenty years from now they are
> going to see that I took a city of dependency and made it into a city of workers!
> **—Mayor Rudolph Giuliani, 1998**

> The new social contract with welfare recipients will require many more
> mothers to take jobs. But who will care for their children while they work?
> **—editorial, *New York Times*, 1996**

Tasha was a twenty-four-year-old resident of Brooklyn, New York, and lone parent of a twelve-month-old baby. Since the birth of her child, she had been receiving cash assistance under the Temporary Assistance for Needy Families program, better known as "welfare." In November 1998, Tasha received a letter from New York City's Human Resources Administration (HRA) advising her to report to a designated welfare office for a workfare assignment. Like thousands of other welfare recipients in New York, Tasha was to work for the city—cleaning parks, filing documents, or sweeping trash in a public housing project—in return for her welfare check.

The letter advised Tasha to make child care arrangements for the day of her appointment and, if necessary, for the period of her workfare assignment. While informed that she was to receive a voucher to pay for the services of a child care provider of her choice, the letter offered no child care information or advice.

Tasha spent the weeks leading up to her appointment in a desperate search for child care. None of her neighborhood's licensed child care centers had openings; in fact, all had lengthy waiting lists. Tasha called centers located in other parts of the city—some as far away as an hour's subway ride—only to get the same results. A friend told Tasha about a local woman who ran a day care out of her basement apartment, but when Tasha paid a visit the woman seemed cold and unfriendly, and, regardless, she refused city-issued vouchers, accepting only cash. Hearing that she was down on her luck, Tasha's neighbor Beverly offered to care for the baby on the day of her appointment.

At the appointment, a welfare caseworker informed Tasha that she had been assigned to work thirty hours a week in the city's Department of Parks and Recreation; she was to comply with this assignment in order to continue receiving cash assistance. After filling out a stack of forms, the caseworker asked Tasha if she had made child care arrangements. Tasha described how difficult it had been securing decent child care. Shaking her head, the caseworker instructed Tasha that she had two weeks to find child care and report to her workfare assignment; otherwise Tasha risked having her benefits reduced. She advised Tasha to ask a friend, relative, or neighbor to watch the baby, "someone who might need the money." Tasha immediately thought of Beverly and hoped her neighbor would be willing to provide child care on a longer-term basis.

To Tasha's relief, Beverly agreed. Beverly was already caring for two children—a toddler and a three-year-old—whose mother was on welfare and who, like Tasha, had been called into the city's workfare program. In the recession of the early 1990s, Beverly had lost her job as an administrative assistant and exhausted her unemployment benefits looking for work. When she went to apply for welfare, a caseworker suggested the forty-year-old mother of two set up a home day care. Beverly had since earned a living combining short-term contracts in administrative work with providing child care to low-income families in her neighborhood. While she was reluctant to take on another child, she knew Tasha had run out of options.

Beverly was just one of twenty-eight thousand home-based child care providers contracted with the City of New York to care for eighty-five thousand of the city's poorest children. She provided the children in her care with meals and snacks, helped them with reading and numbers, and directed safe play. She comforted them when they were upset and praised them for good behavior. Her workday was long, stretching from seven in the morning, when the first child in her care was dropped off, until seven at night, when the last child was picked up—after which she might head out to the grocery store to purchase food for the next day's meals.

Despite the value of her work, the skills involved, and the long hours, Beverly did not have access to a pension or health insurance through her job, nor did she have paid vacation or sick leave. And unlike the six thousand child care workers employed in over three hundred day care centers funded and over-seen by the city, Beverly was not unionized. Indeed, as a home-based child care provider she was considered a self-employed independent contractor under the law and therefore denied basic labor rights and excluded from employment protections.[1]

While Beverly took great pride in her job, she was among the city's lowest-paid workers. For the care of Tasha's baby, the City of New York would pay Beverly the equivalent of $3.63 an hour, far below the federal minimum wage.[2] The previous year Beverly had earned around $15,000, leaving her family of three hovering not far above the poverty line.[3] Delayed payments from the city's welfare administration played havoc with her ability to pay the rent and other household bills on time. Beverly often paid for books, diapers, and other supplies out of her own pocket, knowing the parents of children in her care could not afford them. But neither could she.

Who Will Care for Their Children?

This book is about the policies and politics that shape the intertwined fates of women like Tasha and Beverly. It is about the intersections of welfare reform and child care; of welfare rights activism and labor organizing; and of neoliberal restructuring, resistance, and the value of women's care work. In the broadest sense, it is a book about the politics of social reproduction in neoliberal times and what we might learn about this politics when viewed through the lens of the urban.

In New York City, welfare reform saw thousands of poor single mothers transition from cash assistance into workfare and the bottom of the labor market, escalating the city's already existing child care crisis. As welfare mothers entered the largest welfare-to-work program in the country and low-wage employment, the question of "who will care for their children?" was thrust to the forefront of city politics (*New York Times* 1996).

Under the administration of Mayor Rudolph Giuliani, New York confronted what Jamie Peck has called "a classic neoliberal dilemma over welfare-to-work" (Peck 2001, 251): its failure to adequately fund child care threatened to undermine the very transitions into work it sought to encourage. Put differently, as caring for one's own child is not recognized as "work" under welfare reform, meeting the child care needs of poor mothers on welfare was an immediate condition of their reproduction as labor power—that is, as workers ready and able to engage in workfare and paid employment. How these needs would be met, however—by whom, under what conditions, and to what effect—was the subject of political and social struggle. More than ten years after welfare reform, in the wake of the 2008 economic crisis, and with Giuliani's successor, Michael Bloomberg, in the mayor's office, the answers to these questions remained matters of contestation.

CHILD CARE ON THE CHEAP

Two years before President Bill Clinton made good on his promise to "end welfare as we know it," Rudolph Giuliani was elected mayor of New York City and set about pursuing an aggressive agenda of privatization, deregulation, and welfare state retrenchment designed to restructure local government along neoliberal lines and curtail the power of municipal unions, while handing tax giveaways to the city's financial, corporate, and real estate elite and dramatically expanding the size and role of the city's police force (Moody 2007; A. O'Connor 2008; Vitale 2008).

At the intersection of welfare and child care, this agenda played out in multiple ways. In the name of expanding "parental choice," the Giuliani administration marketized public child care services through the enlargement of what had previously been a small voucher scheme. At the same time, the administration shuttered a number of unionized, city-funded child care centers, reducing the supply of quality, affordable child care in some of New York's poorest neighborhoods and laying off municipal day care workers in the process. Then, upon the introduction of rigorous new welfare-to-work requirements, the city's welfare bureaucracy channeled mothers on welfare into relying on home-based child care providers for the care of their children. While some mothers preferred these child care arrangements, many did not, and a neoliberal discourse of "choice" hid the hand of a coercive, disciplinary workfare state.

For the Giuliani administration, home-based child care was the fastest and most cost-effective route to moving poor mothers off the welfare rolls. Performing public care work while hidden inside the "private" sphere of the home, excluded from key employment protections and labor rights, and without a union to advance their collective interests, women like Beverly delivered a much-needed service on the cheap.

New York was not unique in these regards. In the wake of welfare reform, publicly subsidized home child care expanded across the United States, becoming the fastest-growing segment of the child care industry (Whitebook

2001). Yet New York was situated to meet the rising demand for child care differently. The city was home to the largest publicly funded, center-based child care system in the nation, a system with roots in the New Deal and one that had survived President Richard Nixon's veto of universal child care legislation in 1971, the city's fiscal crisis of the mid-1970s, and the Reagan administration's antiurban, antipoor agenda of the 1980s. This child care system represented a vision, though one never fully realized, of collective responsibility for social reproduction and quality child care as a public good. It was a vision fought for and defended by poor and working-class women over the decades, including socialists and communists in postwar New York, welfare rights activists and advocates for community control in the 1960s and 1970s, and the city's day care workers, who in 1967 became the first child care workforce in the nation to unionize and go out on strike.

Yet in the decade following welfare reform, despite increases in state and federal child care funding, there was little to no growth in New York's unionized, center-based child care system nor any attempt to make this system more responsive to the needs of working mothers. Instead, the Giuliani administration imposed market discipline on welfare recipients, channeling mothers into relying on nonunion, home-based providers to meet their child care needs. More often than not, these child care providers shared the social and geographic location—as women of color living in low-income neighborhoods—as the mothers they served.

The city's response to the child care crisis must be understood as part of a broader project of urban neoliberalization that targeted the institutional legacies of New York's postwar welfare regime, what historian Joshua Freeman has called its "urban social democracy" (Freeman 2000). Conservative policy makers, neoliberal think tanks, and the city's business elite had long argued that the size and scope of local government in New York—particularly the degree to which the city underwrote social reproduction through an extensive municipal welfare state—fostered the dependency of the poor, was a drag on economic competitiveness, and was detrimental to the city's long-term fiscal health (Freeman 2000; Phillips-Fein 2017). These same forces saw New York's powerful public-sector unions as an obstacle to the restructuring of local government and encouraged the city to pioneer "new ways to get public service work done cheaply," including through volunteer labor, workfare, and widespread contracting with nonunion firms (Krinsky 2011, 383).

For proponents of neoliberalism, these efforts had not gone far enough. As the Republican politician Newt Gingrich said of New York in 1992, "Bankrupt welfare statism and rapacious unionism has caused a systemic crisis that requires radical, even revolutionary, change" (Gingrich 1992). Giuliani promised to bring about such change. Against the backdrop of federal welfare reform, his administration's policies at the intersection of welfare and child care, and those of his successor, Michael Bloomberg, reflected the longstanding desires of neoliberal ideologues, conservative politicians, and corporate elites to rid New York of what remained of its social democratic ethos.

I therefore situate politics at the intersection of welfare and child care within the context of New York's historical and contemporary political economy. In foregrounding the place-specific context of neoliberal restructuring, exploring how forms of market-orientated governance are made through local sites (Peck 2001), I take seriously Peck, Brenner, and Theodore's call for a context-sensitive understanding of neoliberalism (2018). Collectively, they have argued that neoliberal projects are "contextually embedded" insofar as they are produced within contextually specific political-economic landscapes "defined by legacies of inherited institutional frameworks, policy regimes, regulatory practices, and political struggles" (Brenner and Theodore 2002, 349). As neoliberalism develops in constant tension with inherited institutional legacies and existing social-political constellations of power in particular locales, "actually existing neoliberalism," or *neoliberalization*, is necessarily path-dependent, uneven, and variegated across space and place (Brenner and Theodore 2002; Peck, Brenner, and Theodore 2018). The resistance neoliberalization engenders is also shaped by context: neoliberal projects "generate specific sorts of opposition depending upon the existing configuration of, and division of labor in, the state and civil society groups in political-economic space" (Krinsky 2006, 159). In other words, contestation is contingent on preexisting and locally variable capacities for resistance (Peck 2003).

While neoliberal forces sought to mediate New York's child care crisis through strategies of privatization, they faced very specific sorts of opposition. This opposition drew on the rich history of poor and working-class women's struggles over social reproduction in New York, struggles that shaped the city's postwar welfare regime from below. As the city delivered child care services on the cheap, welfare rights organizations, community legal clinics, child care advocates, low-income community groups, activist mothers, and labor unions organized to demand just solutions to the child care crisis. These efforts culminated in community- and union-led campaigns to organize the city's home-based child care providers, taking advantage of an important contradiction: by channeling subsidies to home child care, the city expanded the ranks of a precarious but publicly funded workforce. Many previously "private-pay" child care providers now received public funds for the care of children of low-income families, and the welfare state location of their work opened the legal and discursive space to counter neoliberal logics, organize, and make claims on the state as public employees providing an essential social service.[4]

In the wake of welfare reform, home child care providers emerged as a political force in New York, contesting the policies that shaped their work, winning improvements in wages and working conditions, and demanding increased public investment in child care overall. Moving from the "private" sphere of the home into city streets, to city hall, and ultimately to the state legislature, they refused to be a cheap solution to New York's child care crisis.

Social Reproduction and the City

Despite a growing body of scholarship on cities as sites of neoliberal policy experimentation, state restructuring, and resistance, feminist political economy (FPE) and feminist welfare state scholarship have tended to neglect the urban as a scale of analysis.[5] In addition, critical approaches to urban neoliberalization often fail to account for and theorize social reproduction and the shifting relationship between states, markets, and households (Mahon 2005; Mahon 2009).[6] As a corrective, this book aims to advance a feminist political economy of the urban welfare regime, applying the theoretical lens of social reproduction to processes of urban neoliberalization and an urban lens to feminist analyses of welfare state restructuring and resistance.

Following Ann Porter, I understand welfare state regimes as "complex webs of forces in which the relationships between numerous variables—labour markets, unpaid work in the home, family structures, race and ethnicity, political struggles, state policies—can be considered as part of a dynamic whole in which the process of interaction and change is critical" (Porter 2003, 29). As Porter argues, while this complex ensemble can be seen as shaping the direction of a regime, the relationship between production and social reproduction—as manifest through the nexus between the family/household, the market, and the state—is of central importance.

"Social reproduction" refers to the social processes and labors involved in maintaining and reproducing people, specifically the laboring population, and their labor power, on a daily and generational basis (Laslett and Brenner 1989; see also Bezanson and Luxton 2006). It encompasses the work involved in biological reproduction, the reproduction of human labor, and the reproduction of provisioning and care needs, and it occurs at the level of the household through unpaid work and at the level of the state through social transfers such as education and health care (Bezanson and Luxton 2006). Given the racialized gendered division of labor in the US economy, the work of social reproduction, when organized in the market, typically entails low-wage service-sector jobs disproportionately occupied by immigrant women and women of color (see Duffy 2011). Embedded in an FPE framework, social reproduction offers a basis for understanding how various institutions "interact and balance power so that the work involved in the daily and generational production and maintenance of people is completed" (Bezanson and Luxton 2006, 3).

One of the fundamental insights of the FPE tradition is that social reproduction and capital accumulation are fundamentally in tension and often in contradiction with one another, as expressed in the conflict between the standard of living of workers and the profit imperative, or "life-making" and profit-making (see Cameron 2006; Ferguson n.d.; Fraser 2016; L. Vogel 2013). As Nancy Fraser explains, "On the one hand, social reproduction is a condition of possibility for sustained capital accumulation; on the other, capitalism's orientation to unlimited accumulation tends to destabilize the very processes of social reproduction on which it relies" (Fraser 2016, 100). This contradiction or crisis tendency must therefore be mediated and stabilized by the social institutions of the state, the market, and the family/household (Picchio 1992). In establishing the conditions under which social reproduction takes place—by regulating capital and labor markets and providing supports for social reproduction—the state's role is particularly crucial in mediating this contradiction or, put differently, limiting persistent crisis tendencies in social reproduction (Vosko 2006, 147; Picchio 1992).

Yet one need only look to the variegated character of welfare state regimes, both across and within advanced political economies, to see that state-driven efforts at mediation are inherently neither regressive nor progressive but shaped by social and political struggles and the orientation of particular governments (Vosko 2006, 147–48). As fundamentally political in nature, these efforts can be partial, inadequate, and even paradoxical, giving rise to contradictions and opening space for social movements—as was the case in New York—to contest the terms of mediation and secure more progressive forms of social reproduction (Martin 2010; Vosko 2006).

Restructuring, Rescaling, and the Urban Welfare Regime

A central claim of this book is that under neoliberalism, the urban welfare regime is a crucial site of contested state responses to crisis tendencies in social reproduction. Welfare state scholarship has tended toward methodological nationalism, assuming that the national scale is the privileged level for social policy action, contestation, and analysis (Mahon 2006; see also Greer, Elliot, and Oliver 2015). Such an approach obscures dynamic political economies of scale and takes little account of subnational variation in social welfare provision and political-economic relations. In contrast, this study pays particular attention to local context, while acknowledging that the local or urban welfare regime is an intersection of both local and supralocal dynamics (see Andreotti, Mingione, and Polizzi 2012).[7]

The urban dimension of welfare is not new. Across the advanced political economies urban struggles over social reproduction were central in the development of the Fordist-Keynesian welfare regime as national governments intervened in social reproduction, in various degrees, through the creation and expansion of national welfare states. In this way, national states took on some of the costs of and responsibilities for social reproduction previously borne by subnational governments, including cities, and private institutions, namely families, faith-based institutions, and charities. In the interscalar arrangements of the postwar welfare state, cities came to act as relay points for national Keynesian welfare policies and as providers of services, benefits, and facilities to urban populations (Brenner and Theodore 2002; Harvey 1989; Mahon 2005).

Yet since the neoliberal turn of the 1970s, welfare states have undergone twin processes of restructuring and rescaling (Mahon 2005; Mahon 2009; Andreotti, Mingione, and Polizzi 2012). Responsibilities for key aspects of social reproduction have been devolved to subnational states and offloaded through privatization to households, markets, and the nonprofit sector. As responsibilities for program standards and social welfare provision are devolved, cities have become important sites for neoliberal policy experimentation and the rollout of policies and programs that seek to discipline the urban poor and effectively manage the social fallout from state and corporate disinvestment from social welfare, while promoting urban competitiveness and capital accumulation (Peck 2001; Soss, Fording, and Schram 2011; Wacquant 2009a). One such intervention is welfare-to-work programs designed not to reduce poverty but to enforce wage work, individualizing responsibility for social reproduction and increasing poor people's, including poor single mothers', reliance on the low-wage service-sector jobs abundant in urban labor markets (see Collins and Mayer 2010; Morgen et al. 2010; Peck 2001; Soss, Fording, and Schram 2011). As poor working families struggle to make ends meet in the absence of decent work and social supports, crisis tendencies in social reproduction have escalated, including a crisis in child care.

Welfare reform intensified the child care crisis in urban America as millions of poor single mothers exited the welfare rolls, dramatically increasing the demand for care (Polakow 2007). Yet the child care crisis is not simply a matter of supply and demand. In the United States, child care is largely still viewed as women's work, a private responsibility associated with unpaid "labor of love" done in the home. Women are assumed to have a natural ability to care, and this work is typically understood as not requiring the specialized knowledge, training, and skills that are the justification for good wages (Folbre 2012). Furthermore, the limited ability of families to pay for child care, paired with inadequate public investments, constricts wages for care workers (Vogtman 2017). Care work is also strongly associated with the work of women of color, marked by the legacies of slavery, indentured servitude, and guest worker regimes, and gendered and racialized exclusions from basic labor protections (Glenn 2010). The combined outcome of these intertwined economic, social, and historical forces is that child care and care work more broadly remain enormously undervalued (Vogtman 2017).

While millions of American families find the cost of quality child care out of reach, millions of women employed in the child care industry are living just above the poverty line or even below it (Howes, Leanna, and Smith 2012; Vogtman 2017).[8] The median wage for child care workers in the United States is just $9.62 an hour—40 percent less than the nationwide median wage.[9] One in six child care workers lives in poverty, and half rely on some form of public assistance compared to 21 percent of the U.S. workforce as a whole (National Women's Law Center 2018). And only 3 percent of child care workers are unionized and covered by a collective agreement (Howes, Leanna, and Smith 2012).

The relationship between poor job quality and poor care quality is clear: low wages, lack of benefits, and generalized precarity for care workers leads to burnout and high turnover, inadequate training, and a child care system that fails parents, children, and the child care workforce (Grindal et al. 2015; National Women's Law Center 2018; Whitebook, Phillips, and Howes 2014).[10]

In short, the child care crisis can be understood as a dual crisis of social reproduction: poor and working-class families lack access to quality, affordable child care, while women who work as child care providers struggle to provide for their own families.

The National Context

The Personal Responsibility and Work Opportunity Reconciliation Act of 1996 (PRWORA) replaced the sixty-year-old Aid to Families with Dependent Children program (AFDC) with Temporary Assistance to Needy Families (TANF). PRWORA ended the federal entitlement to welfare for people in need, limited welfare receipt to two years consecutively or five years over a recipient's lifetime, made benefits contingent on efforts to get paid work, and shifted provision away from cash assistance and toward an array of employment supports, central among which are child care subsidies (Allard 2009).

As under AFDC, most beneficiaries of TANF are poor families headed by single mothers (Soss, Fording, and Schram 2011). While welfare reform abrogated the right of these women to care for their own children, policy makers recognized that legislation that firmly recasts poor mothers as employable would dramatically escalate the need and demand for nonparental child care (Levy and Michel 2002). Welfare reform's accompanying child care bill, the Child Care and Development Block Grant (CCDBG) Act, tripled federal expenditures on child care and permitted states to allocate a portion of TANF funds toward child care assistance programs (Adams and Rohacek 2002).[11]

Despite a $4 billion increase in federal child care spending, funding levels have never been adequate to cover all subsidy-eligible families (National Women's Law Center 2018).[12] In order to meet federally mandated work participation rates, states have generally targeted child care assistance to poor mothers in receipt of welfare in order to facilitate their transition into paid employment (Levy and Michel 2002). Furthermore, reflecting the devolved, decentralized, and fragmented character of poverty governance under TANF, access to and eligibility for subsidized child care is geographically uneven, varying by state and within states, by city or county (Houser et al. 2014).

For families that do gain access to subsidies, under federal guidelines, state and local social service agencies must allow parents to choose any legal child care provider that accepts state-issued subsidies, which are typically administered through vouchers. In most states, acceptable providers include licensed child care centers and regulated home-based family day cares but also license-exempt and unregulated (or very lightly regulated) informal care, colloquially known as "family, friend, or neighbor care" (Adams et al. 2006).

Despite the rhetoric of "parental choice," low-income families' child care choices are shaped and constrained by key contextual factors, including the availability, accessibility, and affordability of various child care arrangements; parental awareness of child care options; parents' access to information regarding their legislated child care rights; and the existence of numerous bureaucratic impediments to accessing subsidy (Adams et al. 2006; Chaudry, Sandstrom, and Giesen 2012; Houser et al. 2014). While low-income families place a high value on the quality of child care arrangements (Forry et al. 2013), these contextual factors can force parents into less-than-optimal child care arrangements—unstable, unreliable, and of limited quality—that negatively impact child development (Chaudry 2004; Chaudry, Sandstrom, and Giesen 2012).

Furthermore, rather than create the affordable, high-quality day care that feminists and child care advocates have long demanded (see Michel 1999), policy makers in the wake of welfare reform actively promoted home child care as a cost-effective way to rapidly expand the supply of nonparental care in low-income communities, while having the spinoff effect of creating child care jobs for poor women (see Center for the Child Care Workforce 1998; Jones 2014; P. Smith 2007). Thus, as voucher payments increased as a proportion of overall public child care funding, "the lion's share of public resources have flowed to the least-trained, least-regulated and worst-paid sectors of the industry"—that is, to home-based child care (Whitebook 2001, 45).[13] As this book makes clear, understanding this development as an outcome of poor mothers' child care "choices" is problematic.

While there is tremendous variability in home-based settings, studies have found home child care to be, on average, of lower quality than center-based care (Chaudry 2004; Fuller et al. 2004; Hurley 2018; Layzer and Goodson 2006; Paulsell, Porter, and Kirby 2010). Home child care providers generally lack the resources to provide comprehensive early childhood education and care, including access to training and professional development (Chaudry 2004). They typically earn low incomes and often face delayed payment or nonpayment by local and state agencies that cut their checks (Chalfie, Blank, and Entmacher 2007; P. Smith 2008).[14] Reimbursement rates are set so low that many providers fail to earn enough to lift their families above the poverty line, and turnover rates are unsurprisingly higher than among center-based child care workers (Chalfie, Blank, and Entmacher 2007).[15] Furthermore, clas-

FIGURE 1. As Congress debated the reauthorization of TANF in 2002, Dan Wasserman's political cartoon for the *Boston Globe* captured the Republican response to the child care crisis under welfare reform and the exploitation of poor women's care work as a matter of public policy. © 2002 Dan Wasserman. All rights reserved. Distributed by Tribune Content Agency, LLC.

sified as independent contractors under the law—that is, self-employed small business owners—home child care providers are largely excluded from coverage under labor and employment protections, including from minimum wage, prevailing wage, and overtime protections, workers' compensation systems, and the right to organize and collectively bargain (Chalfie, Blank, and Entmacher 2007). As with home health care, the work of home-based child care is thus characterized by a gendered and racialized precariousness constructed and maintained by the state (see Boris and Klein 2008).

The Local Context

In the 1990s, New York became a key site of neoliberal welfare reform, rolling out one of the most punitive workfare programs in the nation (see Krinsky 2007a). For a number of reasons, the city was symbolic for both welfare's defenders and its critics. First, the welfare rights movement of the 1960s and early 1970s had been at its strongest and most effective in New York (see Kornbluh 2007). During this period, thousands of poor mothers previously denied state support for the work of raising and caring for their children gained access to the city's welfare rolls (Piven and Cloward 1993). While the strength of the welfare rights movement ebbed by the mid-1970s, the city remained a hub of antipoverty activism and home to a network of social service agencies, community organizations, and welfare rights lawyers dedicated to advancing poor peoples' rights. For welfare's conservative critics, this "welfare industrial complex" made New York "an ATM machine to non-working unwed mothers, dispensing taxpayer dollars with little asked in return" (Mac Donald 2014).

Second, at its postwar peak in 1995, the city's welfare caseload was larger than that of any *state* bar California (DeParle 1998). The city accounted for around 70 percent of New York State's caseload, while paying 70 percent of welfare's total local cost (CSWL 2001).[16] Additionally, while the majority of AFDC recipients nationwide were white, the racial composition of the city's welfare rolls was used by conservatives to amplify a racially coded rhetoric of dependency, family breakdown, and the urban underclass.[17] The Giuliani administration employed this rhetoric to mobilize public support for a policy agenda that targeted not only welfare recipients but also poor people in general (Wacquant 2009b, 261–69).

The politics of welfare reform also reflected a broader ideological war on postwar urban liberalism, of which New York was the "symbolic capital" (Brash 2011, 28). Between 1945 and 1975, New York came to embody "a particular style of social democratic politics: one that embraced a strong welfare state, a culture of labor power and solidarity, and a belief in the necessity of using government (even city government) to help the disadvantaged" (Phillips-Fein 2013, 25). And despite successive rounds of austerity and restructuring, beginning with the fiscal crisis of 1975, by the early 1990s many of the institutional legacies of New York's "urban social democracy" remained (Freeman 2000). This institutional resilience was largely due to the strength and influence of the city's labor unions and progressive social movements and a lingering social democratic political culture that emphasized collective responsibility for social reproduction (see Freeman 2000; Freeman 2014).

In sum, in New York's urban welfare regime, proponents of neoliberalism—the city's corporate elite, allied think tanks, and policy makers—saw the institutional legacies of the city's social democracy and the residual power of unions and progressive movements. Just as New York had been a laboratory for social democracy, under the Giuliani administration it became a laboratory for an aggressive project of urban neoliberalization (Moody 2007; N. Smith 1998; Wacquant 2009a; Wacquant 2009b). The administration sought

to build on previous rounds of restructuring with a sweeping project of deregulation, privatization, and retrenchment, rolling back the urban welfare state
and the municipal component of the social wage and rolling out a paternalis-
tic program that penalized poverty and the poor (Wacquant 2009b, 10–18).[18]

Notes on Research Methods

At a macro level, this book advances a feminist political economy of urban welfare regimes. Feminist political economy is dialectical, concerned with conflict
and change, and seeks to understand society from a materialist perspective
that puts women, gender, race, and class at the center of its analysis (Luxton
2006). While my objective in this extended case study is to capture the contextually embedded dynamics of neoliberal welfare state restructuring and resistance in New York, it is also to understand these dynamics in the broader
context of poor and working-class women's struggles over social reproduction
that have shaped the urban welfare regime from the New Deal until today. To
meet these objectives, I employed a multi-method approach in my research.

Situating contemporary restructuring and resistance in historical context
necessitated historical research. I made ample use of the archives of the *New
York Times* and the progressive weekly *Village Voice* to gain insights into the
history of the city's child care movement and day care workers' union and
their role in the emergence of New York's child care exceptionalism. I supplemented this research with the secondary literature on welfare and child care
policy in New York. To fill in gaps and round out my historical research, I conducted open-ended interviews with child care advocates and welfare rights
organizers active in the 1970s and 1980s. In sum, this research was integral to
mapping poor and working-class women's struggles over care work and understanding how these struggles shaped the city's welfare regime, in particular
its child care system, from below.

The data employed in the analysis of the city's welfare and child care policies and the resistance they engendered was gained through several methods. In order to document the escalation of the city's child care crisis in the
wake of welfare reform, I conducted secondary statistical analysis, relying on
data from the city's social welfare administrations. Through this analysis, I was
able to trace the decline in the welfare caseload in New York and subsequent
rise in the need and demand for nonparental child care. I completed secondary statistical analysis to chart the child care usage patterns of welfare mothers
by child care type, documenting poor mothers' overreliance on home-based

child care, particularly informal care arrangements. Much of this data was available through the city's Human Resources Administration and Administration for Children's Services. To determine whether overreliance on home child care was the product of city policies and frontline practices and not simply reflective of the preferences of welfare mothers, I analyzed public policy, reviewing municipal government documents and reports on welfare reform and child care produced by nonprofit groups and local social service agencies. I supplemented this data with open-ended interviews with eight city bureaucrats who had differing degrees of oversight of welfare and child care services in the Giuliani and Bloomberg years. As is to be expected, most of these people chose to remain anonymous.

Mapping the city's policies and the resistance they engendered was also done by analyzing media coverage of welfare reform, child care, and contestation. I reviewed and coded just over one hundred newspaper articles on welfare and child care, dating from 1992 to 2010. To understand how progressive forces identified and mobilized around the contradictions produced by the city's child care policies, I conducted semistructured interviews with twenty-one activists and advocates in welfare rights organizations, the day care workers' union, low-income community organizations, and the city's child care movement. In many cases, participants provided access to social movement materials that assisted in charting the multiple resistance strategies developed by progressive civil society actors, strategies that culminated in the campaign to unionize the city's home-based child care providers. Interviews with staff and elected officials from the home child care workers' union, the United Federation of Teachers (UFT), were particularly useful in highlighting the union's strategy to organize home-based providers based on their para-public status.

Outline of the Book

Through a case study of restructuring and resistance at the intersection of welfare and child care in New York City, this book suggests that under neoliberalism, urban welfare regimes are sites of politically contested, state-driven efforts at mediating crisis tendencies in social reproduction. Yet while processes of neoliberalization generate crisis tendencies for poor and working-class households, privatized remedies aimed at their mediation can be contradictory, opening space for social movements to demand a more equitable distribution of the work of social reproduction across the nexus of state, household, and market.

I make my case in six chapters. Chapter 1 establishes the theoretical framework for this study, which aims to further a feminist political economy of the urban welfare regime by applying the theoretical lens of social reproduction to processes of urban neoliberalization and an urban lens to feminist political economy analyses of welfare state restructuring and resistance. In the context of the restructuring and rescaling of welfare states under neoliberalism, the chapter draws attention to the urban as a vital scale for feminist political economy analysis.

Chapter 2 elevates the historical and site-specific context of contemporary restructuring and resistance in New York. Spanning the years 1933 to 1993, from the advent of the New Deal to the election of Giuliani, the chapter explores the historical context of contemporary struggles over the social organization of care work—as part of broader struggles over social reproduction—and demonstrates their centrality in the development and character of the city's unique welfare regime. The neoliberalization of New York's "urban social democracy" began in response to the city's fiscal crisis of the mid-1970s and has entailed the restructuring of the local welfare state through processes of privatization, deregulation, and retrenchment. The second half of the chapter examines the impact of this restructuring, as successive municipal administrations downloaded costs of and responsibilities for social reproduction onto households and communities, reinforcing class, gender, and racial inequalities.

With this context in place, chapter 3 focuses on the Giuliani and later Bloomberg administrations' policies at the intersection of welfare reform and child care. The chapter opens with a sketch of the contours of neoliberal governance in New York, focusing on the transformation of the urban welfare regime. I then turn to detailing the overlapping and mutually reinforcing strategies of privatization that constituted welfare reform and its accompanying child care policy. Finally, I examine how the city's welfare bureaucracy, despite the rhetoric of "parental choice," channeled mothers on welfare into relying on an expanding pool of home child care providers for the care of their children.

These privatized solutions to the city's child care crisis unleashed a set of contradictions, creating openings for contestation and resistance. Chapter 4 begins by exploring the child care activism of New York City's largest anti-workfare coalition and the extensive public outreach efforts of child care advocates, welfare rights groups, and legal aid lawyers as they attempted to make welfare mothers aware of their legislated child care rights. I then turn my attention to the joint efforts of child care advocates and labor movement activists to leverage welfare-to-work grants to establish an innovative child care program that sought to improve the wages and working conditions of home child care providers and care quality. Close to a decade of organizing and activism around welfare and child care laid the groundwork for community- and union-led campaigns to organize the city's home child care workforce. I take up two of these campaigns in the second half of the chapter.

In the book's conclusion, I discuss the urban welfare regime as a central site of contested, state-driven efforts to mediate crisis tendencies in social reproduction under neoliberalism. I argue that resistance to the neoliberal logic of "child care on the cheap" demonstrates that even in the age of the neoliberal city—in which privatization, deregulation, and welfare state retrenchment appear to be hegemonic processes—poor and working-class women and their allies maintain the capacity to shape the politics of social reproduction from below.

Yet with progress have come setbacks. Since the success of the mid-2000s, home child care providers in New York and across the country have had to face new obstacles in the fight to revalue their labor and make gains in wages and working conditions. In the wake of the 2008 crisis, conservative attacks on the welfare state and public-sector unions, aided by a hostile Supreme Court, have dealt severe but not fatal blows to home care worker unionism. And with a shift to the right in national politics, conservatives threaten an already fragile welfare state while enriching the 1 percent at the expense of poor and working-class Americans, deepening class, gender, and racial inequalities.

But in dark times there are reasons to be hopeful. Cities have emerged as political incubators for new coalitions of progressive forces, bringing together care workers—including child care providers, home health aides, domestic workers, hospital workers, and teachers—with new social movements such as the Fight for 15, immigrant rights, and the Movement for Black Lives. With a reinvigorated women's movement that centers the experiences and demands of poor and working-class women—a "feminism for the 99 percent" (Arruzza, Bhattacharya, and Fraser 2019)—struggles on the terrain of social reproduction are at the heart of efforts to build socially just cities and, it is hoped, a more progressive America.

CHAPTER 1

Social Reproduction and the City

Toward a Feminist Political Economy of the Urban Welfare Regime

One of the greatest achievements of feminist political economy
has been to talk about social reproduction, to make visible and to
problematize what would otherwise be invisible or seemingly trivial to
the economy, to society, and even to (liberal) feminist theory.
    —Sedef Arat-Koç, 2006

Partly because of where they live and work, but also because of the many working-
class women's movements that have flourished in cities, socialist feminists
have been particularly interested in transforming the urban environment.
    —Johanna Brenner, 2014

Feminist political economy is a rich tradition of scholarship with roots in Marxist feminism and socialist feminism, in feminist critiques of the gender blindness of political economy, and in critical debates around women's oppression under capitalism and where to locate "women's work," both paid and unpaid, in the economy (Vosko 2002a; see also Luxton 2006). The last decade or so has seen a resurgence of feminist political economy and especially of interest in the tradition's anchoring concept of social reproduction (e.g., Bhattacharya 2017; Bakker and Silvey 2008; Bezanson and Luxton 2006; Ferguson et al. 2016). This scholarship has spanned diverse disciplines and fields of study, from international political economy to critical geography to welfare state studies and to feminist debates around intersectionality as an analytic strategy to address multiple, crosscutting power relations.[1]

Yet despite the analytical breadth and depth of the FPE tradition, feminist political economists have tended to neglect the urban as a scale of analysis. On the other hand, critical geographies of urban neoliberalization have often failed to theorize and address questions of social reproduction and the shifting relationship between states, markets, and households. Situating my contributions within the FPE tradition, the theoretical framework presented in this chapter aims to further a feminist political economy of the urban welfare regime by applying the theoretical lens of social reproduction to processes of urban neoliberalization and an urban lens to feminist analyses of welfare state restructuring and resistance.

I begin by defining a number of core concepts in an FPE approach to welfare regimes, namely social reproduction and its crisis tendencies, the social organization of care, and the notion of a care crisis. I tease out the relationship between these concepts, situating them within a broader FPE understanding of welfare state restructuring and resistance.

Feminist welfare state research has tended to assume that the national scale is the privileged level for social policy action, contestation, and analysis (Mahon 2006). Against this methodological nationalism, in the second section of the chapter I highlight the importance of the urban as sites of both social welfare provision and of poor and working-class women's struggles over social reproduction, struggles that have shaped welfare state regimes from below.

Under neoliberalism, welfare states have been restructured and rescaled as responsibilities for key aspects of social reproduction have been downloaded to subnational governments, including cities, and offloaded via privatization to households, the nonprofit sector, and to the market to provide for a price (Mahon 2005; Mahon 2009). In the third section of the chapter, I explain how these twin processes, along with broader shifts in gender dynamics, have fueled crisis tendencies in social reproduction for poor and working-class households, taking one expression in a crisis of care.

While these dynamics are the broader context for contemporary urban struggles over social reproduction and contested, state-driven efforts to mediate its crisis tendencies, neoliberalization and the resistance it engenders are uneven across space and place. I turn to the concept of "actually existing neoliberalism" to draw attention to the contextually embedded character of neoliberal projects and the ways in which forms of market-orientated governance are made through local sites (Brenner and Theodore 2002; Brenner, Peck and Theodore 2010; Peck, Brenner, and Theodore 2018). An FPE analysis of urban welfare regimes must therefore account for the contextually embedded and often place-specific character of restructuring and resistance.

Welfare State Restructuring and Resistance

Feminist political economists have developed an approach to welfare state analysis that understands welfare regimes as "complex webs of forces in which the relationship between numerous variables—labor markets, unpaid work in the home, family structures, race and ethnicity, political struggles, state poli-cies—can be considered as part of a dynamic whole in which the process of interaction and change is critical" (Porter 2003, 29).[2] While these variables in-teract to shape the character and development of a given regime, of central im-portance within this ensemble is the relationship between production and so-cial reproduction, particularly as it is manifested through the nexus of state, market, and family or household (Porter 2003, 29).

"Social reproduction" refers to the social processes and labors involved in maintaining and reproducing people, specifically the laboring population and their labor power on a daily and generational basis (Laslett and Brenner 1989; see also Bezanson and Luxton 2006). It involves conception and birth; the work of caring for and maintaining people at the immediate daily level (in-cluding child care and the provision of clothing, shelter, food, health care, and conditions of basic safety); the development and transmission of knowledge, social values, and cultural practices; and the construction of individual and collective identities (Laslett and Brenner 1989; Picchio 1992; Luxton 2006). Embedded in an FPE framework, social reproduction offers a basis for under-standing how the state, the market, and the household interact and balance power to ensure the daily and generational production and maintenance of people (Bezanson and Luxton 2006, 3).

The work involved in social reproduction can be taken up by a variety of institutions and actors. Social reproduction occurs at the level of the house-hold through unpaid work, done primarily by women, and at the level of the state through social transfers such as education and health care (Vosko 2006, 456). The market, where services are available for a price, can also provide so-cial reproduction. In the North American context, given the racialized gender division of labor, this typically entails low-wage service-sector jobs—for exam-ple, in health and social care and in food services—disproportionately occu-pied by immigrant women and women of color (Duffy 2011; Glenn 2010; Lux-ton 2014).

How social reproduction is organized is ultimately a question of power. As Meg Luxton explains, "The allocation of responsibility for social reproduc-tion between the different spheres and the standards or quality of life pro-duced vary in different historical periods and in different societies in response to struggles over economic, political, and social priorities" (Luxton 2006, 38). An FPE approach recognizes that these struggles are at the heart of class strug-gle and are central to the oppression of women and racialized and poor peo-ples (Luxton 2014, 154). In short, who bears the costs and responsibilities for social reproduction in a given historical period reflects social, political, and economic struggles and the balance of social forces, most vitally those of class, gender, and race in a given social formation.

CRISIS TENDENCIES IN SOCIAL REPRODUCTION

One of the fundamental insights of FPE is that under capitalism there is a central friction, tension, or contradiction between social reproduction and capital accumulation (Cameron 2006; Picchio 1992). The social reproduction of the working class is a precondition for capitalist production, ensuring a constant supply of labor with the appropriate skills and behaviors. And consumption by working-class households is necessary for the transformation of the value incorporated in goods and services into new and expanded capital that may be invested back into the ongoing process of production (Cameron 2006, 46). Yet, as Sue Ferguson explains, "The relentless drive to exert downward pressure on wages (and also on taxes) means that although capitalism needs workers, it cannot help but undermine the capacity of those workers to reproduce themselves, generating a conflict between the standard of living of workers and the profit imperative, or between 'life-making' and profit-making" (Ferguson n.d.). As profit maximization and standard-of-living maximization are rarely compatible, the relationship between capital accumulation and social reproduction must be mediated and stabilized by the social institutions of the state, the market, the family or household, and potentially the nonprofit sector (Bezanson 2006; Picchio 1992).

In establishing the conditions under which social reproduction takes place—by regulating capital and labor markets and providing supports for social reproduction through social transfers and services—the state's role is particularly crucial in mediating this contradiction or, put differently, in limiting persistent crisis tendencies in social reproduction (Vosko 2006, 147; see also Cameron 2006; Picchio 1992).[3] However, states respond to tensions in social reproduction in various ways, and, like crisis tendencies themselves, state-driven efforts at mediation are inherently neither regressive nor progressive but shaped by cultural norms, politics, and social struggle (Vosko 2006). As such, state interventions can and do vary, and while existing forms of social stratification and inequalities of power are ready conduits for the direction that mediation takes in a given period, "Degrees of political mobilization and/or the orientation of particular governments can 'reroute' the state-household-market circuits of mediation" (Bezanson 2006, 175).

Given their inherently political nature, state efforts at mediating social reproductive crisis tendencies can be paradoxical, giving rise to contradictions and creating space for social movements to contest the terms of mediation (Martin 2010; Vosko 2006). Depending on the structure of political opportunities movements face—that is, the exogenous dimensions of a political environment that influence their emergence and success (see Meyer and Minkoff 2004)—progressive movements may mobilize around alternative political projects designed to secure a viable process of social reproduction on very different grounds than the state. Typically, such projects involve demands for the state to socialize more of the costs of social reproduction and responsibilities for it, easing the burden on households and communities, especially the women in them.

THE SOCIAL ORGANIZATION OF CARE

Under neoliberalism, the social organization of care is one site of persistent crisis tendencies in social reproduction and where contested efforts at their mediation play out. Across the advanced political economies, the "crisis of care"—often linked to ideas of "time poverty," "social depletion," and "work-family balance"—has emerged as a major topic of public debate (Fraser 2016, 99). The Organisation for Economic Co-operation and Development has called for member states to "do better for families" and develop policies that "reconcile work and family life" (OECD 2011). Beyond the global North, the International Labour Organization has called attention to a "looming global care crisis" and the need for increased investment in education, health, and social care to combat gender inequality and address deficits in care work and care quality (International Labour Organization 2018).

Yet at a more abstract level, the relationship between "care" and "social reproduction" is not always straightforward, owing to the various ways in which the concepts have been defined and the relationship theorized (see Duffy 2011, 9–19)—including the tendency of early feminist political economy scholarship to equate social reproduction with women's unpaid work in the household.[4]

Following sociologist Evelyn Nakano Glenn, I understand care work as involving three interrelated activities, comprising both affective and material labor, that entail providing for the needs and well-being of persons and thus facilitate and are central to social reproduction (Glenn 2010). First, there is the direct caring for a person, which includes physical care, emotional care, and the direct services that assist people in meeting their physical and emotional needs. Second, care work involves the maintenance of the immediate physical surroundings in which people live. Lastly, care involves the fostering of people's relationships and social networks, including what Glenn calls the "weaving and reweaving of the social fabric," the mending and maintaining of personal relationships (Glenn 2010, 5–6). When done for pay in occupations such as home health aide, domestic worker, or child care provider, care work typically involves some mixture of these three activities (Folbre 2012; Glenn 2010).

Beyond the particulars of the labor, "social organization of care" refers to the location of this work, the conditions of those who provide it, and the value the work is accorded (Glenn 2010). Like the broader process of social reproduction in which it is embedded, the social organization of care is dynamic and shaped by a range of factors, including the social relations of gender, race, and class, labor markets, and social struggles. And as with social reproduction more broadly, the state plays a crucial role in shaping the organization of care, especially in the degree to which it supports care work in the household, socializes care through the direct delivery or subsidization of care services, or leaves care to be purchased on the market.

In the U.S. context, there are three ways in which the state shapes the social organization of care that are of particular importance to this study. First, as a liberal welfare regime, the U.S. reliance on primarily means-tested social programs fundamentally shapes the entire labor market for care. Women continue to provide a disproportionate share of both unpaid and paid care, and making only a small part of socially necessary care work a public responsibility "serves to perpetuate care as women's work, rendering much of the skill and labor invisible and certainly making it undervalued" (Armstrong and Armstrong 2004, 26). The disparity between the public need for care and the public resources devoted to care results in a "care penalty" for care providers— low wages, lack of benefits, and a reduction in future earnings (Armstrong and Armstrong 2004; Folbre 2012).

Second, home-based care workers—home health care aides, domestic workers, and home child care providers—have historically been excluded from legal definitions of "employee" and from coverage under U.S. labor laws, including the right to organize and collectively bargain. In this way, the state has historically denied home-based care workers status as workers and has refused to recognize the home as a site of wage labor (Boris and Klein 2015). These exclusions have reinforced a gendered ideology that deems women's care work most removed from the public sphere as having the least economic value and as worthy of the least economic reward (Tuominen 2003, 177). And by further devaluing home-based care work, labor law has interacted with social policy to allow the state to deliver home-based care services, including home child care and home health care, on the cheap (Boris and Klein 2006, 2015).

Finally, in the United States, the social organization of care has been rooted in diverse forms of coercion upheld by the state, including slavery, indentured servitude, guest worker programs, and workfare (Glenn 2010). These forms of coercion have tracked poor, racialized, and immigrant women into the work of caring for others beyond their immediate kith and kin. As Glenn has argued, while varying in degree, directness, and explicitness, these forms of coercion have nonetheless "served to constrain and direct women's choices; the net consequence of restricted choice has been to keep caring labor 'cheap,'— that is, free (in the case of family care labor) or low-waged (in the case of paid care labor)" (Glenn 2010, 5).

As an FPE approach to the welfare state makes clear, the state plays a vital role in shaping the social organization of care work and social reproduction more broadly. Yet feminist political economists and feminist welfare state scholars alike have tended to treat the state as a singular entity—privileging the national scale as a level of analysis—as opposed to a scalar configuration of social welfare provision, social infrastructure, and contestation and struggle (Mahon 2006; Mahon 2009). As Mahon contends, such "methodological nationalism" obscures important processes and variations at both transnational and subnational scales, including the local or urban scale (Mahon 2006).[5] In contrast, feminist geographers have asked in what ways state intervention in social reproduction, and struggles over it, are inherently matters of space, place, and scale (Marston 2000; C. Katz 2001; Meehan and Strauss 2015). By decentering the national scale in welfare state analysis, the contributions of feminist geography can help advance a feminist political economy of the urban welfare regime.

Social Reproduction, Scale, and the Urban Welfare Regime

In response to gender-blind answers to questions of capital accumulation, state regulation, and scale, feminist geographers have insisted on the integration of gender relations and the scales of the family or household and the community or neighborhood into debates on scalar politics and political economy (Marston 2000; McDowell 1999; Mitchell, Marston, and Katz 2004). Further contributions have drawn attention to the scalar arrangements governing social welfare provision and social infrastructure and the way these intersect with the "small world" of the neighborhood and the household. For example, welfare state transfers that support care work in the home or provide care services in the community may involve national, regional, and/or local governments in funding and regulatory regimes (Mahon 2009). And depending on the political opportunity structure they face, social movements demanding greater collective responsibility for social reproduction may mobilize and make claims on the state at multiple spatial scales (Mahon and Macdonald 2010).

The concept of scale has proven particularly useful to analyses of welfare state regimes in the context of their restructuring and redesign under neoliberalism. As Paterson observes, "Rather than viewing the state as an ontological given, scalar theory enables researchers to explore the state as a series of socially constructed arenas and associated processes" (Patterson 2014, 182). This approach allows us to question the methodological nationalism typical of much welfare state scholarship and to explore the degree to which national welfare state regimes exhibit variation at subnational scales—with implications for gender equality and women's social citizenship not just across but also within particular welfare states.[6]

Given the centrality of the city in processes of welfare state development, restructuring, and resistance, a feminist political economy of the urban welfare regime is long overdue. I want to make two points in support of this claim. The first is that cities and urban welfare regimes have been and remain vital sites of poor and working-class women's activism and struggles over social reproduction. These struggles have shaped the development and character of welfare states from below—a point that I take up in greater detail in the historical case study presented in chapter 3.

The second point relates to the importance of the urban scale in the development of the postwar Keynesian welfare state regime and the evolving role of local government in social welfare provision. As sites of social policy action and contestation, cities were central in state efforts to mediate tensions between capital accumulation and social reproduction, giving rise to the national welfare states of the Fordist-Keynesian period. By highlighting the role of urban welfare regimes in this period and their relationship to national welfare states, we are better situated to understand their restructuring under neoliberalism and the implications for the social organization of care work and for social reproduction more broadly.

WOMEN'S ACTIVISM AND THE URBAN WELFARE REGIME

Reflecting the methodological privileging of the national scale in feminist welfare state research, Cohen and Brodie remark: "Feminist movements throughout the world have tended to target the national state as the scale at which social reforms could be delivered, supporting the construction of a strong welfare state" (quoted in Mahon and Macdonald 2010, 209). While it is true that women's movements have mobilized to demand *national* policies that advance women's social citizenship, from maternity leave to universal child care, Cohen and Brodie's claim minimizes a history of women's activism at the urban scale and the degree to which campaigns targeting the national state have been grounded in local and specifically urban politics.[7]

This is especially true of poor and working-class women's activism and the anticapitalist current of the women's movement (Brenner 2014). As the sociologist Johanna Brenner has written: "Partly because of where they live and work, but also because of the many working-class women's movements that have flourished in cities, socialist feminists have been particularly interested in transforming the urban environment" (Brenner 2014, 144).[8] In the capitalist city, poor and working-class women have shaped the politics of social reproduction from below, winning concessions from capital and the state through their activism and advocacy, participation in left-wing political movements, and community-based struggles to transform everyday life.

In the absence of adequate social supports from the state, women in poor and working-class neighborhoods have often created cross-household networks through which they share caring labor and the work of social reproduction more generally (Brenner 2014; see also Hayden 1982). As Brenner explains, "These caregiving networks in turn have formed the social base for women's organizing around a variety of issues relevant to their responsibility for sustaining households and families: tenants' rights, consumer issues, welfare policy, environmental justice and community-based healthcare" (Brenner 2014). This activism has also taken the form of the defense of public space and the demand for its expansion. For example, campaigns for safe streets, revitalization of parks and playgrounds, and the preservation of after-school programs all center around the urban spaces of social reproduction (Brenner 2014; see also C. Katz 2001).

Furthermore, unlike social transfers that national states can distribute directly to individuals, many social services are produced and consumed at the local scale—including housing, education, and child care (Mahon 2005). Women's movements have targeted city governments and social planning practices, demanding that such services be made more responsive to their needs (see Wekerle 1984; Wekerle and Peake 1996). In the United States, poor and working-class women have waged campaigns for the inclusion of day care centers in public housing projects and for twenty-four-hour child care services that accommodate the needs of women working irregular or nonstandard hours (see Naples 1998). African American women have a long history of struggle to end institutionalized racism in urban transportation, schooling, recreation, health care, welfare services, and child welfare systems (see Hill Collins 2000; Levenstein 2009; D. Roberts 1997). Black women in poor and working-class communities have mounted campaigns around the politics of public housing and poverty reduction programs (see Williams 2004) and the politics of hunger and food security, challenging gendered and racialized in-equalities in urban space (see Heynen 2009). Through public-sector unions, diverse working-class women have been on the front lines of campaigns to protect and expand municipal social welfare services, including care services (see Boris and Klein 2015). In these ways, the urban welfare regime has been a site of poor and working-class women's politicization.

Furthermore, these urban struggles have mobilized around poor and working-class women's identities and roles as "guardians of social reproduc-tion"—that is, as the majority of welfare clients, welfare state workers, and public-sector union members, as well as unpaid community caregivers who link other women to the state (Abramovitz 2017, 201; see also Abramovitz 2012). Even national movements driven by poor and working-class women's activism—for example, in the United States, welfare rights or the movement for a national child care program—have their roots in urban struggles with the immediate face of the state in local government and street-level bureaucracies (see Kornbluh 2007; Michel 1999, 118–49). And as the feminist urban histo-rian Daphne Spain points out, while male planning professionals have built "grand boulevards and civic monuments," it is poor and working-class women who build "the places of everyday life, the neighborhood institutions without which a city is not a city" (Spain 2001, 13). It is in these very institutions that much of the work of producing and maintaining social bonds, building com-munity and "sustaining the shared meanings, affective dispositions and hori-zons of value that underpin social cooperation" (Fraser 2016, 102)—which are the social-reproductive precondition for the functioning of capitalist cities—takes place.

Taken collectively, these struggles and labors have contributed to shaping the built form of cities, their physical and social infrastructure, and the degree to which urban space is configured in such a way that takes into consideration women's needs as both wage earners and as unpaid caregivers. As Brenner puts it, poor and working-class women's activism has continually "challenged urban policies that assume male breadwinners and privatized care work. They have envisioned new kinds of built environments that offer collective possi-bilities for care" (Brenner 2014). Poor and working-class women have de-manded that the state not only socialize the costs of social reproduction but also take into consideration questions of geographic equity, women's urban mobility, and access to services and social supports more generally. And, as in the turbulent decades of the 1930s and 1960s, through these struggles poor and working-class women have shaped systems of social welfare provision at the local scale in ways that often necessitate the intervention of higher orders of government to underwrite social reproduction (see Piven and Cloward 1977).

FORDISM-KEYNESIANISM, SOCIAL REPRODUCTION, AND THE URBAN WELFARE REGIME

I have argued that the city has been an important site of poor and working-class women's struggles over social reproduction. As I explore in chapter 2, struggles over the social organization of care work contributed to shaping the historical development and unique character of New York's postwar welfare regime, its urban social democracy. In this section, I employ an FPE approach to give a brief and more general account of urban welfare regimes in the development and interscalar arrangements of the Keynesian welfare state regimes that emerged during the postwar boom, highlighting the U.S. context.

As Brenner and Theodore note, across the advanced political economies, the national scale was the predominant locus for state regulation during the Fordist-Keynesian period of capitalist development (Brenner and Theodore 2002, 359). During this period, cities played a largely redistributive role in national welfare regimes, acting as local relays for national Keynesian welfare policies. Municipal governments maintained a "managerial-welfarist" function, concentrating on the local provision of services, facilities, and benefits to urban populations (Brenner and Theodore 2002; Harvey 1989). With some exceptions, including New York, urban welfare regimes tended to reflect the national social policy regimes in which they were embedded.

In the United States, municipal governments were generally guided by the principles of urban liberalism that posited that the local state bears some responsibility for the maintenance of a minimum level of social reproduction for all. Under this paradigm, urban social problems were largely understood as structural in nature and something that could be solved through government intervention (Vitale 2008). To this end, cities actively engaged in the provision of social services while overseeing the administration of social welfare programs established by upper levels of government, in some cases contributing to their financing. This arrangement reflected the evolution of the local state's role in social reproduction from a limited one in the pre–New Deal era to greater involvement under Fordism-Keynesianism. Through an FPE lens we can understand this evolution as the product of state responses to major economic and social crises, and intense political and social struggles in which government intervened to mediate social-reproductive crisis tendencies in the interests of economic, political, and social stability (see Abramovitz 2010; Cameron 2006).

With the emergence of industrial capitalism in the late nineteenth century, urban political machines used public welfare—typically in the form of outdoor relief, as it was called, including cash and groceries—to command the loyalty of poor and working-class voters (M. Katz 1986). However, the household, and women's labor in it, remained the main source of welfare for most poor and working-class families (Gordon 1994). At the turn of the century, urban social reformers, including women in the settlement house movement and labor unions' women's auxiliaries, as well as urban elites concerned with growing social instability, pushed municipal governments to commit to playing a more active role in social welfare provision, establishing children's bureaus, local departments of public welfare and health care, and public works projects to augment the efforts of local relief agencies, charities, and churches (Abramovitz 2000; Spain 2001). Yet as Brenda Parker reminds us, "Because racism so marked the urban landscape, African-American women and white women worked separately in their reform efforts, providing segregated services to European immigrants and Black migrants from the south." Unlike their white middle-class counterparts, African American female reformers "had the additional burden of combining waged and unwaged labor and helping black individuals and communities manage in racist cities and workplaces" (Parker 2011, 434; see also Collins 2000; Gilmore 2007; Spain 2001).

The Great Depression signaled the first major crisis in social reproduction in the twentieth century and demonstrated the inability of private institutions and subnational governments to effectively mediate tensions between social reproduction and capital accumulation (Abramovitz 2010; Cameron 2006). With cities and states overwhelmed by rising social needs and civil unrest, the federal government—pushed by both business leaders and progressive social movements—intervened to directly underwrite social reproduction through the creation of a national welfare state. Under the auspices of the New Deal and the Fordist-Keynesian economic and social arrangements that would come to characterize the postwar political economy, the United States generated conditions for both successful social reproduction and capital accumulation (Abramovitz 2010; Abramovitz 2017).

However, while the federal government promoted full employment and provided a safety net for the white working class, social programs were constructed around a male-breadwinner, female-caregiver family form, which assumed women's unpaid care work in the home and upheld patriarchal authority (Abramovitz 1996). As such, services supporting women's paid employment were limited. For example, what child care services were available were offered mainly through private charities and churches, not public programs (Michel 1999).

Furthermore, the American version of the Keynesian welfare state "embodied racialized gendered hierarchies," favoring the social reproduction of white households, especially married heterosexual couples (Boris 1995, 171; Abramovitz 2010). Social insurance programs provided generous, respectable entitlements for primarily white male workers. In contrast, the majority of white women and people of color were shut out of the social insurance track of the welfare state and overrepresented in means-tested and more miserly public assistance programs (Nadasen, Mittelstadt, and Chappell 2009, 18). In general, people of color did not benefit from social policies and labor protections to the same degree as whites, especially white men. As Abramovitz notes, the welfare state's early programs "excluded African American and Latino families and over the years provided them with lower benefits, reinforced discriminatory labor market policies, disadvantaged single mothers, and implemented other forms of 'welfare racism' that deprived families of color of the resources needed to adequately care for their families" (Abramovitz 2010, 19). And while federal labor law boosted wages and improved working conditions for many white male workers, it excluded occupations in which people of color were employed in disproportionate numbers—most notably, domestic service and agricultural labor (Boris 1995). However, while the welfare state treated both white women and people of color as secondary citizens, as Lipman has argued (2011, 11), the rights discourse that framed social citizenship did provide the grounds on which marginalized groups would make future claims on the state in the name of civil, social, and economic rights.

In the 1960s, progressive social movements mobilized to demand the expansion of civil rights and social citizenship (see the next chapter). This period marked the greatest increase in federal government spending on social welfare since the 1930s, contributing to the growth of urban welfare states and cementing their importance within the interscalar arrangements of the Keynesian welfare state regime (M. Katz 2012). The federal government increased grants-in-aid to municipalities, and state and municipal budgets grew as public-sector spending rose dramatically (Harvey 2007). In major cities, in addition to increased spending on public education and health care, the expansion of social welfare expenditures included the liberalization of poor relief, a direct response to urban insurrections in hundreds of black communities and the organization and mobilization of poor women on welfare (Fording 2001; Nadasen 2005; Piven and Cloward 1977).

As the federal government intervened in social reproduction through increased social spending, urban welfare regimes came to deliver a range of federally funded social welfare benefits and services to the poor and also provided employment opportunities for African Americans in an expanding public-sector workforce (M. Katz 2012, 59–60). As the federal government sought to integrate African Americans into the labor force, public and quasi-public employment proved important for black women in particular (Katz 2012, 58–59). This period was also marked by the growth of public-sector unionism, with municipal workers demanding collective bargaining rights, improved wages and working conditions, and, along with the broader urban working class, the expansion of basic services (Freeman 2015). While I do not want to romanticize the urban welfare regime of this period—in many ways it remained unresponsive to the needs of marginalized social groups—it no doubt emerged as a key site of social movement demands for greater collective responsibility for social reproduction (J. O'Connor 1973; Castells 1977).

Writing at the twilight of the Fordist-Keynesian era, Manuel Castells went so far as to claim that cities had become "the spatial specificity of the processes of reproduction of labor-power and of the processes of reproduction of the means of production" (Castells 1977, 443). For Castells, the urban was primarily a site, or "spatial unit," of collective consumption—that is, the consumption of commodities whose production is not assured by capital, including affordable housing, mass transit, public schools, hospitals, playgrounds, and parks. But, importantly, the urban was also a site of conflicts over these services that had come to define urban politics (Castells 1977).

By the mid-1970s, cities across the advanced political economies illustrated the social-reproductive contradictions of Fordist-Keynesian capitalism, expressed in escalating tensions between the needs of capital on the one hand and the power of progressive social movements and rising expectations, bargaining power, and standards of living of the working class on the other (see Castells 1977; Harvey 2007). As David Harvey has argued, in the United States, perhaps to a greater degree than in any other advanced political economy, these contradictions were expressed as an urban fiscal crisis, owing to a combination of economic restructuring (the shift to a post-Fordist economy); falling tax revenues (due to deindustrialization, suburbanization, and white flight); rising social welfare costs and public-sector wages (reflecting the gains made by the urban poor and municipal unions in the previous decade); and finally by declining transfers from the federal government, reflecting the turn to the right in national politics (Harvey 2007, 5–6).

In how national states responded to these contradictions, however, the United States was not exceptional. As neoliberal ideas and modes of governance gained ascendency, national governments made cuts to social welfare spending and downloaded key responsibilities for physical and social infrastructure to subnational levels (Brenner and Theodore 2002). Central state supports for municipal activities dwindled, and austerity measures were increasingly imposed on local governments from above, putting intense pressure on cities to cut services and generally restructure city government and urban space along neoliberal lines (Harvey 1989; Brenner and Theodore 2002).

Welfare states also faced challenges stemming from changes in the social organization of care. With shifts in gender norms, deindustrialization, the growth of the service sector, and decline in working-class men's wages and family incomes, greater numbers of women entered the paid workforce (Collins and Mayer 2010). Alongside changes to social policy logics, from supporting women as full-time caregivers to promoting maternal employment, these shifts have left a growing number of families struggling to balance the competing demands of paid work and unpaid care responsibilities (Orloff 2006). It is in this broader context that the city has become a central site of contested, state-driven efforts at mediating escalating social-reproductive crisis tendencies under neoliberalism.

Social Reproduction, Privatization, and the
Neoliberalization of the Urban Welfare Regime

As a political project, neoliberalism emerged as a ruling-class response to the crisis of Fordist-Keynesian capitalism and sought to "re-establish the conditions for capitalist accumulation and to restore the power of economic elites" (Harvey 2005, 19).[9] Understood in this way, neoliberalism entails the increased penetration and domination of the state by capitalist-class interests and aims to eliminate barriers to capital accumulation and effectively redistribute income, wealth, and power upward. It does so through a range of policies, including but not limited to the privatization of public assets, the liberalization of trade and removal of restrictions on corporate investment, the lowering of corporate tax rates, environmental deregulation, and the rolling back of costs of social reproduction through welfare state retrenchment and the containment of working-class wage demands through antiunion legislation and labor market deregulation (see Abramovitz 2017; Harvey 2005; Larner 2000). While the political project of neoliberalism suggests an end (i.e., the restoration of capitalist-class power and unfettered accumulation of profit), the "historically specific, fungible, volatile, and unstable process of market-driven sociospatial restructuring" (i.e. *neoliberalization)*, is the means (Peck, Brenner, and Theodore 2018).

At the urban scale, neoliberalization entails the rolling back of the urban institutions of the Fordist-Keynesian order—including public housing and rent control, public monopolies in the provision of standardized municipal services, municipal unions and local collective bargaining regimes, and the redistributive functions of local welfare state apparatuses, including supports for social reproduction. This is done while at the same time rolling out policies and programs that mobilize city space for capital accumulation and elite consumption practices and that discipline and control the urban poor and other marginalized social groups (Brenner and Theodore 2002; Peck and Tickell 2002; Vitale 2008).

PRIVATIZATION

Central to neoliberal restructuring projects at all scales is the ideology and practice of privatization. Narrowly understood, privatization entails the sale of government assets and institutions to the private sector, "opening up new fields for capital accumulation in domains formerly off-limits to the calculus of profitability" (Harvey 2007, 35). "Privatization" can also refer to the adoption of for-profit practices and the introduction of market mechanisms within the public sector and existing state institutions. However, understood at a more general level, privatization entails the reconfiguration of the relationship between states, markets, and families or households, and between public and private spheres, that characterized Fordism-Keynesianism (Fudge and Cossman 2002).

As ideology, neoliberalism replaces collective responsibility for social welfare with the belief that societies function best when individuals are free to pursue their interests in the market without government intervention (Lipman 2011, 8). Privatization is therefore intimately linked to the belief that the market is both a guarantor of "freedom," "choice," and "individual rights" and superior to the state as a mechanism to allocate goods and services in the economy (Harvey 2005). This does not mean, however, a limited role for government. When understood as a process, neoliberalization involves the active intervention of the state to dismantle the institutional infrastructures of

Fordist-Keynesian capitalism and create new policy infrastructure conducive to privatization and capital accumulation (Brenner and Theodore 2002; Peck and Tickell 2002).

Arguments in favor of privatization are typically couched in the neoliberal discourse of expanding market and consumer choice and individual rights to the exclusion of collective rights and public goods. Yet while proponents of neoliberalism cast the state as inflexible and limiting of "choice," the privatization of public institutions and assets works to constrain real choice by undermining the public-sector option and directing citizens toward market-based solutions to social problems and the provision of public goods. In doing so, neoliberal projects relegate the goal of equality—class, gender, and racial equality—to a lesser status compared to the goal of individual liberty of choice (Jenson and Sineau 2001, 241).

Feminist political economy has made important contributions to critical understanding of privatization as a profoundly gendered process (Bakker 2003; Bezanson 2006; Fudge and Cossman 2002). Embedded in an FPE framework, privatization signals the retrenchment of the state in social reproduction as goods owned or delivered publicly are shifted to the market, to the nonprofit sector, and to families and households (Fudge and Cossman 2002). In doing so, neoliberal projects manufacture a new division of responsibility for individual and social welfare and fundamentally renegotiate the relationship between the public and private spheres that characterized the Keynesian welfare state (Fudge and Cossman 2002). As neoliberal states privatize social reproduction, the responsibility for this work disproportionately falls to women, whether as unpaid work in households—heightening tensions between paid employment and unpaid care work—or as low-wage work in the market and nonprofit sector (Bezanson and Luxton 2006). In this way, the reprivatization of social reproduction can be understood as what Isabella Bakker has called a "dual moment": returning the work of social reproduction to where it "naturally" belongs—that is, the household and largely women's unpaid work, or commodified through monetized caring labor or market services (Bakker 2007, 545).

This process is not only profoundly gendered and classed but also often racialized, as privatization builds on existing unequal divisions of social reproductive labor among men and women, social classes, and racialized groups (Fudge and Cossman 2002). While women in middle- and upper-class households can purchase services associated with social reproduction on the market, offloading care work onto low-wage, typically racialized and/or immigrant women through the exercise of market-based "choices," poor and working-class women must respond to privatization through the intensification of unpaid labor in the household or through increased reliance on extended kin and social networks to take up the slack for shortfalls in subsistence provision, income, and the absence of welfare state services (Bezanson 2006, 12). Consequently, while offering the illusion of market-based choice, privatization restricts the vast majority of women's choices in terms of the amount of paid or unpaid work and leisure activities they wish to participate in (P. Kershaw 2004).

It is important here to highlight the links between financialization and an FPE approach to privatization.[10] As Adrienne Roberts has noted, one outcome of wage stagnation, the growing precariousness of work, and the scaling back of state support for social reproduction is that households have increasingly turned to credit as a means to securing the costs of social reproduction that are being offloaded by capital and the state (A. Roberts 2016). Credit becomes a means of obtaining commodities necessary for reproduction—such as food, clothes, and housing—leading to record levels of household indebtedness, particularly in liberal welfare regimes that offer limited social supports. In the United States, these processes reproduce and deepen both gendered and racialized inequalities as female-headed, black, and Hispanic households not only have less access to income and assets, and thus are more likely to be overly indebted. They are also more likely to be targeted by predatory lenders and are therefore more vulnerable to financial expropriation (Murch 2016).

As illustrated in the wake of the 2007–2008 economic crisis, when financial crises are transformed into debt crises and a fiscal crisis of the state, the risks of the financial sector are socialized through state bailout mechanisms and ultimately offloaded onto poor, working-class, and single-parent households that are the most negatively affected by cuts to social spending deemed necessary to reduce government deficits and debts (A. Roberts 2016, 130–34). Public debt also becomes an instrument of "accumulation by dispossession" (Harvey 2007), as public services and assets—from health and water to education and care services—are privatized under austerity programs, further undermining progressive, sustainable forms of social reproduction, while shifting costs of social reproduction and responsibilities for it to poor and working-class households (Fraser 2016; A. Roberts 2016).

NEOLIBERALIZATION OF THE URBAN WELFARE REGIME

The neoliberal restructuring of the welfare state has gone hand in hand with state rescaling (Mahon 2005, 341; Peck and Tickell 2002). National states have increasingly devolved tasks, burdens, and responsibilities to subnational governments, including for key aspects of social reproduction (Mahon 2005). Lacking the fiscal capacities to fund these responsibilities, and with earlier systems of central government support for social reproduction retrenched, cities are forced to decide whether to finance social infrastructure and services through the local tax base, redeploy programs and services in more "cost-efficient" ways, or effectively abandon their role in social welfare altogether (Hackworth 2007, 12).

City governments have also reoriented policy and practices in response to demands from capital. Capitalist-class demands for deregulation, privatization, and welfare retrenchment made at the national level find their urban equivalent in political coalitions of chambers of commerce, neoliberal think tanks, and policy makers that seek to roll back the redistributive functions of local government, privatize urban infrastructures, and contain the power of those social actors most closely connected to social reproduction, namely public-sector unions and poor people (Brenner and Theodore 2002; Allawhala, Boudreau, and Keil 2010). In the name of creating a "good business climate," these coalitions seek "the destruction of the 'liberal city' in which all inhabitants are entitled to basic civil liberties, social services, and political rights," the primary impetus being the mobilization of urban space as an arena both for market-orientated economic growth and for elite consumption practices, dismantling barriers to investment and capital accumulation (Brenner and Theodore 2002, 372).

Cities must also respond to the demands of nonlocal forces, namely finance capital. As Jason Hackworth has noted, cities in the United States are permitted by state law to issue debt to build and repair infrastructure, offset shortfalls in cash flow, and attract business. As federal support for cities has declined, municipal lending has increasingly made up for shortfalls in spending on city services, social programs, and capital infrastructure (Hackworth 2007, 20). As the fiscal fate of municipalities has become tied to capital markets, bondholders and bond rating agencies can and have imposed extra-local discipline on aberrant city governments (and voters)—including New York (see the next chapter)—demanding cuts to social spending, diminishing the redistributive capacities of the local welfare state, and undermining the power of municipal unions (Hackworth 2007; Peck 2015).

Regardless of the political stripe of those in municipal office, with national economies opened up to global markets, cities also increasingly engage in interurban competition for highly mobile flows of global capital and skilled labor (Allawhala, Boudreau, and Keil 2011, 210). Urban governments rely on policies designed to capture these flows, including tax abatements and other measures aimed at subsidizing capital to relocate and invest in the city. This shift, from what Harvey has called a "managerial-welfarist" function for city government to one of "urban entrepreneurialism" (Harvey 1989), has deleterious impacts on poor and working-class households as cities redirect resources from the provision of social services into tax abatements and other corporate subsidies.

In neoliberalizing cities, the privatization of costs of social reproduction and responsibility for it can be witnessed across a range of policy measures and practices, including the expansion of nonprofit and private-sector delivery of urban social services, the abolition of rent control and the privatization of public housing, the privatization of public education and the aggressive expansion of charter schools, the scaling back of community development agencies, and the introduction of user fees for previously free municipal services (Brenner and Theodore 2002; Peck and Tickell 2002; Lipman 2011).

One of the most widespread forms of privatization is the marketization of social welfare services, often through voucher programs, which engineer forms of consumer choice and market discipline in the public sector (Hackworth 2007; Lipman 2011). U.S. examples include managed-care systems for regulating the private provision of publicly funded health care, Section 8 vouchers for subsidized low-income families' participation in private housing markets, education vouchers that subsidize parents' placing their children in private charter schools, and the voucherization of public child care services (see Schram 2018). While such programs are rolled out in the name of expanding "choice"—as clients are turned into "consumers" who apply economic rationality to all their choice-making practices (Schram 2018, 312)—their overall aim is to open up services to market calculus, reduce the size and scope of the state, and shift costs of social reproduction and responsibilities for it to households, communities and to some extent the nonprofit sector. Voucherization also weakens the power of public-sector unions and lowers municipal labor costs, as the direct delivery of services by unionized public employees is replaced by nonunion private-sector entities.

Processes of privatization are also evident in welfare-to-work initiatives that discipline the poor into the low end of the urban labor market, while individualizing responsibility for social reproduction. In the United States, the federal welfare reform of 1996 ended the entitlement status of welfare for poor women and children, capped welfare spending, and mandated work participation, creating a pool of captive and disciplined low-wage women workers forced to accept "the meanest labor at the meanest wages" (Piven and Cloward

1993, 3–4; see also Collins and Mayer 2010; Soss, Fording, and Schram 2011). In doing so, welfare reform expanded the role of the market in the provision of income and care while eliminating caregiving as a basis for making claims on the state (Abramovitz 2010).

National welfare reforms have also typically entailed some form of decentralization and devolution in policy development and delivery systems, as nationally constituted welfare regimes give way to locally constituted workfare regimes (Peck 2001, 11). In the United States, federal welfare reform devolved residual provisions to the states and from some states to the local level, giving subnational governments latitude to experiment with what Soss, Fording, and Schram have called "neoliberal paternalist regimes of poverty governance" (2011). Paired with defunding by national levels of government, the decentralization of welfare creates a financial climate in which subnational jurisdictions, including cities, "must operate under fixed spending limits and in accordance with the (workfarist) dictates of the federal regime . . . or suffer funding penalties" (Peck 2001, 71). This dynamic disciplines local governments who may prefer less punitive welfare-to-work initiatives that emphasize skills building, training, and education and provide necessary employment supports.

The rolling out of punitive workfare regimes at the urban scale has been paired with aggressive policing tactics designed to manage the social fallout from state and corporate disinvestment from social welfare and the rise of precarious work (Wacquant 2009a; Wacquant 2009b). In this context, state surveillance, "zero-tolerance" policing, and the containment of migrants, homeless people, low-income communities of color, and the poorest residents of the city become a function of the "right hand" of the state—that is, the police and the broader criminal justice system (Wacquant 2009a; Wacquant 2009b; see also N. Smith 1998). In the United States, this turn to a penal approach to poverty governance has led to a massive expansion of the carceral state, tearing apart families and urban communities—disproportionately black and Hispanic—and depriving households of the resources needed to carry out the work of social reproduction (Abramovitz 2017, 218; see also Gilmore 2007).

The politics of race has been intimately tied to the neoliberal restructuring of the urban welfare regime in the United States. The inner city and the public institutions with which it is identified have been "pathologized in a racially coded morality discourse that legitimates their dismantling" (Lipman 2011, 12). In the context of an orchestrated right-wing and corporate-driven assault on the welfare state, the mobilization of a racialized logic that equates cities and urban social problems with black people justifies efforts to defund, privatize, and restrict access to services such as public housing, schools, and health clinics and undermine ideas of collective responsibility more broadly (Lipman 2011, 12). While the more generous social insurance programs—in which blacks and Hispanics are underrepresented—are less politically vulnerable, means-tested social welfare services and benefits associated with racialized urban populations have been frequently targeted by policy makers for derision and dismantling (M. Katz 2013; Soss, Fording, and Schram 2011).

This process of racialization is evident in the reframing of urban social problems, namely poverty. In the 1960s and 1970s, poverty was generally understood as structural and material in nature, while under neoliberalism it is reframed in cultural and behavioral terms (M. Katz 2012). The urban poor are racially coded as black (and to a lesser extent Hispanic), and calls for individual responsibility construct poor people of color as an undeserving "urban underclass" mired in a "culture of poverty." Welfare retrenchment has relied on racist and sexist stereotypes of black women in particular, especially the "welfare queen" (D. Roberts 1997). Social welfare programs are understood to encourage the breakdown of the black family, foster "cycles of dependency," and undermine the work ethic, an interpretation that provides policy makers with a rationale to restructure or dismantle social welfare programs and diminish state responsibility for social reproduction (Roberts 1997; Soss, Fording, and Schram 2011; Wacquant 2009a). In this, black women have been particularly targeted as "the vilified beneficiaries of state largess" (D. Roberts 2014, 1777).

While these are long-term dynamics in the political economy of the American welfare state, the neoliberalization of urban welfare regimes has intensified in the wake of the 2008 financial crisis. As the financial crisis was transformed into a state crisis, the state crisis was transformed into an urban crisis as debts and deficits were systematically downloaded to the local level (Peck 2015, 21). While "austerity urbanism" is not unique to the United States, as Jamie Peck writes, "Due to the spatial concentration of unionized labor, communities of color, poor people, and liberal constituencies, cities are favored—and particularly vulnerable—targets of austerity measures" (Peck 2015, 1). And while right-leaning municipal governments embrace austerity imposed from above, progressive administrations must navigate the pressures created by state and federal governments that pass down budget cuts to the local level (Peck 2015).

These dual processes of restructuring and rescaling form the broader political-economic context in which the urban welfare regime has become a central site of escalating crisis tendencies in social reproduction for poor and working-class households. And while these crisis tendencies can be seen across a range of social processes—from rising homelessness to food insecurity—they take one expression in a growing crisis of care.

THE URBAN CARE CRISIS

Across the advanced political economies, three factors make the care crisis particularly acute in big cities, giving it a distinctly urban character. First, as Mahon observes, the impact of postindustrialism on labor markets—and, thus, the intensity and extent to which the need for nonfamilial care is experienced—are likely to be greatest in major urban areas (Mahon 2009, 210; see also Strauss and Xu 2018). Urban deindustrialization, the shift to service-sector employment, and decline in working-class men's wages and family incomes have been paired with demographic shifts—including rising rates of divorce and lone parenthood and demographic aging. As growing numbers of women have entered the paid workforce, fewer are available to provide unwaged care within their households and communities.

Second, big cities across North America and much of western Europe are sites of concentrated, gendered poverty (see Kneebone 2017; URBACT 2019). Social policies designed to promote maternal employment, including those that push poor mothers into the labor market—whether in the name of "labor-market activation" as in Europe or "ending dependency" as in the United States—have escalated the need and demand for nonfamilial care and especially child care in urban labor markets. In liberal welfare regimes, these policies have been matched with only limited state support for caregiving or work-family "reconciliation" (Orloff 2006).

Finally, the care crisis is exacerbated by the neoliberalization of housing policy, especially the retreat from public housing and rent regulation, and the gentrification of poor working-class neighborhoods, which have pushed low-income families farther away from central cities where there is a concentration of jobs (see Hester 2018). This not only distances poor and working-class families from key social infrastructure built in the Keynesian-Fordist period—including child care facilities—and disrupts community ties and networks of mutual support that are central to social reproduction but also lengthens commute times. As Helen Hester points out, longer commutes mean less hours available for unwaged care work (Hester 2018; see also McDowell et al. 2006).

Turning specifically to the child care crisis, in the absence of universal, publicly funded child care and paid family leave policies typical of social democracies, how urban households in liberal welfare regimes manage this crisis largely depends on the resources available to them. In the context of highly polarized urban labor markets, wealthier households' "solution" to the care crisis typically rests on the exploitation of racialized and/or immigrant women's labor (Arat-Koç 2004; Brenner 2014). Middle-class households may do likewise but also benefit from targeted demand-side supports, primarily in the form of child care tax credits. Low-income households, on the other hand, must turn to limited means-tested, publicly delivered child care services, rely on state subsidies in the form of vouchers to purchase care in the market, or turn to the unpaid or underpaid caregiving of women in overstretched kinship and family networks to take up the slack, with many households patching together some combination of the three (see Folbre 2012; Levy and Michel 2002).

The child care crisis is also a crisis for care workers. The designation of child care as primarily a private responsibility, rather than a public good, shapes the entire labor market for care (Folbre 2012). Child care work remains enormously undervalued and, when commodified in the market, woefully underpaid (see Whitebook et al. 2018). In the United States, child care workers, especially racialized women who are overrepresented in the most poorly paid care jobs, struggle to balance the competing demands of paid employment and the socially necessary but unpaid labor essential to maintaining their households and communities (Folbre 2012, xi). For migrant domestic workers who provide care for wealthy families while mothering their children from afar, this labor can be transnational in nature (Arat-Koç 2006). In this way, the child care crisis is a dual crisis of social reproduction: poor and working-class households lack access to high-quality, affordable child care that parents need to work and children need to grow and thrive, while women working as care providers face low wages, limited opportunities, and inadequate benefits and struggle to provide for their own families (see National Women's Law Center 2018; Polakow 2007; Vogtman 2017).

"Actually Existing" Urban Neoliberalism

While I have sketched some general tendencies in welfare state restructuring at the urban scale—highlighting liberal welfare regimes and the U.S. context in particular—neoliberal restructuring projects are geographically uneven not only across but also within national states (Brenner and Theodore 2002; Peck, Brenner, and Theodore 2018). Peck, Brenner, and Theodore's concept of "actually existing neoliberalism" reminds us that these projects evolve within contextually specific political-economic circumstances defined by legacies of inherited institutional frameworks, policy regimes, regulatory practices, and political struggles. Neoliberalism is "always articulated through historically and geographically specific strategies of institutional transformation and ideological rearticulation" (Brenner and Theodore 2005, 102). An adequate understanding of neoliberalization must therefore explore the "contextually specific interactions between inherited regulatory landscapes and emergent neoliberal, market-oriented restructuring projects," marrying abstract theorizing with site-specific, contextualized investigations (Brenner and Theodore 2002, 349).

In keeping with this approach, analyses of "actually existing" neoliberalism must also account for the contextually embedded character of contestation and resistance since, wherever neoliberal governance is tried, "its 'roll-back' moment—i.e. the point at which it uproots the existing social policy infrastructure—generates specific sorts of opposition depending upon the existing configuration of, and division of labor in, the state and civil society groups" (Krinsky 2006, 159). As Leitner, Peck, and Sheppard put it, "anti-neoliberal forces are confronted by spatially differentiated political opportunity structures, just as they draw upon distinct political capacities, cultures, and visions of their own" (2007, 315). In short, the legacies of past struggles and the capacity of progressive forces to wage new ones in site-specific contexts are important parts of any explanation for geographically uneven patterns of neoliberalization across and within national welfare state regimes. As such, contestation and resistance must be at the center of any analysis of "actually existing" urban neoliberalism.

In the United States, a range of progressive social forces have combined in coalitions in numerous cities, with varying degrees of success, to contest the neoliberal restructuring of urban welfare regimes and push back against the privatization of social services, attacks on public-sector workers, and the punitive regulation of the urban poor (Krinsky and Reese 2006; Mayer 2007). In New York City, neoliberalization evolved within contextually specific political-economic circumstances defined by legacies of the city's social democratic welfare regime and its attendant political culture, both shaped by poor and working-class women's struggles over social reproduction. Contemporary resistance to neoliberalization has drawn on the legacies of these struggles. In order to understand restructuring and resistance at the intersection of welfare reform and child care in contemporary New York, we therefore need to foreground geographical and historical configurations, specificities, and path dependencies, engaging in a contextualized investigation into urban neoliberalization and its counter-politics.

CHAPTER 2

From Urban Social Democracy to Neoliberalizing City

Welfare and Child Care in New York, 1933–1993

> At a time when a national consensus condemned the evils of collectivism,
> working-class New Yorkers pushed their city toward a model as close
> to European social democracy as the country had seen.
>
> **—Joshua B. Freeman, 2000**

> [New York City's] malignant combination of machine politics, bankrupt
> welfare statism and rapacious unionism has caused a systemic
> crisis that requires radical, even revolutionary, change.
>
> **—Newt Gingrich, 1992**

On March 8, 1975, against the gloomy backdrop of a global recession, over two thousand women marched down Fifth Avenue, through the heart of Manhattan, in celebration of International Women's Day. Representing a coalition of over fifty women's and labor organizations, including the New York Council of Labor Union Women and the National Welfare Rights Organization, the women chanted demands such as "Equal Pay for Equal Work," "Money for Jobs, Not for War," and "Universal Child Care Now!" Among the hundreds of colorful protest signs on display was one that read, "We Refuse to Be Shock Absorbers for Capitalism's Crisis" (Klemersrud 1975).

By October 1975, New York City teetered on the brink of bankruptcy. In years past, the city had borrowed heavily to cover its widening budget gap, but now Wall Street banks refused to market city debt. As the city's fiscal crisis mounted, the presidential administration of Gerald Ford refused to bail out New York, making any federal aid conditional on deep cuts to welfare and social spending, to basic services, and to public sector wages and jobs—in a word, austerity (Tabb 1982; Phillips-Fein 2017). The services on which poor and working-class families relied—from day care centers and after-school programs to community health clinics and public libraries—would soon face closure, while their largely female workforces faced layoffs and a precarious future. Poor women on public assistance would see their benefits slashed as the city's welfare program became increasingly stingy and punitive (Kornbluh 2007). As urban elites embraced austerity and the opportunity to remake the city in their own image, poor and working-class women across the five boroughs were made the "shock absorbers" for New York's fiscal crisis.[1]

The Giuliani administration's response to the rising need and demand for child care prompted by welfare reform did not occur in a historical vacuum. Nor did resistance to this response. This chapter explores the historical context of restructuring and resistance at the intersection of welfare reform and child care in contemporary New York. It does so by highlighting how popular struggles over the social organization of care work—as part of broader struggles over social reproduction—shaped the historical development and unique character of the city's postwar welfare regime. As I argue in chapter 3, it was the product of these struggles, in the institutional legacies of New York's "urban social democracy" (Freeman 2000), including the city's unionized child care system, that the Giuliani and Bloomberg administrations targeted for restructuring.

Contestation around this restructuring was also situated within a long history of struggle over care provision and the value of women's care work, struggles in which the activism of the city's poor and working-class women has been central. These struggles have taken a variety of forms: from the day care movement's campaigns for universal child care to poor women's fight for a right to welfare and to day care worker strikes for better wages and working conditions. The opposition to the Giuliani administration's welfare and child care policies, discussed in chapter 4, was rooted in these legacies of resistance.

Finally, through the lens of New York, this chapter tracks escalating crisis tendencies in social reproduction for poor and working-class households under neoliberalism. After the city's neoliberal turn in the mid-1970s, successive mayoral administrations emphasized privatized remedies aimed at mediating these crisis tendencies, remedies that were rejected by poor and working-class women organizing and mobilizing for progressive social reproduction.

Rather than provide an exhaustive history of the urban political economy of welfare and child care, the chapter highlights five key moments—covered in five corresponding sections—that shaped the social organization of care and the historical development and character of New York's welfare regime.[2] First it is necessary to provide a brief overview of the city's postwar welfare state. While the local welfare state of the Fordist-Keynesian era generally acted as a transmission belt for national welfare policies (Brenner and Theodore 2002),

New York City was an urban outlier, exceptional in the degree to which local government underwrote social reproduction, providing a wider range of benefits, services, and protections to poor and working-class households than any other city in United States (Freeman 2000).

Urban Social Democracy

Between 1945 and 1975, New York City built what historians have called an "urban social democracy" or "social democratic polity" (Freeman 2000; Phillips-Fein 2013). In the words of Kim Phillips-Fein, the city came to embody "a particular style of social democratic politics: one that embraced a strong welfare state, a culture of labor power and solidarity, and a belief in the necessity of using the government (even city government) to help the disadvantaged" (Phillips-Fein 2013, 25). In response to the demands of the city's poor and working class—as expressed through electoral politics, a robust labor movement, and participation in tenants' groups and neighborhood associations, welfare rights, civil rights, and women's organizations—the city came to "underwrite a vision of urban social citizenship, unique to New York" (Phillips-Fein 2013, 25).

By the early 1970s, New York was home to an extensive system of public and co-op housing, twenty-two public hospitals and a network of community health centers, a tuition-free municipal university system, cheap and easy-to-use mass transit, world-class museums (and libraries and public parks), a wide range of social services and community agencies serving poor and working-class neighborhoods, and, compared to much of the country, generous welfare benefits for poor people (Freeman 2000, 2014). The city also boasted the largest publicly funded, center-based child care system in the country, staffed by a unionized workforce and notable not only for the number of children it served but also for commitment to child care that set national standards in quality and affordability (ACS 2005).

The neoliberal restructuring of New York, initiated in response to the fiscal crisis of 1975, can be understood as an effort by political and economic elites to roll back these gains of popular struggle, diminish the power of the city's progressive social movements and labor unions, and shift costs of social reproduction away from the state and onto households and communities. From 1975 onward, cuts to social services and income supports—including to child care and welfare—and general state disinvestment undermined the social wage and escalated crisis tendencies in social reproduction for poor and working-class households. As the majority of the city's welfare clients, welfare state workers, and public-sector union members, women—disproportionately women of color—faced "triple jeopardy," bearing the brunt of austerity at home, in the community, and at work.

The Roots of New York City's Child Care Exceptionalism

Child care in the United States has largely been considered a private responsibility, and public funding for child care has historically been limited, means-tested, and tied to efforts to move poor mothers from welfare into paid work (Levy and Michel 2002). The lack of public investment has had deleterious consequences for both child care quality and the wages and working conditions of child care workers. Most child care programs in the United States have been considered to be of low to mediocre quality, while child care providers are among the most poorly paid workers in the economy (Whitebook 2001; Whitebook, Phillips, and Howes 2014).

New York City has stood as somewhat of an exception to these national trends, an outlier among municipal child care regimes. At various points in the city's history, social movement struggles—in which poor and working-class women's activism has been central—have pushed the local state to socialize more of the costs of and responsibilities for child care. Partly as a result of these struggles, the city has come to boast the largest municipal child care system in the country—staffed by a unionized workforce—and has traditionally been committed to strong regulations and the delivery of high-quality programs that set national standards (ACS 2005).

FROM THE NEW DEAL TO THE POSTWAR ERA

Public child care in New York has its origins in the New Deal welfare state, a suite of social welfare programs introduced by the federal government in response to social and economic disruption of the Great Depression.[3] During the 1930s, rent strikes, mob looting, bread riots, consumer boycotts, and demonstrations—often led by Communist Party organizers and other left-wing activists—spread across the United States, although much of the unrest was concentrated in major cities (Piven and Cloward 1971; Katz 1986).

Poor and working-class women's activism was central to these struggles. For instance, in New York City, the Progressive Women's Council—a successor of the United Council of Working-Class Wives—led three thousand women in sit-ins at the city's twenty-nine largest relief centers, demanding a 40 percent increase in benefits and cash allowance for clothing, among other things (Abramovitz 2000, 127). Through Housewives' Leagues, black working-class women launched "Don't Buy Where You Can't Work" campaigns in cities across the Northeast and Midwest, demanding jobs for blacks who had become unemployed during the Depression (Abramovitz 2000, 126).

Confronted with mass unemployment and declining tax revenues, local governments and municipal relief agencies were overwhelmed by demands for assistance, and many cities, including New York, were pushed to the brink of bankruptcy. Big-city mayors and other urban elites demanded aid from the federal government to quell social disorder and save cities from fiscal ruin (Piven and Cloward 1977). This social and political instability led to the launch of the New Deal in 1933 and the introduction of social programs such as emergency relief, Social Security, and unemployment insurance.

A key agency created by the New Deal was the Works Projects Administration (WPA). The WPA hired millions of unemployed workers to carry out public works projects across the country. As part of its mandate, the WPA also established a program of "emergency nursery schools" (ENS), under which New York City established fourteen school-based nurseries, the city's first publicly funded child care facilities (Michel 1999). Prior to the New Deal, child care services in the city had taken the form of day nurseries, many of dubious quality, run almost exclusively by private philanthropic and religious organizations (ACS 2005).

The emergency nursery schools met the needs of only a small number of the city's poor families; their primary purpose was to create jobs for unemployed teachers, nurses, and nutritionists, in addition to caring for children while unemployed parents looked for work. As the nation recovered from the Great Depression, federal funding for the ENS program was brought to an end, and the survival of New York's nascent public child care system was put into question (Michel 1999, 194).

With the onset of World War II, rising numbers of women took up jobs in New York's war industries, and the lack of adequate child care prompted Mayor Fiorella LaGuardia to establish the Committee on the Wartime Care of Children (ACS 2005). Through this committee, New York committed to saving its emergency nursery schools, becoming the only city in the United States with publicly subsidized day care services.[4] According to historian Sonya Michel, New York City provided an example to the nation, and between 1943 and 1945 wartime day cares were established in hundreds of cities under the federal government's Lanham Act of 1941 (Michel 1999). At the height of the war, approximately six hundred thousand children in forty-seven states were being served in 3,102 publicly funded day cares; it is the closest the country has come to establishing a universal child care system (Michel 1999; Fousekis 2011).

An anomaly in wartime planning had initially threatened New York's day cares: the city had escaped federal government designation as a "war-impact area," and as a result its day care services—some public, some voluntary— were not eligible for federal funds under the Lanham Act. As growing numbers of women found work in the city's factories, the LaGuardia administration struggled to provide child care services. In the midst of an escalating child care crisis, and as a result of intense lobbying from the city, New York State finally agreed to step in and jointly fund child care, appropriating $2.5 million for day care for children with mothers employed in defense industries (Michel 1999, 193–94).

During this period, New York City was home to over eighty day cares serving the children of working parents, and the municipal role in the administration of child care became firmly established (Day Care Council of New York 2012). Pushed by women in the social reform movement and by child studies experts, city hall committed to establishing and maintaining high standards through the creation of the Day Care Unit in the Department of Health (Michel 1999). The unit was a pioneering institution in the field of early childhood care and education, overseeing the introduction of educational programs, improving hygiene in city day cares, and developing much-needed physical infrastructure (ACS 2005, 38). According to Michel, New York City officials, civic leaders, and parents, upon the conclusion of the war, were all "eager to see that their model system lasted into the postwar period" (Michel 1999, 194).

THE POSTWAR FIGHT TO SAVE CHILD CARE

At war's end, Congress withdrew funding for wartime day care, in keeping with the prevailing view that "the first responsibility of women with young children, in war as in peace, is to give suitable care in their own homes to their own children" (Vogtman 2017, 12). Bureaucrats in New York State's youth authority argued that the city's day care services were too costly and that access should be restricted to needy families, effectively reducing child care to a welfare service (Michel 1999, 195). As such, they recommended the withdrawal of state aid and relegating day care to an issue of local welfare. Many of the city's working-class women strongly opposed these recommendations, and a citywide grassroots mobilization of parents and children—driven by several left-leaning Popular Front groups under the banner of the United Parents Association (UPA)—demanded the continuation of state funding and the preservation of the city's public day care services (Michel 1999, 195).

The UPA consisted of liberals, socialists, and communists and called for child care as a universal right, seeing it as an essential component of women's social citizenship (Michel 1999, 194). The organization was born in the milieu of what Freeman has called "Red New York" (Freeman 2000), as communists and other leftists exerted influence in the social, cultural, and political life of the postwar city.

In the fight to preserve public day care, the UPA was joined by the Day Care Council of New York (DCC). In contrast to the former's working-class base, the DCC found support in the city's upper-class philanthropic and civic circles and emphasized the financial need of the city's poorest families as rationale for ongoing public investment in child care (Michel 1999, 194–95). Despite their ideological differences, as Michel remarks, the joint campaign of the UPA and DCC was "part of a wave of postwar activism in which, for the first time, American parents directly expressed their need for child care in a visible and organized fashion" (Michel 1999, 195).

While the state ignored the burgeoning day care movement's demands, city hall, under intense pressure from the UPA and DCC, agreed to make up the state's portion of the funds and keep New York's wartime day cares operating (Michel 1999, 195). This was a massive victory for the city's day care movement since it marked the first peacetime allocation of municipal tax dollars for child care programs (Day Care Council of New York 2012). The city's New Deal emergency nursery schools—expanded into wartime day cares—were now an established feature of the postwar urban welfare state, funded exclusively through municipal tax dollars.

In the aftermath of this victory, New York's day care movement continued to be an influential actor in city and state child care politics. Activists pressed city hall to expand its commitment to public child care, and by 1950 New York was serving over forty-six hundred children in close to one hundred day care centers, a quarter of which were located in the city's newly constructed public housing projects. Eighty-four percent of child care funding came from the municipal government, with parental fees and participating social service agencies making up the difference (Michel 1999, 195). As evidence of New York City's child care exceptionalism, the state of California was the only other jurisdiction in the nation to establish a postwar, publicly funded child care system (Fousekis 2011).

CHILD CARE POLITICS ENTERS THE COLD WAR

As the country descended into the anticommunist hysteria of the Cold War, the tenuous coalition at the heart of New York City's day care movement began to unravel (Michel 1999, 196). While the movement's radical wing continued to argue for child care as a universal entitlement for working mothers, middle-class women in the DCC found political expediency in emphasizing child care as a welfare service. Subject to red-baiting, the city's radical day care activists were marginalized while municipal officials welcomed more "respectable" advocates into the policy-making fold (Michel 1999, 197). At the national level, the child care coalition established during the war broke apart as moderate groups distanced themselves from the demand for universal child care, fearing being labeled as communists (Fousekis 2011).

The marginalization of the radical left had important implications for local and federal child care policy moving forward. The DCC was to become the dominant force in New York City and national child care politics and emerged as the core of a new national day care movement that framed child care primarily as a welfare service for the poor, not a social right (Fousekis 2011). As Michel has argued, national child care organizations by the beginning of the 1960s "were fighting a losing battle to reverse the dangerous trend toward linking child care with efforts to reduce the welfare rolls" (Michel 1999, 210). In places like New York and California, where the day care movement's ambitions had been high and the goal of universal child care within reach, means-testing came to determine families' eligibility for subsidized day care (Fousekis 2011).

Despite these shifts, publicly funded child care services emerged as a fixture of New York City's postwar welfare state, setting national standards for early childhood education and standing unique in the support it received from city government. While the system fell far short of the vision of New York's radical day care movement, the demand for universal child care would be revived by feminists, welfare rights activists, and advocates for community control in the 1960s and early 1970s.

The Welfare Rights Movement in New York City

From the early 1960s to the mid-1970s, New York was the epicenter of a national movement of poor women demanding reform of welfare policy, greater respect and dignity, and state support for the work of raising and caring for their children (Kornbluh 2007). Though it was an interracial movement, African American women took the lead in the struggle for what became known as "welfare rights" (Nadasen 2005). Black women had long been excluded from poor relief programs by racist local authorities that deemed them "employable" and fit for wage labor. However, amid urban rebellions in hundreds of black communities and the political response they provoked, millions of previously denied poor women and children gained access to welfare (Piven and Cloward 1977). As historian Premilla Nadasen notes, together these women demanded a decent standard of living based on the work they performed as mothers, regardless of behavior or personal morality (Nadasen 2005). But as New York emerged as a symbol of the welfare rights movement's success, it quickly became a target for those who sought to roll back the gains made by poor women and their allies.

WELFARE AND WOMEN OF COLOR'S CARE WORK

To understand why welfare rights mounted a challenge to the prevailing social organization of care work, we need to briefly explore the history of poor relief in the United States. In 1935 the Social Security Act established Aid to Dependent Children (ADC), which along with Old Age Assistance (for elderly poor people), Aid to the Blind, and Aid to the Disabled constituted the public assistance programs of the New Deal. ADC was modeled on state laws and locally administered programs known as "mothers' pensions" that from 1908 to 1935 provided cash grants to poor single mothers and their children (Gordon 1994). Mothers' pensions were based on the principle that the state should underwrite the social reproduction of families lacking a male breadwinner, allowing mothers to remain home to care for their children (Abramovitz 1996). The Social Security Act federalized mothers' pensions, enshrining permanent support for poor mothers in federal law.

However, while the federal government jointly funded ADC with states and local governments, the latter retained administrative authority (Piven and Cloward 1971).[5] State and county governments used this authority to exclude the vast majority of African American, Mexican American, and sometimes poor white mothers from eligibility for ADC, often under the guise of "suitable home" provisions that allowed welfare caseworkers to deny aid based on moral evaluations of a home's "fitness" for raising children (Glenn 2010, 163–64). Yet moralizing concerns about poor mothers' "worthiness" overlapped with the priorities of states and local authorities for the regulation of the labor supply (Piven and Cloward 1971). Since slavery, black women's work outside of their own homes had defined their social role: as Nadasen writes, black women "reproduced for slave masters, nannied white children, worked as wet nurses, yet had little opportunity to nurture and care for their own children on a full time basis" (Nadasen 2010, 116). Their exclusion from poor relief programs reflected their socially defined gender roles as workers, not homemakers or mothers (Nadasen 2005; Nadasen 2010).

The result of these exclusions was a highly racialized social welfare system, which favored social reproduction by white households while channeling poor women of color into low-wage work in the agricultural sector or into service occupations such as hotel and restaurant workers, cleaners, or laundresses, and domestic work in homes of wealthy white families (Abramovitz 2010; Glenn 2010). By 1939, 89 percent of ADC recipients were white; racialized exclusions and lagging state implementation meant two-thirds of all eligible women were not covered by the program (Abramovitz 2000, 65). Until the 1960s, poor black mothers in the South, Mexican American mothers in the Southwest, and many immigrant women were routinely denied access to welfare on the grounds that they were "employable." For women of color who did gain access to ADC, rates were typically set at levels that compelled many to engage in wage work to supplement their benefits.

THE WELFARE EXPLOSION

In the 1960s and early 1970s, black insurgency and the efforts of the civil rights and welfare rights movements challenged welfare racism and expanded poor relief and the boundaries of social citizenship. Between 1960 and 1972, the number of families on welfare more than tripled, going from 745,000 to over three million (Piven and Cloward 1993, 273–75). However, as costs rose, policy makers looked for ways to impose restrictions on access. The welfare explosion would spark debates about the employability of poor mothers and the need for public child care to support their return to the labor market (Quadagno 1994). These debates were shaped by the politics of race: as black women and other women of color increasingly gained access to ADC, politicians declared a "welfare crisis" and called for increased work expectations (Reese 2005).

As Piven and Cloward argued in their classic text *Regulating the Poor* (1971), the relief explosion of the 1960s, particularly post-1964, was primarily a response to black rebellion in the inner cities. In the spring and summer months of 1964, 1965, 1966, 1967, and 1968, riots swept across almost every major U.S. city in the Northeast, Midwest, and California. Poor blacks rose up against police brutality, institutional racism in housing and labor markets, and the deteriorating quality of black urban life (Marable 2007, 90–91; see also M. Katz 2012). While the rise in welfare caseloads occurred across the country, it was greatest in older industrial cities, such as New York, where black rebellion was met with a combination of state violence and federal efforts to restore social order by expanding access to relief (Piven and Cloward 1971; Piven and Cloward 1977; see also Fording 2001).

As Piven and Cloward noted, the federal government intervened in local relief arrangements primarily in three ways: by establishing new services that provided the poor with information about welfare entitlements and gave them assistance in accessing welfare; through federal litigation that challenged local laws and policies that restricted access to welfare; and by supporting new poor peoples' organizations that informed poor people of their entitlements and put pressure on local officials to approve applications for assistance (Piven and Cloward 1993, 250). The latter development fostered the growth of nascent organizations of poor women who, under the banner of "welfare rights," asserted their right to welfare as a citizenship right, part of a groundswell of civil rights activism around economic issues such as jobs and housing (Nadasen 2005; Piven and Cloward 1977).[6]

In 1966 these organizations came together to form the National Welfare Rights Organization, which at its peak had thirty thousand members and nine hundred chapters in cities and states nationwide (Kornbluh 2007; Abramovitz 2000). Demanding higher benefits and a right to a guaranteed annual income, women in the welfare rights movement made claims on the state based on the work of social reproduction done in their homes and communities (Nadasen 2005). They argued that access to subsistence outside of the labor market was emancipatory for women who had otherwise been condemned to low-wage, menial, and sometimes dangerous employment outside of their own homes, while being denied the right to raise and care for their own children on a full-time basis (Federici 2006; Nadasen 2005; Nadasen 2010).[7]

WELFARE RIGHTS IN NEW YORK CITY

While the fight for welfare rights was national in scope, the epicenter of the movement was New York City. As historian Felicia Kornbluh remarks, the city's welfare rights groups were "the largest; they had the greatest network of support from middle-class professionals such as social workers, lawyers, and priests; and they were the most important sources of strategy and personnel for the national welfare rights movement" (Kornbluh 2007, 4). By the early 1960s, activist groups of welfare recipients—predominantly African American and

Puerto Rican mothers—had begun to sprout up across the city, many of them under the auspices of local antipoverty programs funded by the federal government as part of the War on Poverty. These groups worked with middle-class allies to form welfare rights chapters, coming together under the umbrella of the City-Wide Coordinating Committee of Welfare Groups (Kornbluh 2007).

Several thousand public assistance recipients, the majority of them poor women of color, strategized and mobilized to change welfare in New York. The City-Wide Coordinating Committee led protests, marches, and mass demonstrations on the streets and in welfare offices, which led the city to further liberalize relief policies (Kornbluh 2007). As Kornbluh writes: "Activists used tactics that ranged from demonstrations, sit-ins and other forms of civil disobedience, to legislative lobbying, registering voters to participate in elections, and suing welfare department officials in court. By 1970, the City-Wide Coordinating Committee of Welfare Groups had helped welfare families gain cash grants worth hundreds of thousands of dollars" (Kornbluh 2007, 1). Lawyers and grassroots organizers worked with welfare mothers to challenge the arbitrary decisions of their caseworkers. Legal processes such as "fair hearings" were used extensively: for example, in the fall of 1967 alone, welfare rights groups sponsored three thousand fair hearings cases in New York City, a massive number considering the usual fifty per year (Nadasen 2005, 57).

Along with the threat of further social upheaval, the impact of these and other movement tactics was significant: fewer welfare recipients were subject to sanctions; more applicants were able to get assistance as traditional procedures for investigating welfare eligibility broke down; caseworkers began ignoring regulations as they attempted to process a mounting number of applications; and more poor families got access to the full range of benefits—including clothing assistance and furniture allowances—to which they were entitled (Kornbluh 2007; Piven and Cloward 1971). These factors contributed to the significant growth of the city's welfare rolls. By 1973, one out of ten of the nation's welfare recipients resided in New York City (Jackson and Johnson 1973).

For those seeking to roll back the gains of poor peoples' struggles, New York became a symbol of everything that was wrong with the welfare state. Writing in 1973, presidential advisor Daniel Patrick Moynihan argued, "The social fabric of New York City is coming to pieces. It isn't just 'strained' and it isn't just 'frayed'; but like a sheet of rotten canvas, it is beginning to rip, and it won't be too long until even a moderate force will be capable of leaving it in shreds and tatters" (quoted in Piven and Cloward 1977, 338). When New York's mayor, the liberal Republican John Lindsay, ran for reelection in 1969, his opponents made welfare spending a central issue of the campaign, claiming his administration had allowed poor people to "defraud the city." As white working- and middle-class voters became increasingly conservative on issues of racial equality, Lindsay abandoned his commitments to the city's poor and pledged to cut the welfare budget and tighten eligibility requirements (Kornbluh 2007, 4–10).

By the mid-1970s, the national welfare rights movement had lost momentum (Nadasen 2005). As the urban rebellions and protest movements of the previous decade ebbed, national politics took a turn to the right. With the election of Richard Nixon in 1968 and passage of federal legislation that tied welfare receipt to participation in paid work, women on welfare faced severe cuts in benefits and new restrictions on their eligibility. According to Kornbluh, the city's welfare rights activists confronted "a new set of strategies by the city and state that undercut their organizing efforts and ultimately decimated their membership ranks" (Kornbluh 2007, 4). The epicenter of the movement would become a focus of national backlash against welfare mothers and the urban poor in general.

THE LEGACY OF WELFARE RIGHTS

The legacy of welfare rights in New York is threefold. First, over a period of twelve years, thousands of the city's poorest mothers—predominantly women of color previously denied access to welfare—won financial support for the work of raising and caring for their children. Due to the militancy of the movement and the city's liberal political culture, New York's welfare system came to provide some of the most generous benefits in the country, easing the poverty experienced by poor mothers and their children.

Second, women in the welfare rights movement reframed their unpaid care work as legitimate work worthy of a wage; in this they laid the groundwork for struggles by women of color and some white women—in movements such as Wages for Housework—for the recognition of domestic work and child care as work (see Federici 2012). Finally, in their militancy and success—given the sheer number of families that gained access to assistance and to the full range of benefits to which they were entitled—welfare rights redrew the boundaries of urban social citizenship to include poor black and Puerto Rican women and increased the extent and reach of the city's postwar welfare state.

Social citizenship in New York was buttressed by federal and state funding to cities under the Great Society and War on Poverty programs (Phillips-Fein 2017, 24), and New York's urban social democracy by the early 1970s included free tuition in the city university system (CUNY), health care for all, affordable public housing, and a vast network of community agencies and economic development projects in low-income neighborhoods. With its comparatively generous social programs and large welfare caseload, the city became the scourge of conservatives (Freeman 2000). Never ones to shy away from hyperbole, conservative critics took to referring to New York as "Moscow-on-the-Hudson" (Magnet 2004). The city would be a symbolic target of the neoliberal project to come, and within a few years many of the historical achievements of poor and working-class New Yorkers, and the social movements they built, were under threat.

Care Workers' Unionization and the Fight for Universal Child Care

While welfare rights activists demanded state support for the work of raising and caring for their children, the movement also sought the creation of day care centers to support mothers' employment.[8] However, according to Premilla Nadasen, movement leaders warned that the fight for child care "should ensure that it did not create 'a reservoir of cheap female labor' that 'institutionalized partially self-employed Mammies,'" for while day care services "could potentially free some women from the constraints of child care, they could just as likely increase exploitation of other women" (Nadasen 2010, 115–16). In this the movement leveled a critique of the race and class blindness of a mainstream (white, middle-class, and liberal feminist) women's movement that demanded day care but paid little attention to the wages and working conditions of child care workers.

Perhaps owing to the strong left-wing presence in New York's women's movement, the child care demands of welfare rights activists complemented the political thrust of the city's day care movement. Day care activists made important gains in the mid- to late 1960s and saw levels of mobilization reminiscent of the fight to preserve funding for wartime child care (Interview 14). An important element in this wave of activism was the struggles of the child care workers employed in the more than four hundred publicly funded day care centers in the city, which offered free or subsidized child care to poor and working-class families. Given their poverty-level wages, these workers were that "reservoir of cheap female labor" to whom welfare rights activists sought to bring attention. Like the poor women they served, day care workers set about collectively organizing to assert the value of their care work.

DAY CARE WORKERS UNIONIZE

While postwar New York was a center of labor movement power, union membership was concentrated in the private sector, especially in manufacturing and construction. By the early 1960s, most municipal workers still did not belong to a union, and pay and working conditions in many city agencies were poor (Freeman 2015). In January 1965, eight thousand of the city's welfare workers went out on strike, demanding improvements in their pay and benefits and also in the city's treatment of their welfare clients (Freeman 2000, 205–6). On the picket line for twenty-eight days, the welfare workers sparked organizing by other municipal employees and led the city to set up a new system of labor relations that formalized collective bargaining.[9] The American Federation of State, County and Municipal Employees (AFSCME) District Councils 37 and 1707 would go on to win organizing drives in city-run hospitals and with school lunch workers, building cleaners, librarians, and court reporters. Many of the newly organized workers were African American and Puerto Rican, and collective bargaining lifted their families out of poverty for the first time (Freeman 2015).

As part of this wave of public-sector unionism, the city's day care workers set about organizing, and by 1967 they had become the first child care workforce in the nation to unionize, forming AFSCME Local 205 Day Care Employees (District Council 1707 2012). After a bitter three-week strike, in which 1,100 workers shut down 113 of the city's day care centers, members of Local 205 voted 643 to 65 in favor of their first contract (New York Times 1969). The contract included recognition of a union shop, the introduction of a welfare fund, and a series of pay increases paralleling then-recent settlements won by other city employees. Perhaps most importantly, the wage scale for day care workers was made comparable to that offered to elementary teachers in the city's public school system (Clines 1969). Day care workers were incorporated into one of New York's growing municipal workers' unions, Local 1707 of the Community and Social Agency Employees.

It did not take long for the newly unionized workers to exercise their political muscle. In 1969, after intense lobbying by Local 205, New York City introduced the first for-credit training program to upgrade the skills of day care workers (Day Care Council of New York 2012), making the link between child care quality and the wages and working conditions of child care providers. And as was the case in the 1940s and 1950s, what happened in New York child care politics had ripple effects beyond the Big Apple. The success of Local 205 sparked a wave of day care organizing across the country: child care workers joined social service employees, auto workers, and even painters' unions in states such as Massachusetts, Michigan, and Wisconsin (Blank, Chalfie, and Entmacher 2007).

While unions such as the American Federation of Teachers and the Service Employees International Union (SEIU) would go on to organize day care centers in scattered cities across the country, by 2004 only 3 percent of the nation's child care workers were covered by a collective agreement (Blank, Chalfie, and Entmacher 2007). In this regard, Local 205 was a trailblazer in the fight for dignity, respect, and better wages and working conditions in the sector, and to this day it remains the largest day care local in the United States (District Council 1707 2012).

In addition to the struggles of day care workers, growing child care activism led by feminists in the New Left, civil rights activists, and early childhood advocates pushed the Lindsay administration to initiate the Task Force on Early Childhood Development, putting child care squarely onto the city's policy agenda (District Council 1707 2012). Many of these activists would coalesce into the Day Care Forum, a coalition of child care interests, which emerged as the city's most prominent and progressive child care advocacy organization—a 1960s version of the UPA (Interview 14). While the Day Care Forum organized for the expansion of public investment in child care throughout the late 1960s and early 1970s, it would come to play a crucial role in the struggle to resist day care cuts in the wake of the city's fiscal crisis.

THE FIGHT FOR UNIVERSAL CHILD CARE

After New York's day care workers organized in the late 1960s, their ranks expanded in the early 1970s when the city's publicly funded day cares proliferated at an extraordinary rate (Brozan 1979). The cause of this expansion was fourfold. First, under the Great Society and War on Poverty, federal aid to cities had provided local government with the means to expand social services, including day care. Second, in the late 1960s and early 1970s, black and Latino struggles for "community control" of social services led to growing enrollment in day care programs in what had been previously underserved communities.[10] Third, the push for community control overlapped with a resurgent child care movement, which found its voice in the Day Care Forum and the Committee for Community Controlled Day Care. Child care activists worked alongside the day care workers' union to pressure city hall to expand quality, affordable child care. And finally, the day care movement found a sympathetic ear in the city government as feminists and child care advocates entered a newly created municipal agency expressly devoted to "children's services" (Interview 14). The confluence of these factors led not only to the expansion of day care services in New York but also to a push for universal child care.

Much of the child care activism and advocacy of this period centered on the Agency for Child Development (ACD). In 1969, Mayor Lindsay appointed the noted African American social worker Georgia L. McMurray to head the newly created Early Childhood Task Force (Carney Smith 1996). Along with child development experts, the task force included a number of prominent feminists from the civil rights movement, including child care activist and cofounder of the feminist *Ms.* magazine Dorothy Pitman Hughes (Love 2006). The task force recommended the creation of an agency to deal exclusively with children's services, focusing particularly on the needs of preschool children and their families, and in 1971 the ACD was founded, with McMurray appointed its first commissioner. Under McMurray's leadership, New York City went from serving fifteen thousand children in 260 day care centers in 1969 to forty-five thousand children in well over 300 centers some five years later (Carney Smith 1996, 461).

With input from the city's day care movement, the ACD introduced a number of pioneering reforms, including ten-hour-a-day child care services to meet the needs of parents working nonstandard hours—although the more radical demand of "around-the-clock" day-and-night care, supported by McMurray, was deemed too costly by the city (Carney Smith 1996, 461). The ACD also established public outreach programs to encourage immigrant and non-English-speaking communities to place their children in the city's high-quality day cares, contributing to expanding enrollment in the public system (Interview 14). In addition, the ACD introduced citywide counseling resource centers for parents—to provide child care information and advice—and expanded the number of home-based day care programs to serve the needs of families in underserved neighborhoods. Finally, as a step on the path toward universality, McMurray established a number of state-subsidized child care programs for working- and middle-class families that could afford to pay a portion of program operating costs (Carney Smith 1996, 461).

While the day care movement welcomed these reforms, activists pushed McMurray and her agency to fulfill their vision of universal child care (Interview 14). From 1969 to 1971, a coalition of feminists, early childhood advocates, and labor and civil rights leaders had worked with Congress to legislate universal child care policy that would have provided cities with substantial funding to set up child care centers open to all on a sliding fee scale and provide nutrition and medical services in addition to high-quality care for young children (Vogtman 2017, 13). Their efforts came to a halt when President Nixon vetoed the Comprehensive Child Development Act of 1971 on the grounds that it would, in his words, "commit the vast moral authority of the National Government to the side of communal approaches to child rearing" (quoted in Polakow 2007, 9).

The makeup of the national child care coalition was mirrored in New York, as organizations such as the Day Care Forum and the Committee for Community Controlled Day Care—harking back to the days of the UPA—demanded a universal, publicly funded, high-quality child care system, even if the federal government refused to fund one (Interview 14).[11] New York's day care movement sought to build on the city's tradition of child care exceptionalism, but, in the absence of a significant increase in state and federal funding, city hall claimed activists' vision of universal child care was simply too costly to realize (Interview 14). New York was already on the hook for a substantial portion of the welfare and Medicaid costs that had risen rapidly in the 1960s and early 1970s (Boris and Klein 2015).

The tensions between the city and the day care movement came to a head when the ACD sought to impose new child care eligibility requirements handed down from the state. Against the backdrop of President Nixon's veto and federal efforts to more closely tie child care funding to welfare-to-work initiatives, these new regulations were designed to restrict access to the city's publicly funded day cares to the poorest of the poor. Furthermore, the ACD required program directors to behave like welfare caseworkers, recording the details of their clients' lives, including marital status, income, health, and their "addictive habits" (Feigelson 1973). Both parents and day care directors found the new procedures "outrageous and demeaning" (Feigelson 1973, 41). Sixty day care centers, all members of a coalition called the Committee for Community Controlled Day Care (CCCDC), refused to comply with the new regulations. In response, the ACD threatened to withhold funding, and the CCCDC duly replied by taking the city to court, claiming the agency was violating the terms of its contract (Feigelson 1973).

At stake in this fight were competing visions of New York City's child care system. McMurray, the respected child care advocate and feminist, was presumably sympathetic to the idea of universality. However, she was no longer an advocate; she was now a city commissioner accountable to the mayor and ultimately to the state, which held the ACD's purse strings. As federal child care funding—administered by the state—had grown during the 1960s, it had come to account for 75 percent of the city's total child care pot, with the city and state each contributing half of the remaining 25 percent (Lacks 1971). Federal funds were dispensed under Title 4A of the Social Security Act, which defined day care as a social service for which parents must be "income eligible." To their credit, McMurray and Mayor Lindsay had lobbied the state to relax the new regulations, but to no avail (Lacks 1971). With limited funds at the ACD's disposal, McMurray argued that the city's priority had to be on serving the neediest families (Feigelson 1973, 42).

On the other side were the CCCDC and the Day Care Forum, both driven by a vision of a universal child care. In keeping with this vision, community-controlled day care programs, of which there were seventy-five in the city (out of a total of two hundred publicly funded day cares), had been enrolling children based on a loose definition of "community need." These programs, run by parents but funded by the city, did not require families to disclose their earnings, "considering such questions an invasion of privacy and a means of reinforcing class distinctions" (Lacks 1971, 11). As Bob Gangi, a coordinator of the CCCDC, said, "When a parent tells us they need day care for their children . . . we take their word. It's not our province to dictate what families have a right to day care" (quoted in Lacks 1971, 11). For the city's day care movement, the CCCD's programs were the building blocks of a municipal, universal child care system and vehicles for fostering social solidarity across class, ethnic, and racial boundaries.

The push for community control in child care services had challenged the old system in which established nonprofit agencies, such as the YWCA, operated the city's publicly funded day care centers. As African Americans and Latinos organized to have a say over social services, most notably public education, the old system was giving way to "newer organizations that were emerging from low-income communities, communities of color, coming together to provide child care as the system expanded" (Interview 14). The CCCDC opposed New York State's new child care regulations and resented the city for adhering to them, on the grounds that low-income eligibility cutoffs effectively excluded middle-income families from public day care, cut existing programs that were economically and racially integrated, and rendered child care services a "holding operation for the very poor" (Lacks 1971). Shirley Johnson, a prominent African American child care activist, summed up the day care movement's egalitarian vision:

> We think everyone should be allowed to put his or her kids in day care. If you want to leave your kid to go downtown to look in Macy's window you should be able to . . . I know lots of women got off welfare because day care allowed them to work. Not made them. Allowed them. But I don't believe a day care center should be a welfare center. That would change our whole movement. That's what's at stake in

our fight with the city. We want the classes to come together. . . . That's why we're having so many problems. [Day care] is good for me and the lady down the street whose husband makes $15,000, or even $25,000, and that lady she goes and has tea—like some people still do that you know—it's good for us all to talk together. And our kids talk together. If you got kids together in day care really sharing, you got okay kids. And then you got an okay society (quoted in Feigelson 1973, 41).

Day care activists like Johnson were incensed that Georgia McMurray, whom they considered an ally, had threatened to defund their programs for failing to comply with regulations she herself had opposed. One activist said she felt "betrayed" by the commissioner: "I'd always thought of her as a friend. . . . She had always seemed to support us. What was she doing? How could she smash us in such a personal way?" (quoted in Feigelson 1973, 42).

As the battle between the CCCDC and the city dragged on, only thirteen of the original sixty day cares refusing to go along with the regulations held out. The CCCDC staged a demonstration on the city's Triborough Bridge, temporarily tying up traffic and later set up a one-day "model day care center" on the lawn of city hall (Feigelson 1973). At a press conference, an impassioned Dorothy Pitman Hughes, who had sat on the task force that led to the ACD's creation, said the state and city's policies were tantamount to creating day care "concentration camps for minority children" (quoted in Feigelson 1973, 42).

Despite the protests and fiery rhetoric, the CCCDC and its coalition of community-controlled day cares, unable to operate without ACD funding, ultimately lost their battle with the city. The ACD forced all publicly funded day cares, including community-controlled programs, to fall in line with the new state regulations. As with the left-wing day care activists of the late 1950s, the dream of a universal child care system in New York City had been crushed. According to the CCCDC's Bob Gangi, the ACD's tough stance was evidence that New York—like the nation—"had swung to the right" (quoted in Feigelson 1973, 42). The likes of Gangi could not foresee that the political climate would become even more hostile to those who envisioned a city built around collective responsibility for social reproduction and more democratic and egalitarian ways of organizing care.

Child Care, Fiscal Crisis, and New York's Neoliberal Turn

Throughout the 1960s and early 1970s, progressive social movements in New York made numerous claims on local government. Alongside other movements, the struggles of working-class women, particularly poor women of color—whether through the welfare rights movement, the day care movement, or women-dominated unions like Local 205 Day Care Employees—pushed the city to expand social welfare programs and underwrite more of the costs of social reproduction. As with the postwar fight to save public child care, the social organization of care work had emerged as a key site of contestation within the urban welfare regime.

With the rollout of the federal government's Great Society and War on Poverty programs, the rapid expansion of social services, and open admissions in the municipal university system, New York's urban social democracy had reached its apex. Over a period of a decade, the city government had dramatically increased its spending on welfare, child care, health care, education, and the municipal payroll (Moody 2007). Nationally, these programs had come to make up the largest portion of big-city budgets (M. Katz 2012). But as politics took a turn to the right—and as the day care movement's fight for universal child care had clearly demonstrated—the project of building a social democratic "welfare state in one city" was pushing up against serious political constraints. In microcosm, New York City illustrated the heightening contradictions of the Fordist-Keynesian order, pitting the needs of capital against popular demands for more progressive forms of social reproduction.

The fiscal crisis of 1975–77 marked a turning point in the history of postwar New York and the urban politics of social reproduction. As David Harvey remarks, in the early 1970s New York City was "heading towards becoming a social democratic, almost socialist, kind of municipality. The big businesses were terrified politically. So they launched a financial coup against the city. . . . New York City had to be disciplined into a new kind of economic future" (Harvey 2007, 8). In the midst of the fiscal crisis, governance of the city was effectively transferred from democratically elected politicians to state-appointed technocrats and financial elites insulated from popular pressures (Phillips-Fein 2017). According to Harvey, the terms on which the crisis was resolved "pioneered the way for neoliberal practices both domestically under Reagan and internationally through the IMF in the 1980s" (Harvey 2005, 48). In other words, New York City was the staging ground of a global neoliberal counterrevolution.

While the causes of the crisis are complex, economic elites and conservative politicians blamed the city's fiscal woes on its extensive welfare state, the "dependent" (i.e., nonwhite) poor whom it benefited, and "greedy" public-sector unions, whose members delivered a range of municipal services (Freeman 2000; Phillips-Fein 2017; Tabb 1982).[12] When the city needed loans to meet its debt obligations, Wall Street bankers refused to continue lending unless New

York curtailed some of its "generous" social policies and generally restructure its welfare, state offloading costs of social reproduction onto households and communities. When John Lindsay's successor as mayor, Abe Beame, bypassed Wall Street and went to the White House to ask for federal financial aid, President Gerald Ford refused (Harvey 2005, 46). Ford offered "as support for his decision the data on supposed welfare frauds that had become common fodder in the city's political discourse" (Kornbluh 2007, 181).

The federal government, the state, and Wall Street demanded austerity and a reorientation of the role of municipal government in return for bailing out the city (Harvey 2005; Phillips-Fein 2017). Treasury Secretary William Simon declared that federal aid to New York ought to be "on terms so punitive, the overall experience made so painful, that no city, no political subdivision would ever be tempted to go down the same road" (quoted in Freeman 2000, 259). The primary role of city government was no longer to be looking after the needs and well-being of the population at large but creating a "good business climate" (Harvey 2007, 9). Tuition was charged for the first time in the city's university system, user fees were introduced for previously free public services while other services were privatized outright, fire stations were closed, social welfare spending was significantly curtailed, public sector wages were frozen, and city employees were laid off en masse (Freeman 2000; Phillips-Fein 2017). Poor women on welfare were subject to increasingly punitive reforms, and new eligibility restrictions were enforced by the city's welfare bureaucracy (Kornbluh 2017). As for the day care programs many poor and working-class families had come to rely on, they were first among the city services targeted for cuts.

DAY CARE DEFAULT

At the onset of the crisis, New York State froze $23.8 million in child care funding to the city (*New York Times* 1975). State administrators charged the ACD with falling behind on its licensing regulations and health and safety standards. But the primary source of tension between city and state was the gradual expansion of day care services to include a growing number of children from working-class families, whose incomes exceeded subsidy eligibility limits under the federal Social Security Act—the main source of child care funding. While the income eligibility ceilings had been raised in the early 1970s, some publicly funded centers had begun to operate using even higher income thresholds, leading to expanding enrollments and rising municipal day care costs (*New York Times* 1975, 24). Although the fight between the ACD and the Committee for Community Controlled Day Care demonstrated that the city had reined in this practice, in the midst of the fiscal crisis the state pushed for drastic action, instructing the ACD to phase all non-eligible children out of the system by attrition (Weisman 1975). The *New York Times* called it a "day-care default" and "a blow to a city desperately in need of more and speedier state and Federal assistance for a wide range of services" (*New York Times* 1975, 24).

The ACD commissioner, Georgia McMurray, was criticized for her "mishandling" of the agency's finances (Weisman 1975, 1). Of course, this "mishandling" was really McMurray's willingness, at least for a time, to heed day care activists' call to expand the city's public child care system beyond the narrow parameters set by the state and federal government. In the midst of the fiscal crisis, state and federal child care funding, as with other social services, became conditional on the city imposing austerity measures. This forced the ACD to roll back the expansion of public child care and further contain the ambitious agendas of the CCCDC, the Day Care Forum, and Local 205, the day care workers' union.

Austerity measures would severely impact New York's child care sector and the ability of poor and working-class families, particularly single mothers, to meet their child care needs. For instance, the ACD reported a "rising fear by many day care mothers that they would be forced to return to welfare rolls for lack of an alternative [to child care]" or turn to care by relatives or neighbors (*New York Times* 1976a, 33). Other women said they would scale back their work hours from full-time to part-time in order to stay home with their children (Sheppard 1976a, 35). In desperation, McMurray and the city's day care movement made the case that cutting child care funding ran counter to the other major plank in the austerity agenda: slashing the city's welfare rolls (Sheppard 1976a). Their argument was ultimately ignored, and, as the fiscal crisis escalated, further efforts were made to restructure the city's child care system along neoliberal lines and privatize responsibility for care.

In September 1975, the state legislature enacted "emergency" arrangements for governing the city that effectively weakened the power of the mayor and city council. Control of city finances shifted from city hall and the mayor's office to a new state agency known as the Emergency Financial Control Board (EFCB). The EFCB's seven-member board included the governor and comptroller of New York State, the mayor and comptroller of the city, and three corporate executives (there was no labor representative or representatives from the city's largely poor and working-class black and Latino communities). The EFCB was "empowered to order the city to reduce its spending, to evaluate and audit the city's records, and to override labor contracts agreed to by the city's elected officials" (Phillips-Fein 2017, 152–53).

With city finances now under the control of the EFCB, the cuts came fast and furious and had an immediate impact on social services. By late 1975, the ACD's $159 million budget was cut by 20 percent, or $31 million, forcing the city to close twenty-eight day care programs (Maitland 1975, 18). New subsidy eligibility limits eliminated seventy-two hundred children from the city's day care programs, rolling back the gains made by the community control movement (Maitland 1975, 18).[13] A mayor-appointed special task force on child care—the first since the Lindsay administration's Early Childhood Task Force—was tasked with "cutting waste" in the system and transferring responsibility for determining eligibility for subsidies from local day care programs to a newly disciplined ACD (Maitland 1975).

In addition, rather than adopting administrative measures that would ensure the full use of existing day care spaces, programs running under capacity had their funding cut or were threatened with closure. According to members of the special task force, these measures were enacted in the name of "efficiency" and aimed to "address mismanagement" and "improve productivity" (Sheppard 1976b, 27). The city's extended-day (ten-hour) child care programs, one of the most progressive reforms of the early 1970s, were eliminated. Furthermore, the state introduced parental co-payments for families now deemed ineligible for free child care, effectively imposing user fees and further shifting the costs of care onto households (*New York Times* 1976a, 32).

ERODING QUALITY CARE AND QUALITY CARE WORK

By the spring of 1976, the city had closed another forty-nine day care centers that served close to three thousand children. Seventy-five percent of these children were transferred to "underutilized" day cares, resulting in severe overcrowding (Kihss 1976a). These measures undermined the high standards the day care movement had long fought to establish, threatening New York's child care exceptionalism. The closures also meant that close to fifteen hundred unionized day care workers, members of Local 205, lost their jobs (Kihss 1976a).

An audit by the city's comptroller concluded that day cares were "required to have too many employees with overly high qualifications" (quoted in Kihss 1976b). ACD subsequently increased staff-child ratios, impacting both working conditions and the quality of care provided. Furthermore, the audit quoted research reports that found that high qualifications and low staff-child ratios had "little impact" on care quality and openly questioned ACD's adoption of professional qualifications for program directors and child care providers that exceeded those of New York State (and most other state) requirements (Kihss 1976b). Austerity in child care was taking the form of cuts to services, erosion of program quality, and an attack on day care workers, eliminating jobs and undermining wages and working conditions, while questioning child care providers' skills and professional status.

Day care activists and Local 205 organized to resist this agenda (Interview 14). In May 1976, just over one thousand angry day care workers, activists, and parents—children in tow—took to the streets and marched on the headquarters of the Emergency Financial Control Board to demand it stop what activists called "the hatchet job on the day care program" (quoted in New York Times 1976b, 40). Two months later, an even larger crowd of around four thousand marched near city hall in defense of child care services, chanting slogans such as "We want day care! No more welfare!" (Phillips-Fein 2017, 206). Energized by the turnout, Local 205 and the Day Care Forum worked to bring together child care activists, providers, parents, and unions to fight the cuts and lobby the state government in Albany (Interview 14). They framed their struggle around the common interest of ensuring that children had access to good quality care, which required protecting the city's traditional commitment to high standards and tough regulations. As one activist involved in the Day Care Forum put it, "The union's vested interest was they didn't want their members to lose their jobs. The Forum was very focused on parents losing access to subsidies. The Day Care Council of New York, representing the boards of directors, was concerned with the agencies losing resources to provide the services in their communities. So, while each organization had something they were concerned about, they all agreed that they would be stronger working together. The union would bring its political clout, the Forum its ability to organize parents and low-income communities, and the Council its ability to interface with the 350 or so program sponsors to get them behind whatever efforts were going on" (Interview 14).

The most powerful of the coalition's three partners appeared to be organized labor. Despite the fiscal crisis, New York's municipal unions had made some headway in the child care sector. In 1976, DC 1707 organized and chartered Local 95, a union of child care providers—primarily women of color—employed in agencies of Head Start, a federally funded early childhood education program with origins in the War on Poverty (DC 1707, 2012). Union power in the sector expanded further when the Council of School Supervisors and Administrators, the union representing principals and vice principals in New York's public school system, organized directors and co-directors in the city's publicly funded day care centers (CSA 2012).

Yet these successes were countered by union trade-offs with city hall and the political elite overseeing New York's exit from financial ruin. One condition of federal aid to the city was a guarantee that municipal unions agree to no increases in wages or benefits. In return, state legislation granted municipal unions an agency shop, guaranteeing a regular flow of dues (Moody 2007, 47). Municipal union leaders had also been convinced to invest their members' pension money in city debt in return for some say—very limited compared to that of the city's financial elite—over New York's future (Freeman 2000, 269). This decision effectively locked the city's powerful municipal unions into the logic of austerity: either moderate their demands or lose their pension funds through municipal bankruptcy (Harvey 2005, 45). While city unions had initially organized large demonstrations against the banks and the EFCB and even hinted at a general strike, they ultimately fell in line with the program of austerity and welfare state retrenchment (Freeman 2000).

The weakness of the city's municipal unions, illustrative for Local 205 in particular, was demonstrated in the tepid response to state changes to child care funding arrangements. Two years into the crisis, New York State withheld federal child care dollars from the city until it developed its family day care sector—that is, unlicensed, untrained, and dramatically underpaid nonunion care providers, who required less state funding than center-based programs. In addition, the ACD had to agree to contract with private, for-profit day care operators (*New York Times* 1977, 43). Overall, these changes allowed public funds to escape the unionized municipal child care system for for-profit day care chains and nonunion home child care providers. As part of a municipal labor movement on the defensive, Local 205 did little to resist these changes. In addition to service cuts, day care closures, staff layoffs, and erosion in standards, the city's child care system was being increasingly deregulated and privatized.

FROM THE "BEST LEGACY WE HAVE" TO NEOLIBERAL NORMAL

By 1979, New York City's day care programs had adjusted to neoliberal austerity, learning to "do more with less." Georgia McMurray's successor at the Agency for Child Development, Lewis Frankfort, said the city's child care system had undergone a metamorphosis that "it was ill prepared for when the fiscal crisis first struck" (quoted in Brozan 1979). While Frankfort called New York's public day cares "the best legacy we have of the 1960s Great Society," the state and the EFCB continued to impose retrenchment in social provision and cuts to standards. While some federal funds had become available for child care, enrollment had only recovered to 1974 levels, and inflation ate up much of the new funding (Brozan 1979).

The impact of neoliberal restructuring on the city's child care system was clear: in addition to outright closures, twenty day care centers that lost their funding in 1976 were three years later receiving a two-year start-up grant from the state to "demonstrate economic alternatives to publicly funded day care" (Brozan 1979). In other words, public funding had become increasingly premised on the privatization of service delivery. Furthermore, subsidy eligibility ceilings remained low, and, while some money for training had bolstered the child care workforce, staffing cuts had not been reversed. These cuts intensified the workload of day care workers and eroded child care quality. As one program director explained, "[Child care] aides have been cut from working 38 hours a week to 20, so instead of having three adults per classroom, we have two and a half" (quoted in Brozan 1979). And like those of all municipal employees, the wages of city day care workers did not grow in either nominal or real terms during this period (Moody 2007, 81).

In the midst of austerity, the victories of the child care movement were defensive ones. As one advocate put it, "We were successful in staving off a number of cuts; they weren't as bad or as draconian as they would have been if there was no action at all" (Interview 14). There were some important victories: for instance, the city committed to contribute more of its own tax dollars for child care to complement federal and state funds—essentially a modest renewal of funding arrangements won by child care activists after the war. Through groups like the Day Care Forum, activists and advocates had been successful in beating back a wholesale withdrawal of municipal support for child care services (Interview 14).

Beyond public child care, the neoliberal discipline imposed on New York's urban social democracy had overwhelmed the political forces of the left (Freeman 2000; Moody 2007). With the federal government steadily withdrawing aid from big cities, cuts were imposed on a range of municipal services, and the city's public-sector unions were weakened as a result. Cuts impacted the municipal university system, the city's public hospitals and public housing, and the provision of other key social services, including home care (Moody 2007). In terms of the municipal payroll, the city's public workforce shrank by 69,672 (Phillips-Fein 2017, 207). Across the spectrum of city services, cuts disproportionately affected workers of color, who in the wake of civil rights legislation and the expansion of public-sector employment in the Great Society years had found municipal jobs to be powerful vehicles for economic mobility (M. Katz 2012). According to one account, two-fifths of African American municipal employees and half of Latino employees were dropped from the city payroll (Kornbluh 2007, 182).

In 1975, Beulah Sanders—a tenacious community organizer and leader in the welfare rights movement—had led the city's International Women's Day march, demanding that child care be available twenty-four hours a day, regardless of a family's income (Kornbluh 2007, 182). Five years later, in the context of austerity, a weakened welfare rights movement, and a day care movement on the defensive, Sanders's vision seemed little more than a pipe dream. The city's fiscal crisis had afforded New York's political and business elite the opportunity to roll back the gains of popular struggle, restructure the urban welfare regime, and neutralize the power of once mighty public-sector unions.

The ramifications of the city's restructuring went far beyond the five boroughs. As Piven has argued, "New York City was only the exemplary case, the means that was used to instruct poor and working-class groups in other cities not to resist similar and even more drastic cost-cutting campaigns by local elites" (Piven 2011, 159). Elites sought to retake urban space for the purposes of capital accumulation and reassert control over municipal government, for it was at the local level that popular struggles by poor and working-class people had forced concessions in the 1960s and early 1970s (Piven 2011, 160).

With the presidential election of Ronald Reagan in 1980, the neoliberal project begun in New York was scaled up to the national stage, with deleterious consequences for the city's poor and working-class people. Through the day care movement, welfare rights struggles, and care workers' unions, the city's poor and working-class women had asserted the value of their care work and mobilized to demand state investment in social reproduction with some success. Through retrenchment, deregulation, and the increasing marketization of social welfare, the neoliberal restructuring of New York had reprivatized costs of social reproduction and responsibilities for it, shifting them back onto households and communities, especially the women within them.

Federal State Restructuring and Child Care and Welfare in New York

With New York City as neoliberal test case, Reagan's presidency marked the beginning of a full-scale assault on the Keynesian welfare state (Piven and Cloward 1985; Block et al. 1987). Reagan attacked organized labor, cut taxes for the wealthy, deregulated labor markets, eliminated environmental controls, and made significant cuts to federal funding for cities, limiting the scope of services they could provide to urban populations (Katz 2008).[14] Social supports for the poor diminished significantly throughout the 1980s as the federal government slashed income support programs and cut funding for social services.[15]

While pursuing policies that negatively impacted all poor and working-class families, Reagan mobilized white racial backlash against the urban poor—racially coded as black—to win popular support for privatizing care and redistributing income and wealth upward (Briggs 2017). As Laura Briggs has noted, Reagan was particularly fond of telling the story of a Chicago-area "welfare queen" who drove a pink Cadillac and bilked hardworking taxpayers by using multiple names and addresses to collect food stamps, Social Security, and AFDC (Briggs 2017, 51). As feminist scholar Wahneema Lubiano has pointed out, the administration employed this racist and sexist trope as a "cover story" for reducing government provision for social reproduction in general, cutting vital supports for households and communities (quoted in Briggs 2017, 50).

Neoliberal restructuring at the national scale began in earnest with the Omnibus Budget Reconciliation Act (OBRA) of 1981, "probably the most significant piece of social legislation since the Great Society" (Boris and Klein 2015, 152). The act restricted eligibility for welfare, cut benefit levels, and reduced funding for a range of social services. It also marked a significant shift in urban policy as the federal government dramatically withdrew support from cities, ending a federal aid program that provided more than half the money for some municipal budgets (Katz 2008). Furthermore, in place of matching state expenditures, after an across-the-board cut of 22 percent, the OBRA capped federal funding for social programs and introduced block grants, giving states the means to displace social welfare programs run by big cities.[16] Lastly, the act placed the funding of community services directly under state governments, reversing a key legacy of the Great Society and War on Poverty in which the federal government bypassed states to directly fund urban antipoverty initiatives (Piven and Cloward 1985).

As Boris and Klein remark, the OBRA "blindsided big cities and rebuffed their recently mobilized constituencies of African Americans, Latinos, poor people, feminists, and public employees." Under the new funding arrangements, states had to choose which social services to reduce or eliminate, and administrators shifted costs to users through increased fees and eligibility restrictions until programs served only the poorest of the poor (Boris and Klein 2015, 152). By the end of Reagan's second term in office, federal assistance to cities had been slashed by 60 percent, starving municipal governments of the revenue needed to provide even the most basic social services. These cuts had a disastrous effect on older industrial cities especially; with their high levels of racialized poverty and limited property tax bases, many depended on federal aid to provide services. Schools and libraries, municipal hospitals and day care centers, and sanitation, police, and fire departments "were forced to shut their doors" (Dreier 2011).

It is important to note the degree to which neoliberal restructuring was engineered through state rescaling. The Reagan administration downloaded the costs of and responsibilities for key aspects of social reproduction from the federal to state and local governments. In turn, state and local governments cut social spending and welfare services and shifted costs of social reproduction to families/households and communities. For poor and working-class women, this restructuring meant less state support for their social reproductive labor—whether the unpaid work of care in the household and community or as workers in the urban welfare state providing services such as education, health care, and child care (Abramovitz 2010).

NEW YORK CITY CHILD CARE UNDER REAGAN

The impact of the OBRA on New York City's public child care system was far-reaching. New York's public day care programs lowered their nutritional standards for children's meals, raised parents' co-payments, and further reduced the income level at which families qualified for child care subsidy (*New York Times* 1982). At the time, in 1981, the city was serving forty-three thousand children from low-income families—down from forty-five thousand in 1975—70 percent of whom were near or below the poverty level. Over seven thousand families were on the waiting list for subsidized care, and that number would grow steadily throughout the 1980s (CCI 1990). More and more of New York's low-income families had to rely on exclusively private means to meet their child care needs.

In addition to funding cuts, the Reagan administration sought to use public dollars to expand the private child care market, privatizing social services by marketizing their delivery. To this end, the federal government passed legislation permitting states to use federal funds for child care voucher programs (Interview 4).[17] Federal regulations governing social service provision had previously mandated that states spend federal dollars on either government-operated day care centers or contracts for child care spaces with nonprofit community agencies. In the name of "parental choice," federal policy makers ended these restrictions and encouraged states to expand what were previously small voucher programs. The move reflected the neoliberal emphasis on deregulation, privatization, and "consumer choice," profoundly altering public financing for child care (Meyers 1990). Privatization was accompanied by a reduction in child care standards, monitoring, and enforcement, as for-profit child care chains mushroomed (Meyers 1990, 562–67; Whitebook 2001, 23).

In New York City, these changes had their intended effect. In 1984, the Agency for Child Development introduced child care vouchers for low-income families for the first time, citing the agency's desire to make subsidized care available in neighborhoods with few or no city-run day care programs and to maintain service levels in the face of budget constraints (Interview 4). For the city, vouchers were one way of containing both capital and labor costs. Public dollars would increasingly be channeled away from the city's unionized, center-based child care programs and toward for-profit day cares and a growing number of home-based child care providers, both lightly regulated family day cares and informal child care provided by family, friends, and neighbors (Interview 4). While the number of vouchers offered by the city was initially small, ranging from one thousand to fifteen hundred annually, it marked an important shift in how the city dealt with rising demand for child care (McCall 1997). The new emphasis on vouchers stood to erode the city's public child care infrastructure forged in the New Deal, saved after the war, and expanded during the 1960s and early 1970s.

However diminished, New York City's public day care centers did weather Reagan's antiurban, antipoor agenda. While voucher use expanded as a percentage of overall subsidies, New York, unlike other cities, continued to contract with nonprofit agencies for the provision of child care services. In the few big cities that had managed to hang on to their New Deal and wartime day nurseries and expand quality center-based child care services under the auspices of the Great Society and War on Poverty, the federal government's neoliberal turn to vouchers marked the end of this model of service delivery (Interview 14). While battered by years of cuts, New York's unionized day care centers now stood almost alone in the country.

CHILD CARE AND THE FAMILY SUPPORT ACT

Throughout his time in the White House, Reagan employed race-coded euphemisms regarding "welfare dependency" and the "urban underclass," promising to restore the "work ethic" to the poor. As was the case throughout the program's history, the majority of women and children on welfare remained white, and caseloads had declined significantly since the early 1970s (Mink 2002). Nevertheless, politicians looking to endear themselves to southern white voters and so-called Reagan Democrats in the North were not satisfied with the draconian OBRA, and in 1988 Congress passed what was arguably the most important welfare legislation since the Social Security Act of 1935 (M. Katz 2008, 57). The product of a compromise between conservatives and moderates, including rightward-drifting Democrats, the Family Support Act (FSA) transformed welfare from an income maintenance program designed to help single mothers stay home to care for their children into a mandatory work program designed to channel poor women into the low-wage labor market (Rose 1990).

The FSA expanded federal requirements for states to shift their welfare caseloads into work-related programming and increased obligations on welfare recipients to work in subsidized and unsubsidized jobs, enter job training, or enroll in school (Peck 2001, 97). The legislation also increased state discretion in the design of welfare-to-work programs, provided they met federally set participation rates of 7 percent of their welfare caseload by 1991 and 20 percent by 1996 (S. Collins and Goldberg 2004). States were threatened with funding cuts for failing to meet these aggressive targets, and in states where counties and municipalities had always maintained a significant degree of autonomy in program design and delivery, including New York, cities were given more room to experiment with workfare programming, intensifying state involvement in the lives of poor women (Krinsky 2007a).

The FSA also marked a shift in the definition of employability for poor mothers. Work-related activities were made *mandatory* for welfare recipients whose youngest children were three years of age or older.[18] However, the federal government gave states the option to include mothers with children as young as twelve months (Naples 1991). In addition, all teenage parents were required to participate in a "learnfare" component regardless of the age of their children. Abrogating the right of many poor mothers to care for their own children, the legislation revisited the paradox of cost-cutting welfare reforms that required public investment in child care to be successful (Levy and Michel 2002).

To meet rising demand for child care services, the FSA required states to provide subsidy for up to one year for families transitioning from welfare to paid work, known as transitional child care (TCC). In addition, states were required to guarantee child care to welfare mothers participating in training or education programs approved by the state under another federal program, called AFDC–Child Care (Levy and Michel 2002). Under both programs states were authorized to operate their own day care programs or issue grants and contracts with for-profit and nonprofit child care providers. But in keeping with the reforms of the OBRA and increasing marketization of child care services, states were also authorized to provide parents with vouchers or even cash for child care (Besharov and Samari 2001, 196).

Despite these policies, a significant increase in federal child care funding was not forthcoming, and by 1990 the TCC and AFDC–Child Care programs were so limited that the implementation of the FSA was at a standstill in many states (Levy and Michel 2002). As historians Denise Levy and Sonya Michel put it, "The very political forces that were intent on reducing welfare rolls were also opposed to expanding government services like child care" (2002, 256). As a result, local welfare bureaucracies exempted many welfare recipients with children younger than school age from welfare to work. A growing number of participants were placed on child care waiting lists (Levy and Michel 2002).

The lack of federal funding for the FSA meant that only a small fraction of welfare mothers actually participated in locally administered workfare programs (M. Katz 2008, 75). However, the failure to adequately fund child care should not be understood as a failure of welfare reform. If the goal was to reduce the welfare rolls and discipline poor mothers into the low-wage labor market, the FSA was a success (Reese 2005). As benefits became stingier and states were emboldened to make life on welfare more difficult, workfare participants and welfare leavers were often reliant on family, friends, and neighbors for the care of their children (Levy and Michel 2002, 244).

Despite the child care rhetoric that accompanied the FSA, almost all of the increases in federal child care spending during the Reagan administration went to middle- and upper-income families (Michel 2004). Forms of indirect support to these families in the form of tax incentives and deductions increased, stimulating the growth of for-profit child care across the country (Michel 2004, 156). In contrast, by the end of the decade, only 18 percent of low-income families used child care centers or preschools, with home-based child care the primary option for the poor (Levy and Michel 2002). This meant a large percentage of poor children were in minimally regulated or unregulated home settings and without the educational and developmental care that middle- and upper-class families could purchase at accredited preschools and child care centers.

MANDATING MARKETIZATION AND THE RISE OF "PARENTAL CHOICE"

Despite the shift toward workfare, the Family Support Act did not have the drastic impact on the welfare rolls that policy makers had anticipated (Quadagno 1994). For many, the law's failure to move welfare mothers into paid work demonstrated that "successful" welfare reform had to include significant levels of public investment in child care. Without this key employment support in place, many policy makers argued, any attempt at far-reaching welfare reform was doomed to failure (Levy and Michel 2002).

With this in mind, in 1990 Congress passed the Child Care and Development Block Grant (CCDBG) Act, allocating $825 million to individual states for child care services (Michel 2004). While child care advocates had high hopes for the legislation, it did little to reverse the funding cuts of the 1980s (Michel 2004, 156).[19] In addition, the act meant further deregulation and marketization of public child care. Under the block grant, a portion of child care dollars transferred to the states had to be made available to parents in the form of vouchers (Besharov and Samari 2001, 196). Unlike under the Family Support Act, in which states were *authorized* to provide child care vouchers, under the CCDBG the federal government made vouchers mandatory.

In essence, the CCDBG Act marked the deregulation and privatization of local and state child care programs from above. By the late 1980s, fewer and fewer states and cities could offer poor families the option of child care in a nonprofit, regulated, center-based setting. Informal child care and family day care had become the default "choice" for many poor families (Levy and Michel 2002). And while the portion of funds subject to these new regulations was initially small, by 1997 nearly half of all federal child care dollars fell under the "parental choice" requirement (Besharov and Samari 2001).

These changes also had an impact on the child care workforce. As researcher Marcy Whitebook has pointed out, with voucherization public dollars once the exclusive domain of better-paying nonprofit or government-operated center-based programs "were now diffused across all sectors of the industry, fueling expansion not only of child care services but [also] of lower-paying child care jobs" (Whitebook 2001, 26). With this shift, the proportion of women of color caring for and educating young children increased (Whitebook 2001; see also Duffy 2011, 97–100). These providers tended to be concentrated in urban neighborhoods where the need and demand for subsidized child care was most acute. Child care activists and advocates began to think through how best to provide training and support services to this growing sector of the child care workforce (Whitebook 2001, 23).

For the conservative policy makers and neoliberal think tanks pushing these measures, the CCDBG Act marked a significant victory. In the words of researchers affiliated with the free-market American Enterprise Institute, the legislation marked "the end of government instructing parents on how to care for their children" (Besharov and Samari 2001, 217).[20] In reality, the CCDBG

Act left poor families with few choices in a child care market dominated by expensive accredited preschools and day care centers at the high end, and unlicensed, untrained, and vastly underpaid home-based providers at the other.

THE CCDBG IN NEW YORK CITY

The impact of the CCDBG Act in New York was significant. The number of child care vouchers issued by the Agency for Child Development grew from between 1,000 and 1,5000 annually from 1984 to 1990 to 12,660 in 1995, just six years after the passage of the law (McCall 1997). Not all of the city's child care advocates were opposed to vouchers. Some argued that vouchers made subsidized child care a reality in poor neighborhoods historically underserved by city-funded day care centers (Interview 14). As urban sociologist Pauline Lipman has persuasively argued, "While the neoliberal discourse that links vouchers to 'choice' is shaped by free-market ideologues and political elites, it is nonetheless materialized on the ground in the wake of the failure of public options to serve poor and working-class communities" (2011, 141). Thus, even for child care advocates and activists committed to high-quality public child care provision, in the context of a municipal child care system weakened by years of cuts, voucherization held a compelling—if neoliberal—logic.

Yet the federal mandate for "parental choice" would contribute to a fundamental reshaping of New York City's child care system, perhaps far beyond what some child care advocates imagined. Up until 1994 ACD had prohibited the use of child care subsidies for informal or "family, friend, and neighbor" care, reflecting its historical commitment to regulated and developmentally appropriate care. However, the agency was forced to change this practice after the passage of the CCDBG Act (Interview 14). Parents could now use vouchers for informal child care, and the city's commitment to high-quality center-based programs, undermined by over a decade of austerity and restructuring, had suffered yet another blow.

From New Deal to Neoliberal New York

Popular struggles over the social organization of care work—as part of broader struggles over social reproduction—profoundly shaped the historical development and character of New York City's postwar welfare regime. From the postwar campaign to save public day nurseries and the efforts of the United Parents Association to the fight for community control and universal child care in the early 1970s, poor and working-class women's activism played a central role in fostering New York City's child care exceptionalism. While the principle of child care as a social right was never fully realized, between 1945 and 1975 these women helped build the largest publicly funded child care system in the nation, one recognized for its commitment to high-quality programming delivered by nonprofit community-based agencies.

By the late 1960s, the women on whose labor this system rested had formed a union and struck for three weeks, part of the wave of public-sector unionism that swept New York in the latter half of the decade. The city's day care workers came to set national standards for wages and working conditions in the child care sector. In its combination of affordable, quality care and decent work, New York's municipal child care regime reflected the city's social democratic political culture.

Like the city's day care workers, the women of the welfare rights movement demanded that their care work be socially recognized and valued, while also insisting on access to child care services and an end to the exploitation of women who worked as professional caregivers. Against the backdrop of nationwide urban unrest, poor women of color claimed a right to welfare on the basis of the work of raising and caring for their children. Their militancy contributed to the liberalization of welfare policy in the late 1960s and early 1970s, as thousands of poor single mothers gained access to the city's welfare rolls.

These social movements—welfare rights, care worker unionism, and the child care movement—were part of broader struggles over social reproduction. From the New Deal to the Great Society, popular struggles shaped the urban politics of social reproduction from below, pushing New York City to underwrite more of the costs of and responsibilities for social production than any other municipality in the United States. Supported by federal funds but also the local tax base, New York's urban social democracy came to include an array of social welfare programs and services. Yet the fiscal crisis of 1975 revealed the escalating contradictions in the urban welfare regime and in Fordist-Keynesian capitalism more broadly. The crisis was seized upon by political and business elites as an opportunity to roll back the gains of popular struggle, contain the power of progressive social movements and municipal unions, and reprivatize social reproduction.

With the election of Ronald Reagan to the presidency, the neoliberal practices pioneered in response to New York's fiscal crisis were elevated to a national scale. As Laura Briggs has said of the neoliberal turn, "Decades of activism to expand the time and resources communities had for reproductive labor had given way to a conservative movement to reduce support for it by privat-izing wealth and care" (2017, 47). As went New York, so went the nation. The Reagan administration drastically cut aid to cities, reduced funding for so-cial welfare programs, and passed welfare reforms that tied benefits to par-ticipation in welfare-to-work programs, while at the same time failing to ad-dress basic issues of social reproduction, including child care. Reflecting the broader neoliberalization of social policy, when the federal government did make limited investments in child care, funding was framed by the discourse of "choice." The voucherization of child care reflected increasing marketiza-tion and privatization of urban social services, cutting labor costs and under-mining the power of public-sector unions. State disinvestment in social repro-duction, including in the city's public child care infrastructure, coincided with the entry of greater numbers of poor and working-class women into the urban labor market, a response not only to shifting gender norms but also to declines in working-class men's wages (the product of deindustrialization and weak-ened unions) and in the real value of welfare benefits. As Collins and Mayer point out, many of the jobs these women entered—in areas such as nursing, home health care, child care, and food and restaurant work—substituted for labor formerly performed at home (Collins and Mayer 2010, xi).

Yet despite more than a decade of neoliberal restructuring, by the early 1990s many of the institutional legacies of New York's social democratic wel-fare state remained, however weakened. Welfare rights struggles had contrib-uted to making public assistance more accessible in New York than in any other locale, and by 1993 the city was home to one in ten of the nation's wel-fare recipients (DeParle 1998). Poor New Yorkers continued to have access to a range of social welfare services and supports not available in other big cities. And whereas most municipal child care systems had withered away—the leg-acy of wartime child care and the 1960s Great Society all but erased—thanks to the strength of New York's child care movement the city's publicly funded day cares had weathered successive rounds of austerity. As for city workers, unions such as Local 205 Day Care Workers, while disadvantaged, remained influential actors in local politics and continued to defend public services and fight to protect the wages and working conditions of their members.

These were the institutional legacies of popular struggle at which the Giu-liani administration would take aim. For the political and economic elites who had driven the neoliberalization of New York, the city's welfare state remained too generous, its poor people too dependent, its taxes too high, and its pub-lic-sector unions too powerful. In an era of urban neoliberalization and the entrepreneurial city, New York was a reminder of politics done differently. As presidential candidate Bill Clinton campaigned on a promise of "ending welfare as we know it," the Republican politician Newt Gingrich said of the Big Apple: "The malignant combination of machine politics, bankrupt welfare statism, and rapacious unionism . . . is contributing to the slow-motion suicide of the world's once greatest city" (Gingrich 1992). Against the backdrop of federal welfare reform, thousands of the city's poor single mothers would soon be called into a punitive workfare program designed to push them to take the meanest work at the meanest wages, heightening the need and demand for child care. As welfare reform escalated the city's already existing child care crisis, the neoliberal push for privatization and a militant anti-unionism would combine as a new mayor sought to provide child care on the cheap.

CHAPTER 3

Restructuring
Welfare Reform and the
Neoliberalization of Child Care, 1994–2005

In the Bronx, a city caseworker searching for licensed babysitters finds only six names in her computer, and all six have let their certification expire. She prints the useless list for a welfare mother with worried eyes and says, "You'll just have to do the best you can." In Brooklyn, a harried caseworker refuses to even hunt for openings, offering her welfare clients an outdated child care directory instead. But of the providers listed in Brownsville, where nearly nine hundred children need care, the only two available centers have room for fifteen. And in Queens, a caseworker nods impatiently as a nervous mother ticks off the twelve places she has called, none of which could watch her baby son. But instead of excusing the mother from workfare, the caseworker leans across his desk and threatens her, slowly and deliberately and in violation of state law. "They're going to reduce your benefits if you can't find anyone," says the worker, Anthony Sweeny. "Can you survive on less money? No? Well, you have to find somebody—a neighbor, a friend, somebody. You have 10 days. No more excuses."
—**Rachel Swarns, 1998**

Prior to welfare reform, New York had a shortage of quality, affordable child care. Despite boasting the largest child care system in the country, the supply of quality child care in the city had not kept up with rising demand. Despite the best efforts of welfare rights activists, child care advocates, and day care workers, neoliberal austerity had worked to limit poor and working-class families' access to child care subsidies and put downward pressure on the wages and working conditions of the city's child care workforce and on care quality. The steady erosion of "the best legacy New York had of the 1960s"—to recall the words of former ACD commissioner Lewis Frankfort—had also undermined experiments with round-the-clock and extended-day child care services, which, with more women working nonstandard hours and irregular schedules, had become a necessity for many families. In short, as one of New

York's leading child care advocates put it, "long before welfare reform, this city had a child care crisis" (Interview 4).

As welfare reform dramatically increased the need and demand for child care, escalating the crisis, the city revisited "a classic neoliberal dilemma over welfare-to-work": its failure to adequately fund child care provision threatened to undermine the very transitions into work it sought to encourage (Peck 2001, 251). As thousands of poor mothers entered workfare and the low-wage labor market, the question of who would care for their children was thrust to the forefront of New York City politics. This chapter maps the development and analyzes the impact of the Giuliani and later Bloomberg administrations' policies at the intersection of welfare reform and child care.

"Actually Existing Neoliberalism" in Giuliani's New York

In November 1993, Rudolph "Rudy" Giuliani won New York City's mayoral election, beating the incumbent David Dinkins, a liberal Democrat and the city's first African American mayor. Under the mayoral administrations of Abe Beame (1974–77) and Ed Koch (1978–89), the neoliberal transformation of New York had taken the form of cuts to social spending and basic city services, and, under Koch in particular, subsidizing big business and privatizing public space (Soffer 2012). Dinkins had promised a more socially just city—emphasizing community development, economic opportunity, and racial justice—yet his administration was effectively "disciplined by a resurgence of elite mobilization aimed at safeguarding New York's neoliberalization" (Brash 2011, 31). In the context of this opposition and the recession of the early 1990s, Dinkins adopted an increasingly neoliberal approach to urban governance, freezing the city's corporate tax rate while cutting social services (Vitale 2008, 105). As Alex Vitale has argued, the Dinkins administration failed to provide progressive solutions to social crises wrought by two decades of neoliberalization, including sharp rises in homelessness, street crime, and public disorder (Vitale 2008). Giuliani's electoral success signaled voters' reaction against the perceived failures of urban liberals to resolve these crises and mitigate their impact on the quality of everyday life in the city (Vitale 2008).

Giuliani relied primarily on white electoral support. His electoral coalition consisted of conservatives, disaffected upper- and middle-class Manhattan liberals, and enough outer-borough Jewish voters and white Catholics to secure a narrow victory over Dinkins (Moody 2007, 127–32). The first Republican mayor of the city in over a quarter-century, his campaign had the support of key factions of New York's ruling class, including the backing of powerful corporate and real estate interests, the endorsements of former mayors Ed Koch and Robert Wagner Jr., and the intellectual support of neoliberal think tank the Manhattan Institute (Moody 2007). As the city struggled to recover from the recession, Wall Street's powerful bond rating agencies rewarded the new administration's commitment to austerity (Hackworth 2007, 35).

TRANSFORMING THE URBAN WELFARE REGIME

Politically, the Giuliani administration sought to roll back what remained of New York's Keynesian welfare state, its "urban social democracy," and roll out a punitive, neoliberal workfare state (see Krinsky 2007; Wacquant 2009a; Wacquant 2009b).[1] Many of the administration's interventions in "the social" were introduced under the guise of a campaign to improve the "quality of everyday life" in the city. The Manhattan Institute had promoted "quality of life" as a political concept beginning in the late 1980s as part of its neoliberal approach to urban social problems (Vitale 2008, 43; see also Peck 2010). Following the intellectual lead of the Manhattan Institute, Giuliani took what he called a "zero-tolerance" approach to the behaviours of the so-called urban underclass, deploying aggressive policing tactics against marginalized populations, including homeless people, sex workers, "squeegee men," and black and Latino youth in the city's low-income neighborhoods—sometimes to deadly effect (N. Smith 1998).[2] Under the auspices of "broken-windows policing," the mayor and his police chief William Bratton pledged to "reclaim" the city's public spaces for the "tax-paying, law-abiding" New Yorker (Wacquant 2009a, 10–18). Social services for the most marginalized segments of the urban poor were cut, and new methods of social control—such as strict, letter-of-the-law enforcement around "quality of life offenses" such as loitering, panhandling, sleeping in public spaces, and graffiti writing—were rolled out in their place (Wacquant 2009a; Wacquant, 2009b). In these ways, Giuliani shifted the focus of local government from reducing poverty and providing a minimum level of social reproduction for all to maintaining order and protecting the welfare of the city's middle- and upper-class residents (see N. Smith 1998; Vitale 2008).

Welfare featured prominently in the new mayor's public pronouncements and policy discourse. In his 1993 election and 1997 reelection campaigns, welfare reform was a key plank in Giuliani's platform, employed to rally the support of white working-class New Yorkers (traditionally Democrats) to the corporate-friendly agenda of a Republican mayor. Harking back to the fiscal crisis of the mid-1970s, and with direct echoes of Reagan's racially coded rhetoric, Giuliani publicly denigrated the "welfare dependent" poor, blaming them, and the public assistance programs on which they relied, for the city's fiscal ills. Lacking personal responsibility and individual initiative, welfare recipients were contrasted to New York's hardworking taxpayers. In a major address in 1998, the mayor promised to end welfare by the year 2000 and "restore the work ethic to the center of city life and transform New York City from the former welfare capital of the world to the work capital of the world" (Giuliani 1998). As he later proclaimed in a town hall meeting, "I want to be remembered as the man that took a city of dependency and made it into a city of workers!" (quoted in Cole 2006).

The Giuliani administration blended a neoconservative approach to family and community life—elevating the white hetero-patriarchal family while emphasizing law and order, public civility, and personal responsibility—with a neoliberal preference for market solutions to problems of urban governance (see Vitale 2008). With the exception of the city's police force, under Giuliani's watch the city adopted strategies to reduce the size and cost of local government through deregulation, privatization, and managed competition for public services (A. O'Connor 2008; Weikart 2001). In the language of neoliberalism, the mayor aimed to improve city services by "dissolving state monopolies" and introducing "competition" and "choice" for the "consumers" of services (see Savas 2002).

To this end, Giuliani implemented more than eighty privatization initiatives during his two terms in office, including the contracting out of city services and the sale of city-owned assets to private business (Cooke 2008).[3] In the area of social welfare alone, the city contracted out service delivery to private providers in home health care, homeless shelters, and employment training. Voucher programs were either introduced or expanded in a wide range of services, including in child care, public housing, public education, employment, and homeless services (Weikart 2001). Welfare offices, formerly called "income support centers," were renamed "job centers" and worked closely with private for-profit employment agencies mandated to assist welfare recipients with job search and skills development on a pay-for-performance basis.

The restructuring of public services had a devastating effect on the municipal workforce. Thousands of full-time city jobs were eliminated through layoffs and severance programs (Cooke 2008). Municipal labor costs were lowered by the contracting out of custodial work in public schools, security guard services, vehicle maintenance, data-entry services, tax billing, medical lab work in the public health department, road resurfacing, and a host of other public functions (Savas 2005). In some agencies, such as the Parks Department, city employees were replaced with workfare participants, slashing the municipal payroll while weakening public-sector unions (Krinsky 2006; Weikart 2001). In sum, the Giuliani administration relied on a range of strategies to reach a singular goal: get public service work, including the work of social reproduction, done cheaply.

This restructuring disproportionately impacted African Americans who had gained access to city jobs in the 1960s and 1970s as a result of civil rights legislation and affirmative action policies (Taylor 2011). By the early 1990s, one-third of African American employment in New York was government related, and black women in particular were overrepresented in the agencies Giuliani targeted for cuts, including the Human Resources Administration, youth services, municipal hospitals, and the City University system (see Podair 2011). Given some of the shared characteristics of home health care and home child care work, including as sites of employment for women of color, the Giuliani administration's approach to the restructuring of home care services is instructive. In 1993 there were over sixty-seven thousand unionized home care attendants employed in the city's $1.2 billion home care program (Ness 2009). Home care services are covered under the federal Medicaid program—overseen by the state and city—and jointly funded by all three levels of government. Giuliani argued that the program was "much too generous" and imposed costs that the city could not afford (quoted in Ness 2009, 59). With the mayor's backing, New York State governor George Pataki cut home care spending by a whopping 30 percent, a move that saw thousands of homebound elderly and disabled New Yorkers lose their eligibility for services and thousands of unionized home care workers either lose their jobs or work too few hours to support their households (Ness 2009, 93).

The administration sought to lock in such reforms by pairing welfare state restructuring with property tax reductions and ongoing subsidies to corporate and real estate interests—despite inheriting a $2.3 billion deficit from the previous administration (Moody 2007). Giuliani's fiscal policies worked to limit the city's capacity to spend on social welfare and respond to rising social need (Brash 2011, 37–39). Thus, as the city government withdrew from underwriting costs of social reproduction—by, among other things, raising tuition in the municipal university system by one-third, slashing the homeless services budget, gutting antipoverty programs and community services, and even making a failed attempt to privatize the city's public hospitals—the administration augmented capital accumulation with tax giveaways to corporations, developers, and the superrich (Brash 2011; Moody 2007; Sites 2003).

In sum, the restructuring of New York's welfare state was marked by an emphasis on privatization and market models of service delivery, a shift from redistribution to punitiveness, and offloading of costs of and responsibilities for social reproduction onto households and communities. This transformation had markedly gendered and racialized impacts, with women—and particularly women of color—disproportionately represented among both the beneficiaries of the welfare state and as frontline providers of city services. In the wake of these transformations, poor and working-class households, and especially the women in them, were left to take up the social reproductive slack left by a retrenched and reprivatized welfare state, intensifying their unpaid caregiving work in the household and community (see Davis et al. 2002). And as workers in the urban welfare state, women had to cope with rising levels of precariousness as public-sector jobs were slashed and service delivery contracted out to nonunion private providers.

Child Care Policy before Welfare Reform, 1993–1995

Ten months before Giuliani was elected mayor, and three years prior to federal welfare reform, four-year-old Matthew Hintzen and seven-year-old Terrance Fisher died in a fire in an unlicensed home day care in the working-class neighborhood of Hollis, Queens. The day care was run by eighty-two-year-old grandmother Eleta Brown. Brown cared for up to six children or more at a time, charging parents just sixty dollars a week for her services. Firefighters found Hintzen and Fisher in the cellar, next to a pile of mattresses near a nonworking smoke detector (*New York Times* 1993).

At the time of the tragedy, New York City was home to 178,000 children whose parents were in paid work and who were cared for outside of the home. The number of regulated child care spaces in the city—including private day care centers, publicly funded programs, and licensed family day cares—was around 51,000, leaving 127,000 children "at risk in places that are too often unsafe and under-supervised" (*New York Times* 1993). For every New York child under the age of three in regulated child care, fifteen were cared for in unregulated settings (see CCI 1990).

After the tragedy, the *New York Times* set about documenting what it called "Nannygate for the Poor." Armed with statistics wrested from city hall, inves-

tigative reporters revealed the extensive use of unregulated child care by poor
and working-class families, putting a spotlight on the city's burgeoning underground or "illegal" day care industry. According to reports, subsidized child
care served only 13 percent of the city's eligible families. An estimated twenty-
five thousand day care providers in New York's low-income neighborhoods operated, like Eleta Brown, without official oversight or licenses (Richardson 1993).

In a scathing editorial, the *Times* decried the lack of child care choices available to the city's poor and working-class families and urged policy makers to
do better: "If parents weren't so desperate, they could demand more from their
caregivers. If an understaffed City Health Department were better able to register, train and monitor caregivers, they would certainly be able to give more.
'It doesn't matter if they make $500,000 or $5,000,' a union official said about
the Queens tragedy, 'parents have to have child care.' True. But parents who
make $500,000 have the kinds of choices that the parents of Matthew Hintzen
and Terrance Fisher did not have" (*New York Times* 1993). As the editorial acknowledged, for moderate and low-income New Yorkers, choice in child care
was a fiction; for these families, choices were constrained by their economic
realities and the failure of government to deliver affordable, accessible, quality
child care.

By the time Giuliani was sworn in as mayor, the names of Hintzen and
Fisher may not have been forgotten, but the call for investment in quality child
care certainly was. Making good on a campaign commitment to privatize city
services, Giuliani announced a "tuition-voucher plan" for child care. The
mayor defended his plan to the public like this: the city could cut costs, serve
a greater number of children, and give parents more "choice" by diverting
scarce resources from expensive city-contracted unionized day care centers to
vouchers for parents (Treaster 1994). The plan sought to shift the city's child
care dollars from maintaining buildings and operating programs—supply-side
subsidies—to an emphasis on demand-side subsidies that would in theory increase parents' purchasing power in the child care market. The plan clearly
framed child care as a private, not public, responsibility—a service to be purchased on the market, not delivered by the state.

One of Giuliani's earliest and most outspoken critics, the city's public advocate Mark Green, predicted that the voucher plan would force the closure of
a significant number of the 445 child care centers funded and overseen by the
city. "While promising more choice and less bureaucracy," Green explained,
"the proposal would actually provide less day care in poor neighborhoods and
less choice" (quoted in Treaster 1994).[4] As the city's child care advocates ar-

gued, vouchers were set at rates significantly below the real cost of child care in a center-based setting. With direct public funding withdrawn in place of vouchers, capital and operating costs would have to be covered by increased co-payments for parents, many of whom could not afford to pay more than they already did. From the perspective of child care advocates, it was clear that the new administration sought to increase the flow of public dollars to the private child care market, and particularly to underpaid and minimally regulated home-based providers, while defunding the city's unionized day care programs (Treaster 1994).

Despite opposition from child care advocates, City Council adopted the voucher plan (Treaster 1994). It was a clear victory for Giuliani and his neoliberal vision for child care. While the city's Human Resources Administration had previously issued only a small number of vouchers to welfare mothers transitioning to employment, for the first time in its history the Agency for Child Development—with its historic commitment to quality, center-based care—would issue child care vouchers with no conditions on how they were spent. While ACD vouchers could be used to purchase care from city day cares, the more likely scenario was that they would be used for home-based family day care and license-exempt informal care, often provided by family, friends, and neighbors (Kolben 1997, 2). The administration had effectively channeled public dollars away from the city's unionized, center-based child care infrastructure and toward the private child care market and its patchwork of low-cost home child care. Public resources were to increasingly flow to what child care advocates noted were the least-regulated, least-trained, and worst-paid sectors of the child care industry (see Whitebook 2001).

The introduction of the voucher scheme came in the wake of a widely reported national study on home-based child care. According to the New York–based Families and Work Institute, home child care "often fails children," providing only moderate to mediocre care and little of the programming necessary for healthy early child development. The report was the first nationwide study of home-based child care in more than a decade and explicitly made the link between care quality and the wages and working conditions of child care providers. "The more the provider was paid," researchers found, "the better care tended to be," with low-income and black and Hispanic children tending to be in lower-quality care. In addition, the study confronted the neoliberal language of "choice" that surrounded debates about family child care, finding that 65 percent of mothers said they had no other choice of care, while 28 percent said they would use other care if it was available (Chira 1994).

FROM VOUCHERS TO CLOSURES

Despite being heralded by New York's child care community, the Families and Work Institute study had no impact on the Giuliani administration's child care policies. In fact, just a year after the city's voucher plan was rolled out, and on the eve of federal welfare reform, the Human Resources Administration proposed the closure of ten of the city's unionized day care centers. The closures added up to a loss of nineteen hundred child care spaces in some of the highest-quality programs the city had to offer. In the face of opposition, the administration reiterated the logic behind its child care agenda: closing centers saved on rent and capital costs, displaced children could be moved to other day cares, and more parents would be provided with vouchers to pay for the child care services of their choice (D. Hevesi 1995).

At one of the day care centers targeted for closure, a mother who had recently transitioned from welfare to work pleaded with the mayor to keep the facility open: "It took me twenty years to come off welfare and I refuse to go down that road again. Self-respect, self-esteem, and independence, because I'm a single parent, that's what this center has done for me" (quoted in D. Hevesi 1995). The administration proved unconcerned that the realities of child care did not match its rhetoric of "parental choice." Nor did it seem to consider the shrinking number of spaces in the city's publicly funded centers a threat to poor single mothers' transition from public assistance to paid work.

These early policy shifts signaled the approach the administration would take as federal welfare reform rolled out the following year. By the time President Bill Clinton signed the Personal Responsibility and Work Opportunity Reconciliation Act (PRWORA) into law, thousands of single mothers on welfare were being called into the city's workfare program, putting massive pressure on New York's child care infrastructure, as welfare leavers competed with working poor families for regulated child care spaces. The expansion of vouchers early in Giuliani's first term was clearly made with an eye to welfare reform. Indeed, as two supporters of the mayor's child care policies put it, the administration sought to create "a responsive market for child care," encouraging the entry of unlicensed, informal providers into the market, "increasing supply and improving parental choice during a period of sudden demand for child care services" (Besharov and Samari 2005, 9).

Under the ideological cover of "parental choice," the city was expanding a low-wage labor market in home-based child care providers who could deliver a necessary social service on the cheap. And in closing a number of the city's publicly funded day care centers, the administration had made clear its preference for the privatized delivery of social services and disregard for the unionized workers who had historically fought for and defended public provision of quality child care in New York.

Child Care and Welfare Reform in New York, 1995–2005

In 1996, President Clinton made good on his campaign promise to "end welfare as we know it." Federal welfare reform, under the auspices of PRWORA, created the Temporary Assistance to Needy Families (TANF) program, ended welfare as a federal entitlement, limited welfare benefits to two years consecutively or five years over a recipient's lifetime, and made benefits contingent on efforts to get paid work (Bashevkin 2002, 74). The federal government set a target of 50 percent of welfare mothers to be in work or training thirty hours a week by 2002. TANF replaced AFDC, which had provided cash welfare to poor mothers since 1935. As a block grant to states, TANF further devolved responsibility for welfare programming to states, giving state governments and, through second-order devolution, local governments broad flexibility in determining eligibility, methods of assistance, and benefit levels (Soss, Fording, and Schram 2011). In order to receive federal funds, states had to spend some of their own dollars on programs for needy families or face fiscal penalties if they failed to do so.

PRWORA introduced a series of measures designed to regulate the conduct of poor single mothers on public assistance. Welfare mothers now had to disclose the paternity of their children, teenage parents had to live with an adult, and states were offered various incentives to reduce out-of-wedlock births without increasing abortion rates (Mink 2002). The legislation framed marriage as an institution that promotes the interests of children and the foundation of a healthy society and emphasized responsible fatherhood and motherhood as essential to children's well-being. In essence, PRWORA told the poor single mother that "if she doesn't participate in a father-mother family, she surrenders her right to care for her children" (Mink 2002, 103). As Leah Vosko puts it, "it's mandatory marriage or obligatory waged work" (2002b, 165).

On the child care side, welfare reform involved a major reconfiguration of federal child care policy and funding streams. Four pre-TANF child care programs were merged into a single block grant called the Child Care and Development Fund (CCDF). Prior to 1996, funding for three of these programs (serving AFDC families, families at-risk of requiring public assistance, and families transitioning from AFDC to work) was open-ended: states were required to put up matching funds in order to draw down federal dollars, but there was no maximum amount they could access (Levy and Michel 2002, 250). Under TANF, the three categories of recipients were absorbed into the larger groups of those who are *eligible* for benefits under federal law but not *entitled* under state regulations, leaving these groups to compete for a share of limited child care resources. Welfare leavers are typically granted the highest priority by state and county welfare administrations (Levy and Michel 2002, 250).

In keeping with the devolved, decentralized, and fragmented nature of poverty governance under TANF, state-level decision-making has become a key determinant of how much subsidized child care is available and how it is distributed. Need, state fiscal capacity, and fiscal effort all factor into the availability and quality of subsidized care. In addition, states vary on income eligibility limits, parent co-payments, and maximum payment rates to child care providers. Furthermore, while states are given the option of using surplus TANF funds for child care, not all states choose to do so (Levy and Michel 2002).

According to the CCDF, all families receiving child care subsidy are to benefit from the health and safety requirements, consumer education, parental choice, and other provisions of the statute (Levy and Michel 2002). Yet notwithstanding overtures to quality, the CCDF allows funds to go to relatives and/or child care providers who are exempt from licensing, and only a 4 percent share of overall child care funding can be used for quality improvements (Whitebook 2014, 10). While all children under age thirteen in families with incomes below 85 percent of a state's median income are eligible for child care services, funding levels have really meant that only a fraction of those eligible are actually served (Levy and Michel 2002, 247). Despite increasing federal child care funding by $4 billion, it is estimated that CCDF has only ever covered 15 to 20 percent of all eligible children, leaving many low-income families without access to subsidized child care (National Women's Law Center 2018).

WELFARE REFORM, GIULIANI STYLE

New York City anticipated federal welfare reform by a year, initiating the nation's most ambitious "work-first" welfare program in 1995. Without waivers from the federal government, the Giuliani administration expanded an existing—but relatively small—municipal workfare program, the Work Experience Program (WEP), tightened eligibility procedures for new applicants, and introduced a strict sanctions regime to enforce compliance (Krinsky 2007a).

At the state level, New York's welfare reform process concluded in the summer of 1997. As New York City was home to over 70 percent of the state's wel-

TABLE 3.1. New York City AFDC/TANF Caseload by Year

Year	Number of cases	Number of people
1993	293,962	792,263
1994	312,127	842,246
1995	312,220	845,910
1996	293,303	794,876
1997	258,387	695,648
1998	225,651	609,126
1999	202,764	556,158
2000	178,821	480,259
2001	153,239	403,013
2002	97,487	227,084
2003	89,247	202,425
2004	88,811	201,199

TANF replaced AFDC in New York in 1998.
Source: New York State Office of Temporary and Disability Assistance.

fare caseload, state-level welfare reform was necessarily conceived with an eye to the city (CSWL 2001, 327). For the state to meet federal work participation requirements under TANF and continue to draw down federal dollars, the city would have to drastically cut its welfare rolls and, as such, New York State's Welfare Reform Act reproduced much of what was already on the ground in the city (CSWL 2001). The Giuliani administration was successful in convincing the state to certify nearly all aspects of the WEP, and by mid-1998 New York City's TANF regime was fully operational (Krinsky 2007b).

The WEP was part of the broader welfare reform scheme known as Work, Accountability and You (NYC-WAY). NYC-WAY's stated goal was to engage the city's entire welfare caseload in "activities that reduce dependency and increase employability," a strategy known as "full-engagement" (Besharov and Germanis 2005, 146). Before 1998, the program was heavily reliant on public-sector work placements. The program went from requiring just under ten thousand welfare recipients to be engaged in work-related activities—including education, training, or job search—in 1995 to requiring up to forty thousand recipients to do work for city agencies and contracted nonprofit organizations three years later (Krinsky 2007a).

As John Krinsky notes, the WEP was designed with "enormous disincentives to remain on welfare, and created more opportunities for the state to sanction—or cut off—welfare recipients' grants" (Krinsky 2006, 158). In David Dinkins's last year in office, 13.1 percent of recipients were thrown off the city's welfare rolls for failure to comply with program requirements. Between 1995 and 1996 the rate more than doubled to 30.2 percent (Krinsky 2006). As the program expanded, WEP workers became increasingly noticeable around the city: sweeping streets, cleaning parks, and picking up trash while sporting bright orange vests. In keeping with what Piven and Cloward (1971) call "degradation rituals," the Giuliani administration sought to publicly humiliate welfare recipients, thereby discouraging potential applicants from applying for public assistance (Krinsky 2007a).

However, as New York State and New York City moved to comply with TANF, the WEP was scaled back and NYC-WAY became increasingly focused on a "work-first" approach that prioritized rapid labor force attachment by denying aid to new applicants until they had completed an initial job search and by emphasizing strategies of "diversion" and deterrence designed to discourage poor people from applying for benefits altogether (Krinsky 2007a). The arrival of Wisconsin's welfare guru, Jason Turner, to head the city's Human Resources Administration in 1998 and subsequent conversion of welfare offices into "job centers" marked this shift.

DETERMINING THE EMPLOYABILITY
OF POOR SINGLE MOTHERS

Initially, NYC-WAY applied only to recipients of the state-funded general welfare program (known as Home Relief), who were by definition able-bodied childless adults and disproportionately men. In the spring of 1996, the program expanded to mothers with children over the age of three (Krinsky 2007a, 38).[5] Women in this category were assigned to a six-month, twenty-hour-per-week WEP assignment, followed by four weeks of job search (typically thirty to forty hours a week) at an approved employment services program. If a recipient had not secured employment at the end of the job search period, she was assigned to another six months in the WEP.

By the end of 1997, the city had expanded its work requirements to include TANF recipients with children three months or older. Despite massive shortages of infant and toddler spaces in the city's center-based child care system, the administration chose not to follow the lead of states and counties with more generous exemption policies.[6] According to one of Giuliani's key policy advisors, New York City (and by default, the state) could not meet federally mandated work participation rates if it exempted mothers with preschool-age children (Lawrence Mead, personal communication, June 12, 2009). Such a scenario, the argument went, would jeopardize the state's, and thereby the city's ability to draw down federal TANF funds. However, according to the city's Independent Budget Office, due to the aggressive nature of work-first welfare reform in New York, by early 1998 the city was already exceeding TANF work participation rates by some measure (IBO 1998).

By 1998, Jason Turner—one of the architects of the pioneering Wisconsin Works (w-2) program—had been recruited to head the HRA and oversee New York City's welfare-to-work regime. According to Turner, the city's decision to treat welfare mothers with children as young as three months as "employable" had to do with "replicating, to the extent possible, the conditions and expec- tations of workers with those of recipients." Turner argued that, for working mothers, a three-month paid maternity leave "is usually the maximum com- panies provide, so we did the same. . . . After three months, mothers would be required to participate in activities up to 40 hours, the same as the working population" (Turner, personal communication, August 29, 2009). If working mothers had to struggle to balance the competing demands of paid work and unpaid caring responsibilities, why shouldn't poor single mothers on public assistance?

The administration was unconcerned by the city's shortage of infant and toddler care or general lack of regulated child care spaces. An aggressive "work-first" approach for all but mothers with the youngest of children was intimately tied to the administration's aim to further privatize costs of and re- sponsibilities for caregiving by facilitating the expansion of home-based child care, partly through frontline practices that pushed TANF mothers to either "choose" this care or divert them from public assistance altogether, leaving them to rely on exclusively private means to meet their child care needs. As Turner himself said, "there was no shortage of child care in New York City. There was ample care, for example paid care in the homes of others, or un- paid care with grandmothers" (Turner, personal communication, August 29, 2009). Child care was to be secured with minimum state support (in the form of vouchers) via the market, or with no state support at all.

This perspective was echoed by one of welfare reform's key intellectual architects, the political scientist Lawrence Mead, a sometime-advisor of Gi- uliani. Mead, who spent his Wednesdays consulting at the HRA (C. Vogel and deMause 1998), argued, "A lot of [welfare] mothers were already working off the books so they had child care arrangements, familial or kinship networks" (Mead, personal communication, June 12, 2009). Mead had studied Wiscon- sin's w-2 program, which also relied on the expansion of home-based care— both family day care and informal care—to meet rising demand (see Mead 2004). Through w-2, Wisconsin provided need-based subsidies to mothers of children under twelve for market-based care. The state reimbursed the child care provider at market rates. As Jane Collins and Victoria Mayer remark, "In providing these subsidies, the state hoped to entice new providers to enter the market . . . and the program succeeded dramatically in this respect," as home-based child care proliferated in low-income neighborhoods where need was greatest (Collins and Mayer 2010, 70; see also Jones 2014). Reacting to critics of child care outcomes in Wisconsin and New York, Mead said: "The assumption of child care advocates is that all child care must be public or there is no care and that is false. A lot of the care is private; it's informal. The belief that child care would not be available should these mothers go to work turned out not to be true. . . . Many mothers had family members at home who could take care of their children; they made informal arrangements with friends and neighbors" (Mead, personal communication, June 12, 2009).

Such logic cannot be divorced from the politics of race. In 1998 the racial composition of New York City's TANF rolls was 5 percent white, 33 percent African American, and 59 percent Hispanic (DeParle 1998). In their book *Disciplining the Poor: Neoliberal Paternalism and the Persistent Power of Race*, Joe Soss, Richard Fording, and Sanford Schram find that race continues to shape the administration of welfare and that under TANF the racial composition of a state or county's welfare caseload is a strong predictor of welfare restrictiveness and "get tough" policies. States and counties with larger black caseloads generally make their benefits more meager, impose sanctions at higher rates, and have tougher eligibility and work requirements (Soss, Fording, and Schram 2011, 128–40). In contrast, the small number of states in which a vast majority of TANF recipients are white—for example, Oregon and Vermont—usually run the most generous welfare programs and are more likely to waive work requirements for poor mothers with young children.

Other states that, like New York, exempted only mothers with children three months old or younger from mandatory work requirements included Alabama, Arkansas, New Jersey, Michigan, Florida, and Wisconsin (Urban Institute 2002), all states in which a high percentage of the TANF caseload was black and/or Hispanic (Soss, Fording, and Schram 2011).[7] Thus, under the cover of policies that were officially race-neutral, the evidence suggests that New York City perpetuated the racialized (and gendered) logic engrained in the U.S. welfare state since the New Deal. The city required single mothers with very young children to work because a higher percentage of its TANF caseload was black and Hispanic, mothers who had long been treated as employable and undeserving, subject to racist exclusions from poor relief, and for whom kith and kin had traditionally provided child care in the absence of state support, as Mead himself suggests. Understood alongside the administration's approach to policing, it becomes clear that the city's workfare regime was one side of a racialized "double regulation of the poor" (Wacquant 2009b).

For the likes of Mead and Turner, how New York City was going to meet rising demand for child care services was never in doubt. Despite parents' right to choose among a variety of child care options, the cost of and responsibilities for care were to be borne primarily by low-income households and communities in the form of home-based child care and the unpaid or underpaid women—disproportionately women of color—who provided it. Welfare reform "worked" because these women picked up the social reproductive slack left by a stingy, punitive workfare state that assumed that low-income women of color's capacity to do the work of social reproduction at home and in the community was endlessly elastic. However, one of the obstacles to realizing the Giuliani administration's preference for home child care was TANF parents' legislated child care rights, including their right to choose regulated center-based child care.

WELFARE RECIPIENTS' CHILD CARE RIGHTS

Under the new TANF regime, New York State and federal social welfare law established certain child care rights for welfare recipients. These laws were intended to ensure adequate child care for parents engaged in welfare-to-work programs (Powell and Cahill 2000).[8]

Under both New York State and federal law, parents on welfare with children under the age of thirteen who are required to participate in work-related activities are guaranteed child care assistance. When a parent is called to participate in workfare, the law requires her caseworker to assess her ability to work and her need for supportive services, including child care. Under the law, caseworkers must address child care issues with their clients to make sure they will be able to comply with work requirements. If a parent demonstrates that she is unable to find adequate child care, caseworkers are obligated to provide her with two choices of child care providers, at least one of which must be a regulated provider. In addition, if a parent needs help obtaining a regulated provider, her caseworker must find two accessible and available providers with openings. Should a parent demonstrate that she is unable to secure appropriate child care and therefore is unable to meet her work requirement, and her child is six years of age or younger, federal TANF regulations prohibit states from sanctioning the parent or terminating assistance (Powell and Cahill 2000).

Furthermore, under both New York State and federal social welfare law, parents who participate in welfare-to-work activities and receive federally funded child care assistance have a right to choose from a variety of child care options. According to Powell and Cahill, Congress promoted "parental choice" in the name of "empower[ing] working parents to make their own decisions about child care so that they could ensure that their children were cared for in a safe and positive environment" (2000, 8–9). Welfare recipients engaged in welfare-to-work have the option of either enrolling their children with a provider that has a grant or contract for the provision of child care services, or receiving a child care voucher in order to pay directly for child care services. Under federal law, if a parent is in receipt of a child care voucher, she must be allowed to choose from a variety of child care types, including center-based care, regulated family day care, and unlicensed, informal care. Finally, should a parent successfully transition into paid employment, she has a right to transitional child care support for up to one year after leaving public assistance (Powell and Cahill 2000).

With states given a great deal of discretion over the administration of child care, access to subsidized care is ultimately determined at the local level, "where widely varying bureaucratic practices can determine who receives services and who does not" (Levy and Michel 2002, 251). This is especially true for a state like New York, which devolved much of its welfare and child care policy-making authority to counties and cities. As the case of New York City demonstrates, how TANF child care works in law is not always the reality experienced on the ground. Even in states that consistently draw down maximum federal child care funds, the frontline practices of local welfare bureaucracies have led to the denial of benefits and a lack of availability of child care (Levy and Michel 2002, 252; Houser et al. 2014). Despite guarantees of "parental choice" in federal and state law, the local welfare regime is clearly an important site of policy making and administration at the nexus of welfare and child care (Houser et al. 2014).

Prior to 1998, a number of state and civil society actors warned of the imminent escalation of the city's child care crisis and impact of welfare reform, Giuliani-style, on New York's historical commitment to high-quality, center-based child care. Many of these reports drew on the experiences of welfare mothers who had been called into the city's NYC-WAY program in 1996 and 1997. The reports documented the shortage of spaces in publicly funded day care centers (including very few slots for children under two years old), the lack of social planning around child care in the leadup to federal welfare reform, the disorganized nature of the city's child care system, and the child care experiences of welfare mothers participating in the WEP.

A Crisis in Progress, a Crisis Foretold

In 1995, at the behest of child care advocates, city council, and officials in the Agency for Child Development, New York City undertook an analysis of the potential impact of federal welfare reform on the city's child care system. The Temporary Task Force on Child Care Funding (TTF) was to "suggest ways to maximize and enhance the availability, quality, effectiveness and efficiency of child care services in New York City" (New York City Temporary Task Force on Child Care Funding 1996). The task force's members were appointed by both the mayor and council and reflected the input of the council's Democrats: in addition to high-ranking civil servants in the HRA and ACD, the TTF included representatives from the city's child care community and unions representing day care workers and directors.

The basic assumptions guiding the TTF's work in part reflected the city's historical commitment to quality child care and the framing of child care as both a developmental service for children and as an employment support for working families. The report stated that the quality of child care and early education offered by the city had "a decisive effect on how well they [children] do in school and in their later lives" and that "child care and early education must be viewed in a broader context as an issue with workforce, economic, social, and educational implications" (New York City Temporary Task Force on Child Care Funding 1996, 3). Yet reflecting input from the mayor's office, the report was inflected with the language of "efficiency," "cost-effectiveness," and mentions of "public-private partnership" as a solution to the city's child care crisis.

The report noted that in the context of rising demand for child care, the city should ensure use of "all available sources of funds," including increasing funds through "private sources." In addition, the discovery of "system efficiencies" and the "streamlining" of administration could result in the delivery of "increased services at lower costs *without* compromising quality." The report acknowledged that there had never been sufficient funding to meet the child care needs of all subsidy-eligible families. Yet despite the growing gap between needs and resources in the early 1990s, the TTF noted that the Agency for Child Development had "achieved its mission admirably: its high-quality assurance standards and its educational programs are exemplary. The city's licensing requirements for all center-based early childhood programs ... *are among the highest in the nation*" (New York City Temporary Task Force on Child Care Funding 1996, 5, emphasis added twice).

Looking ahead to federal welfare reform, the TTF warned that welfare families might push out low-income working families from subsidized care as the city sought to meet federally mandated work participation rates. The report thus urged the city to maintain its financial commitment to child care "at its current level of funding" and "continue to serve low-income working families who need affordable care so that parents can stay employed and children can be safe and well cared for" (New York City Temporary Task Force on Child Care Funding 1996, 1). The TTF also observed that child care services had not kept up with new needs, such as the growing number of parents working irregular and unpredictable work schedules (New York City Temporary Task Force on Child Care Funding 1996, 7). The system was further flawed by the relationship between the multiple agencies involved in providing and regulating child care, causing miscommunication and a lack of coordination between agencies and difficulties in effectively gathering data and implementing and evaluating services. These "inefficiencies," the report suggested, should be addressed prior to the rollout of federal welfare reform.

Perhaps most importantly, the report highlighted the lack of regulatory oversight of informal child care. Referring to the city's "historical commitment" to quality child care, and touting its strong licensing standards for publicly funded care, the report stated, "Much of the child care used by welfare recipients paid for by public funds is unregulated, 'informal' care, which requires neither inspection nor licensing. It is unknown whether this care meets with basic health, safety, and education standards." The report acknowledged that there were "profound concerns about the quality of this care and its effect on children" (New York City Temporary Task Force on Child Care Funding 1996, 8).

The report framed informal care as a little more than a stopgap employment support for single mothers. In doing so, it reaffirmed the ACD's strong commitment to quality, center-based care, recognizing its developmental value for children. It is here that the report most strongly shows the influence of child care advocates and AFSCME Local 205, the day care workers' union. The task force stressed, "As welfare reform continues to expand, the need for quality child care and early education will increase." "In response," the report continues, "the City must develop a plan for prioritizing how funds will be spent and must increase capacity by recruiting providers who offer *quality* services" (New York City Temporary Task Force on Child Care Funding 1996, 8, 9, emphasis added).

Overall, the TTF represented the views and sense of urgency of both child care advocates and civil servants in the ACD. While the influence of the mayor's neoliberal agenda is evident in some of the report's language, the TTF concluded with a series of progressive recommendations designed to reshape New York City's existing child care delivery system "to create one that is high quality, efficient, consumer-driven, and responsive to communities' needs." These recommendations included expanding quality child care services, delivering center-based care outside of traditional working hours, and requiring assurances that all health, safety, and regulation standards were updated and complied with (New York City Temporary Task Force on Child Care Funding 1996, 9). While the report acknowledged that the early 1990s was a time of "fiscal restraint," little in the report could be interpreted as a call to deregulate and privatize the city's public child care infrastructure.

The TTF was not the only actor predicting an escalation of the city's child care crisis. In late 1997, the city's Independent Budget Office (IBO)—a publicly funded agency that provides nonpartisan information about the municipal budget to the public and elected officials—also chimed in on welfare reform's implications for child care. In a report titled "The Fiscal Impact of the New Federal Welfare Law on New York City," the IBO took account of TANF's work participation requirements to project the increase in demand for child care and welfare reform's broader impact on the system (IBO 1997). The IBO estimated that by the year 2002, when federal work requirements hit 50 percent, "between 33,000 and 84,000 full-time equivalent child care slots (40 hours per week) will need to be created, depending upon whether the two year work requirement is enforced" (IBO 1997, 22). The annual cost of a regulated child care space in the city was estimated at $5,000, meaning additional costs per year would range from $212 million to $599 million by 2002. While the IBO recognized that TANF would increase federal funding for child care, the report predicted that the new funds would be insufficient to meet rising demand (IBO 1997, 23).

Of particular significance was the IBO's observation that in response to welfare reform, "city officials have *publicly stated their intentions to increase the use of lower-cost informal daycare* by work program participants" (IBO 1997, 22, emphasis added). As indicated by the tenor of the TTF report, child care advocates understood that the city would move in this direction given the voucherization of ACD subsidies in 1994 and the high reliance on informal child care providers by those mothers called into welfare to work prior to 1998.

Thus, despite "parental choice" being guaranteed by federal and state regulations, the Giuliani administration had publicly announced its intent to meet rising need by pushing poor women on welfare to use informal child care.

The Citizens Budget Commission (CBC)—a nonpartisan, nonprofit civic organization and fiscal watchdog—also reported on the state of child care in the city. A 1997 CBC report noted, "Since informal care institutions are typically less reliable and have less educational content, it appears that children of parents who are participating in welfare-to-work activities or who have recently left welfare for work are receiving inferior care" (CBC 1997, 39). Furthermore, the CBC stated that the city's welfare administration was failing to ensure that all families eligible for subsidized child care were receiving it: lack of communication, inadequate delivery of applications, and insufficient publicizing of the availability of subsidies all contributed to HRA's provision of access being "deficient" (CBC 1997, 37). The city's welfare agency was systematically denying child care subsidies to eligible families; according to the commission, the HRA was "neither assisting parents in securing high quality child care for their children nor enabling them to find the type of care they prefer" (CBC 1997, 39).

The CBC also commented on the potential impact of increased reliance on informal care by low-income families: "Relying on allowances for informal care could provide cheaper care for larger numbers than would expansion of subsidies for center-based and other regulated care. But the former type of care is generally less reliable, has far fewer educational benefits, and is virtually unregulated. In the face of significant new demand, careful consideration should be given to the choices of how to expand child care subsidies and to ensure adequate quality of informal as well as formal care" (CBC 1997, 40). Finally, the state deputy comptroller, Carl McCall, echoed many of the findings of the IBO and CBC. McCall doubted the city's preparedness to keep up with the demand for child care unleashed by federal welfare reform while also keeping care affordable, safe, and reliable. The city was already operating at capacity, with long waiting lists for both low-income working families and families transitioning from welfare to work. "If the system is poorly designed or badly implemented, and parents cannot find a dependable child care placement," he argued, "the objectives of welfare reform are undermined" (McCall 1997, 2). Furthermore, McCall confirmed what many of the city's child care advocates had already observed: whereas vouchers had once been a small part of the city's child care subsidy program, the Giuliani administration had ramped up their use, from 3,900 in 1996 to over 12,600 the following year (McCall 1997).

"ON THE BRINK OF A MAJOR CRISIS"

By early 1998, the city was "on the brink of a major child care crisis" (OPA 1998, 1). The Office of the Public Advocate summed up the concerns of many in the child care community, and of poor single mothers themselves, when he asked, "While parents on welfare get the education and skills they need to work, who will take care of their children? How can the City best insure that these children get safe, reliable, enriching care that sets them on the course toward becoming healthy, capable adults? Ignoring these issues jeopardizes both the safety of children and the success of the City's welfare-to-work program" (OPA 1998, 1). As the TANF regime rolled out in New York, it was apparent: "Now, more than ever, the City is counting on the expansion of unregulated, informal child care to serve as the primary solution to the child care shortage" (OPA 1998, 25).

In sum, these crisis reports documented the city's increasing reliance on informal child care in the years leading up to the implementation of federal welfare reform in New York. The criticisms contained in the reports had a dual focus. First, without affordable, quality care for the children of welfare mothers, the potential developmental benefits of child care would be lost. The reports saw developmentally appropriate care—as provided in the city's unionized, publicly funded centers—as essential to breaking the "cycle of poverty" (see Chaudry 2004). This argument had undergirded liberal support for programs such as Head Start since the 1960s (Michel 1999), and it was central to critics' support for the expansion of regulated child care and warnings about the increased flow of public dollars to informal providers.

Second, the criticisms focused on the fact that without stable child care arrangements, the success of welfare reform would be jeopardized. Here the argument against informal care was that it was unstable, unreliable, and would not allow welfare mothers to engage in work or work-related activities and meet the necessary participation requirements under TANF. A corollary to this argument was that the children of mothers transitioning from welfare to work stood to displace the children of low-income working families, leaving the latter to turn to welfare as their child care costs rose with declining subsidies, increased parent co-payments, and an overall lack of child care spaces. Last, as all of the reports note, while focusing on the questions of quality and stability, the question of cost was paramount. Informal child care was attractive to the city because it was two-thirds the cost of regulated family day care and far less costly than unionized, center-based care.

As federal welfare reform rolled out at the local level, there was no shortage of voices drawing attention to the impending escalation of the city's child care crisis. Numbers differed from report to report, but most estimates put the projected number of New York City children needing nonparental care as a result of welfare reform at over one hundred thousand by the year 1999 (CBC 1997). The Office of the New York City Public Advocate argued that under TANF approximately seventy-four thousand New York City parents receiving public assistance were to be working by 2002. By 1997, already thirty thousand eligible families were on waiting lists for child care subsidies (CCI 1998). These projections assumed that all such families would not only qualify for subsidies—which they would—but also that they would receive them—which they did not.

The writing was on the wall as to how the city would meet the increased need and demand for child care. As the *New York Times* observed: "New York City spends millions of dollars a year paying for child care for welfare recipients without any quality control, safety oversight or basic information about the people being paid to care for thousands of the city's most vulnerable children" (Sexton 1996). One-quarter of the children in subsidized child care were already cared for in unlicensed, informal settings (CCI 1996).

The *Times* echoed Giuliani's critics who questioned the wisdom of allowing public dollars to flow to informal care "without a concentrated effort to improve the early development of many of the city's impoverished children" (Sexton 1996). As President Clinton signed welfare reform into law, Barbara Blum, president of the Foundation for Child Development and former high-ranking official in social services, had said, "The tendency for public administrators will be to create the cheapest kind of care, and that is exactly the opposite of what these children need" (quoted in Sexton 1996). But creating "the cheapest kind of care" is exactly what the Giuliani administration had been doing. And to defend its strategy it relied on the neoliberal discourse of "choice."

BY CHOICE OR NECESSITY?

In response to the mounting public criticism of the administration's child care policies, Mayor Giuliani repeated his mantra of parental choice. "Decisions on day care are made by parents themselves," the mayor exclaimed (quoted in Sexton 1996). The mayor's spokespeople argued that expanding the number of city-contracted child care centers was both costly and difficult; as such, informal care had to be part of solution to address rising demand (Sexton 1996). The administration's position mirrored that of state officials in Albany who argued that expanding state-subsidized informal care would have to be part of any plan to put more welfare mothers to work. According to the director of Early Childhood Services in New York State's Social Services Department, "The reality is that well over half of the subsidized child care used in the state is informal. Those decisions we feel rest with parents" (quoted in Sexton 1996).

Officials at the HRA tried to assuage critics, pointing to state laws that said welfare recipients reporting for workfare assignments were to be provided with the names of two registered day care providers—including a regulated option—and welfare recipients could not be sanctioned for lack of adequate childcare (Sexton 1996). Yet day care providers, elected officials tasked with investigating the city's welfare-to-work program, and welfare mothers themselves all said that frequently referrals to regulated care were not offered or recommended providers had no vacancies. Welfare mothers described the experience as a "bureaucratic nightmare, replete with misinformation, misdirection, even outright hostility" (quoted in Sexton 1996). A *New York Times* editorial bemoaned the shift in the city's child care policies: "Historically, New York City has been a leader in providing adequate child care for low-income children whose parents need to leave the home for education or training. It will face a formidable task as the workfare experiment proceeds" (*New York Times* 1996).

By mid-1998, it was evident that the Giuliani administration was facilitating the expansion of home-based child care, channeling dollars away from the city's center-based system, in order to meet the growing demand for nonparental child care fueled by welfare reform. The administration had ignored the recommendations of its own child care task force, and child care advocates, municipal budget watchdogs, the city's public advocate, and the New York State deputy comptroller, and the *New York Times* roundly criticized its policies. More than 80 percent of welfare mothers called into the city's welfare-to-work program were relying on informal child care arrangements (CCI 1998). While in some cases poor mothers preferred these child care arrangements, in many cases they did not, and the neoliberal rhetoric of "choice" hid the hand of a coercive, disciplinary welfare apparatus.

TANF Child Care Rights and the Welfare Bureaucracy

After their participation on the Temporary Task Force, and as the city ramped up workfare, child care advocates found municipal policy-making channels closed. Openly critical of the administration's child care policies, advocates had an increasingly difficult time accessing city data on welfare and child care (Interview 4). Nancy Kolben, director of New York City's foremost child care advocacy organization (Child Care Inc.), summed up the views of advocates, saying, "Right now, government officials have gone behind closed doors, and child-care experts are on the outside. I don't think the city really knows what it is going to be doing with day care. But if they plan to expand the informal care system used by their welfare-to-work office, it is going to be a tremendous waste." A former deputy commissioner of the ACD echoed Kolben's remarks: "No one would argue that informal care is developmental child care. We're spending tens of millions of dollars in purchasing that kind of care, and it is an awful waste" (quoted in Sexton 1996).

Shut out of city hall, between 1998 and 2003 welfare rights groups, child care advocates, and women's organizations set about documenting the routine violation of TANF recipients' legislated child care rights and questioned the administration's repeated insistence that the growth of publicly subsidized informal care was simply a matter of poor single mothers' preferences. Advocates also worked with TANF recipients to inform poor mothers of their child care rights, assist with child care referrals, and push HRA to acknowledge and address, albeit with limited results, the growing number of poor children in informal care.

NEW YORK CITY'S STREET-LEVEL BUREAUCRATS

Welfare reform in New York City saw the further separation of what were essentially two parallel child care subsidy systems. In contrast to the small increase in funding made available to the Administration for Children's Services (ACS)—as ACD was renamed—between 1996 and 2003 HRA's child care expenditures more than tripled, rising from $43 million to approximately $143 million (CCI 2003). The ACS is responsible for administering public funds for child care subsidies, including Head Start services, for low-income parents not on welfare. The HRA operates a separate child care subsidy system for welfare recipients. HRA job centers are welfare mothers' primary source of child care information and advice.

The job center was a key component in the administration's workfare regime. Under TANF, changing the culture of the "street-level bureaucracy" (Lipsky 1980)—the caseworkers who are the primary face of decision-making authority for welfare recipients and those seeking assistance—was an object of policy makers and administrators across the country (Soss, Fording, and

Schram 2011). Case managers are responsible for evaluating client cases, distributing services and supports, and applying penalties and sanctions. In a city like New York, with a welfare administration long considered one of the most liberal in the country, "culture change" among street-level bureaucrats took on an added impetus (see Turner 2005).

Jason Turner and his team were tasked with replicating the "Wisconsin miracle"—that is, a steep decline in the welfare rolls over a short period of time—in New York City. While Turner inherited the Work Experience Program, under his guidance a number of changes were made to the appearance, organization, and operation of the city's welfare offices (see Turner 2005). First, welfare offices were converted into job centers, physically refurbished with new computers and furniture, and run on a new data management system that measured welfare-to-work outcomes. A series of new public management practices were also introduced: for example, merit pay for mid-level bureaucrats and caseworkers, along with new performance measures to govern promotions. For frontline welfare caseworkers, productivity was measured by how many cases they closed in a given period of time. A caseworker with high productivity could earn up to a 20 percent bonus on top of one's regular pay (Turner 2005). In line with the principles and objectives of neoliberal public administration, these changes aimed to create a competitive culture both within and between job centers.

Under TANF, caseworkers are under intense pressure to push clients off the welfare rolls in as short a period as possible, while deterring potential applicants from applying for assistance (Watkins-Hayes 2009; Soss, Fording, and Schram 2011). Under politically conservative administrations, these pressures are unsurprisingly even greater. As Soss, Fording, and Schram have observed, caseworkers are subjected to new tools for securing compliance with benchmarks and outcomes that are tied to financial incentives and penalties, "grounding governance in a market calculus designed to raise the odds that preferred paths will be freely chosen" (Soss, Fording, and Schram 2011, 207). In this way, new techniques of management are intended to shape the ways caseworkers govern themselves. This was the on-the-ground context for the delivery of child care services to welfare mothers in New York.

CHOICE IN LAW, COERCION IN PRACTICE

New York clearly opted for cheap child care provisions for poor children, while their parents, mostly poor single mothers, were coerced into the low-wage labor market. But what did this look like on the ground in the face-to-face interactions between welfare mothers and their caseworkers? The process by which HRA "activated" welfare recipients typically proceeded as follows: recipients received a call-in letter from HRA advising them to report to a designated job center for assessment and work activity within two weeks of the date of notification. The letter advised clients to make child care arrangements for the day of their appointment and, if necessary, for their work assignment. The letter did not, however, provide child care information or advice (CCI 1999, 5).

If a client reported to her appointment without child care in place, she was given two days to make arrangements. As per state and federal welfare law, caseworkers were required to provide clients with two child care referrals, one of which was to be a regulated provider. Typically, caseworkers had a list of regulated programs from which they were to make a referral in addition to a list of women on public assistance that the agency had designated to care for the children of other welfare recipients (CCI 1999, 5).

Protocol required new applicants to conduct a job search on the day of application—an up-front strategy of hassle—while searches were to continue throughout a WEP placement for those already on the rolls. In New York, TANF applicants were encouraged to seek cash or in-kind assistance from private sources, such as kith and kin, charities, and churches, prior to filing an application. Such diversionary tactics left many applicants unaware of their procedural rights under welfare law, including their right to child care assistance (CSWL 2001, 330).

As a series of reports released between 1999 and 2003 concluded, the HRA systematically violated the child care rights of TANF recipients and provided inadequate child care supports (CCI 1999; CCI 2003; CSLW 2001; Powell and Cahill 2000; Powell and Cahill 2001; Scharf and Carlson 2004), producing a high reliance on informal care among TANF families (see table 3.2). The Office of the Public Advocate observed as early as 1997 that caseworkers were channeling increasing numbers of parents to use informal child care arrangements and, to a lesser extent, licensed family day care providers (OPA 1997, 26). Under New York City's TANF regime, these practices continued.

The findings of these reports can be summarized as follows.[9] Given the shortage of regulated, subsidized child care in New York City, the two-week timeline allotted to parents to search for and evaluate child care options was grossly inadequate. Furthermore, TANF mothers' call-in letter provided no information or advice in regard to child care. There was also no guarantee that

TABLE 3.2. Use of Informal Care: TANF Recipients vs.
ACS Low-Income Working Families (1995–2011)

Year	TANF		ACS	
	All children enrolled	Percentage of children in informal care	All children enrolled	Percentage of children in informal care
1995	20,634	83	46,660	>1
1998	14,458	83	63,613	3
2000	38,000	89	56,549	2
2002	30,824	84	55,962	not available
2003	40,779	77	61,643	7
2007	45,766	71	56,754	14
2011	47,533	47	48,485	12

TANF replaced AFDC in New York in 1998.
Source: Child Care, Inc.

the timing of a welfare mother's summons to the job center would correspond with the enrollment schedule of child care programs, making securing regulated care extremely difficult (CCI 2003).

Caseworkers also failed to assist TANF parents in securing child care services. NOW's Legal Defense and Education Fund (NOW-LDEF) found that more than half of parents surveyed received no assistance (Powell and Cahill 2000, 2). If caseworkers asked a client "Do you have care for your child?" and the client replied in the affirmative, no further child care options would be discussed (Powell and Cahill 2000, 2). Clients may have secured temporary arrangements for the day of their first appearance at the job center, yet caseworkers systematically interpreted this response as indicating that a client's child care needs were met (CCI 1999; CCI 2003).

Furthermore, NOW-LDEF found that 79 percent of respondents were not shown the mandated "Important Information about Child Care" notice that accompanied TANF enrollment forms (Powell and Cahill 2000). Many TANF mothers reported leaving job centers thinking that there were no alternatives to informal care arrangements (CCI 1999, 4). Indeed, the HRA's guidelines for caseworkers read: "Encourage the client to consider family, friends and neighbors," with the proviso that caseworkers should show parents "how to identify licensed child care, if needed" (Richie and Epstein 1997). In failing to provide adequate child care information, the city was routinely violating state and federal laws regarding the distribution of information and assistance in finding appropriate child care.

Additionally, in contravention of welfare regulations, TANF recipients were routinely sanctioned or threatened with sanction if they were unable to engage in work activities for lack of adequate child care. NOW-LDEF found that almost half of surveyed parents reported being threatened with sanctions if they could not secure child care arrangements (Powell and Cahill 2000; Powell and Cahill 2001). Furthermore, 95 percent of surveyed parents were not informed of their right not to be sanctioned for failure to secure adequate child care (Powell and Cahill 2001, 2). A report by the Office of the State Deputy Comptroller found that caseworkers at one of two HRA job centers visited by the office were unaware that mothers were exempt from work-related requirements if unable to find appropriate child care (McCall 2000, ii), suggesting the regulation had not been adequately communicated to job center staff by senior bureaucrats in HRA.

Finally, TANF mothers whose cases were closed were not given information about transitional child care, to which they were entitled under federal and state law (CCI 1999; CCI 2003; Scharf and Carlson 2004; Stohr 2002). Although an entitlement, TCC benefits were available only on request. Thus, if a client had not been informed of them, the benefit would not be issued. A study by the Community Service Society of New York found that seven out of ten public assistance recipients were not aware of their eligibility for TCC or were outright denied the benefit (Stohr 2002). In addition, parents had to reapply for TCC, adding yet another administrative hurdle to receipt. In some instances, caseworkers closed cases improperly, leaving transitioning recipients ineligible for TCC benefits (Scharf and Carlson 2004).

According to reports, the above issues were exacerbated by the inadequate training of HRA caseworkers, high turnover in job center staff, and antiquated child care information systems (CCI 1999; CCI 2003). Caseworkers were found to have "a very limited understanding about the City's complex child care system and the range of regulated programs and services that are available to parents" (CCI 1999, 4). Caseworkers' workload, the time constraints in which they operated, and the intense pressure to close cases all factored into the lack of information they passed on to mothers regarding child care options and availability.

The reports stressed two other factors, not directly related to frontline practices, which figured into welfare mothers' high reliance on informal care. First, regulated child care providers were discouraged from serving TANF recipients due to ongoing delays in payments from the HRA. Delays and nonpayment for services were common, and providers were often paid retroactively. Regulated providers reported having to write letters, make telephone calls, or obtain legal assistance to receive payment from the city (CCI 1999). While there is no evidence that this mismanagement was intentional and designed to discourage regulated providers from taking on TANF children, it unquestionably had some impact.

Second, not a factor particular to New York, there was simply a lack of regulated child care spaces. Although the growth in family day care met some of the demand for regulated care, openings in family day care programs and child care centers became increasingly difficult to find in low-income communities such as the South Bronx, parts of Upper Manhattan, and poorer sections of Brooklyn (CCI 1999; CCI 2003). This lack of supply was exacerbated after 2000 when the Giuliani administration announced it would expand workfare participation beyond federal requirements, despite the fact that WEP participants were already experiencing great difficulty obtaining regulated child care (Powell and Cahill 2000, 2).

The research reports included a number of recommendations. The first was that TANF parents be provided with written information concerning child care, including TCC, a month in advance of their "activation" so that they would have ample time to consider their options and make arrangements. The second was that welfare caseworkers be trained about their clients' child care rights. Written procedures were inadequate, and caseworkers ought to be required to undergo specific training to ensure they provided written and oral information regarding child care and also informed parents that they could be sanctioned for failure to find child care. Third, the reports recommended that some form of advisory committee or ombud position be created to ensure that the city lived up to its mandate to fully inform parents of their child care rights and options. These specific recommendations accompanied more routine calls for the expansion of regulated child care slots in family day care and center-based programs, for the regulation of informal providers, and for the resolution of payment problems that discouraged regulated providers from accepting TANF children.

Far from being a matter of "parental choice," the very high reliance on informal child care arrangements (and to a lesser extent family day care) by welfare mothers in New York was the product of Giuliani administration policies and frontline practices of its welfare bureaucracy. While in some cases mothers may have preferred these child care arrangements, in many cases they did not, and the neoliberal rhetoric of "choice" hid the hand of a coercive, disciplinary workfare regime. The administration engaged in a deliberate strategy to channel public child care dollars to a precarious home child care workforce, effectively deregulating and privatizing the city's publicly funded child care services, while shifting costs of and responsibilities for caregiving onto low-income households and communities, especially the women in them.

The Municipal Retreat from Child Care Funding

The Giuliani administration's commitment to an agenda of privatization was further illustrated by the city's retreat from child care funding amid escalating demands for services. To understand this final point, it is necessary to examine some of the minutiae of the child care funding formula. In New York, subsidized child care services have always been financed through a mix of city, state, and federal dollars. Under the Child Care Development Block Grant, and most of the federal child care programs that preceded it, the city and state must each spend a fixed amount of its own money in order to draw down federal child care dollars (these funds are referred to as "maintenance of effort" or "matching funds"). Historically, one of the markers of the city's commitment to public child care has been its record of consistently spending more municipal dollars on child care than is required under its maintenance of effort (IBO 2002, 3).

In the initial years following the passage of federal and state welfare reform, New York City spent more municipal dollars on child care than was required under the CCDBG and the corresponding state child care program (IBO 2002). Between 1996 and 1999, federal dollars paid for a third of the city's child care needs, with the city paying two-thirds (Nyary 2004a). However, citing municipal budget "constraints," the Giuliani administration reversed this pattern in 2000, withdrawing municipal dollars from the overall funding mix (IBO 2002).

The year 2000 marked a period of particularly heightened demand for child care as the Giuliani administration ramped up welfare participation rates beyond those required under TANF. By 2003, under Giuliani's successor Michael Bloomberg, New York exceeded the federally set target to reduce welfare rolls by 50 percent and was providing ninety-six thousand children with subsidized child care (IBO 2002). However, since 2000 almost all of the growth in child care spending had been attributable to rising levels of federal funds. In the years 2000 and 2001, the city's contribution to the municipal child care pot fell below 1999 levels (IBO 2002).

Between 1998 and 2003 federal funds grew from 34 percent to 64 percent of the city's child care budget (IBO 2002). By 2004, federal funds made up 75 percent of all spending on child care in New York, with the municipal government paying only a quarter—down from two-thirds—of the costs (Nyary 2004a). This trend showed no sign of abating. For the fiscal year 2005, for example, New York City was slated to receive another $65 million increase for child care under the CCDBG. However, rather than put this money into improving child care quality and access, the city proposed using approximately $40 million of federal funds to reduce the city's share of child care expenditures, shrinking the city's burden of child care costs even more (Kaufman 2004).

These cuts had a significant impact on the availability of child care for poor families in New York City, both welfare mothers and low-income working families. For example, from 1999 to 2003, overall enrollment growth in ACS and HRA child care was limited to 8 percent (CCI 2004). The number of slots allocated to TANF families actually declined from 37,569 in 2001 to 35,563 in 2002 (IBO 2002). While the city was projected to expand child care capacity by around ten thousand slots in 2002, after the city cut its contributions to the child care funding mix the expansion was limited to just three thousand—a difference of seven thousand subsidized child care spaces (IBO 2002).

The cumulative effect of the city's retreat from child care funding was expanding waiting lists. By 2003, there were forty-six thousand eligible families on the waiting list for subsidized child care services (CCI 2003, 6). The retreat had an impact on the city's unionized day care workers as well. According to union officials, Giuliani and Bloomberg both fought giving fair and equitable contracts to all unionized municipal employees, but day care workers and center directors were particularly vulnerable (Interview 12). As the city's child care budget was scaled back, day care workers and center directors went four years without a contract—from 2001 to 2005.

The union accused the Giuliani and Bloomberg administrations of siphoning off funds allocated to childcare in order to pay for other budget items (Nyary 2004b). As union officials argued, federal funds from the CCDBG were intended not only to allow local governments to increase the supply of child care but also to ensure that child care workers' compensation levels kept pace with the cost of living. And as Sandy Socolar, a senior policy analyst with AFSCME Local 205 Day Care Employees noted, the administration's failure to invest in New York's center-based system produced a staffing crisis: "People who stay in child care do it by choice, but how long can they stand it if their pay is frozen at levels four years old? If you can't attract qualified people, there's higher turnover and the children pay for it with teachers who have inadequate preparation" (quoted in Nyary 2004b). The siphoning off of federal funds intended to boost center-based child care workers' wages was clear evidence of the administration's antipathy to this unionized workforce.

Child care advocates and Local 205 were incensed at the municipal retreat from child care in the midst of an escalating crisis. Child Care Inc. criticized the city for its "pronounced pattern of divestment of local funds" (CCI 2003, 5–6). As Nancy Kolben noted, the city had lost an opportunity to expand subsidized care: "If we started at the base at the time we got additional funding and all that funding had gone to child care, we would have been able to serve *30,000 more children*" (quoted in Kaufman 2002, emphasis added). Bill de Blasio, then chairman of the city council's general welfare committee, echoed Kolben's concerns: "For years now, federal and state money has come into New York to create more slots, but the city has been supplanting those dollars" (quoted in Kaufman 2004).

In sum, at a time of peak demand for child care services, the Giuliani and then Bloomberg administration disinvested from child care, allowing federal and state dollars to increasingly supplant city funds in the municipal child care pot. These administrations refused to expand subsidized child care, illustrating their preference for market solutions to the city's escalating child care crisis. Furthermore, they refused to bargain with the unionized workforce so essential to that system's reputation for quality child care.

For the thousands of low-income families on the city's child care waiting list, the thirty thousand subsidized spaces—mentioned above by Kolben—could have eased the tensions between paid work and social reproduction. Instead, these families, poor single mothers among them, were left to meet their child care needs through private means, either purchasing care on the market or relying on the unpaid labor of grandmothers, sisters, aunts, and neighbors. For those families who did gain access to subsidies, the city's failure to invest municipal dollars in the center-based child care infrastructure left them with few real choices in child care.

Child Care on the Cheap

Seven years and two mayoral administrations into New York's workfare regime, Nancy Rankin of the Community Service Society said of the city's child care system, "One wonders sometimes whether the system is intentionally complicated. The administrative systems can—and do—pose barriers even when [the child care placements] are guaranteed and the funding is there" (quoted in Stohr 2002). The evidence presented in this chapter suggests that New York's child care system was not only "intentionally complicated"—diverting thousands of poor families from accessing benefits to which they were entitled—but also that the HRA, through frontline practices, channeled welfare mothers into relying on low-cost, informal child care. While some mothers may have preferred informal arrangements, the neoliberal rhetoric of "parental choice" hid the hand of an increasingly coercive and disciplinary welfare apparatus.

Not much had changed since the last days of AFDC when the Citizens Budget Commission proclaimed, "It appears that HRA is neither assisting parents in securing high quality child care for their children nor enabling them to find the type of care they prefer" (CBC 1997, 39). Reflecting on these trends, perhaps the city's most authoritative voice on child care, Nancy Kolben, expressed deep disappointment at what she and other advocates saw as a missed opportunity: "By spending limited public resources on informal care, we are failing to invest in the programs that give the poorest children the best opportunities for gaining fundamental learning skills. We could have created child care centers with trained teachers, equipped playgrounds and enriched learning environments. Instead, more children are in unsafe environments or parked in front of a TV" (quoted in Kaufman 2004). Echoing these sentiments, one of the architects of the federal Head Start program, child psychologist and early childhood education expert Edward Zigler, called the city's approach to child care "a disaster in the making." "What good does it do to keep telling people about the importance of the first few years in life," Zigler asked, "when policymakers in New York tell people, 'Here's some money. Go find something'?" (quoted in Kaufman 2004). Responding to the criticism, officials at the HRA repeated the claim that poor single mothers preferred leaving their children in unregulated child care settings "despite encouragement from social workers [to use licensed care]" (quoted in Kaufman 2004). Behind closed doors, officials inside HRA acknowledged that some welfare caseworkers may have been failing to inform clients of their child care options but insisted that the administration worked hard to build a regulated child care system that supported mothers transitioning into the labor market (Interview 16). But others intimately familiar with the city's child care system disagree. Ajay Chaudry was the ACS deputy commissioner for child care and Head Start from 2004 to 2006. He led the first comprehensive study and redesign of New York City's child care system in the post-Giuliani era and conducted extensive research on welfare mothers' experiences with child care (see Chaudry 2004). Chaudry sums up the Giuliani and Bloomberg administrations' policy logic like this:

The cost of regulated, quality child care is a lot more than the cost of welfare so the only way it [welfare reform] was going to work was to encourage the cheapest kind of care possible. It [the expansion of informal care] was a conscious choice. First, you give parents very little time to arrange child care. And so any type of child care you can get will do. So there was a huge push toward informal child care . . . mothers were pushed to use as inexpensive child care arrangements as possible, pushed to use informal care and they had very little or no time to arrange child care before beginning work (Chaudry, personal communication, December 5, 2010)

Chaudry acknowledges that federal funding levels were inadequate, but, had funding substantially increased, "they [the Giuliani administration] wouldn't have expanded it [regulated child care] regardless. Even if the funding was two or three times as much. . . . Neither the Giuliani nor Bloomberg administrations demonstrated a strong will to expand the formal child care market in New York." He continues: "The administration's preference for informal care was because a) it's easier to turn on and off and b) *they had no desire to increase public sector care. They were ideologically opposed to the public sector.* If they could [have], they probably would have said to TANF mothers 'we are providing you with no child care assistance and you still have to go to work.' It just so happened to be federal law that a family had to get child care assistance in order to meet work requirements . . . so essentially they said 'we're going to set it up that your only real option is informal care but you have no excuse, whether you find care or not you're going to work'" (Chaudry, personal communication, December 5, 2010; emphasis added). And while Chaudry notes that welfare reform incentivized the choice of informal care—as poor families could keep subsidy money within their kith-and-kin networks, making up for reductions in cash assistance (or "child care as the new welfare")—all in all, he determines that "from how the city budgeted for anticipated increased demand for subsidies to how it structured, facilitated, and encouraged child care enrollment by WEP families, it was an *intentional policy of HRA to push TANF clients to use informal care*" (Chaudry personal communication, December 5, 2010; emphasis added).

One of the city's most well-respected child care advocates and social policy analysts agrees. During Giuliani's time in office, this former city staffer worked in the Office of the Public Advocate. Responding to the city's claims that the HRA did not direct TANF mothers to informal care, this person said: "The city's primary concern was with getting mothers off of welfare. HRA was not concerned with ensuring very young children were in environments that are going to foster healthy child development. . . . *The city created a substandard child care voucher system for welfare families* rather than looking at child care resources overall and what makes most sense for families, welfare reform, and kids. . . . It [child care] was not the focus of the city or mayoral administration"

(Interview 3). Like other child care advocates, this source argues that the increase in federal child care funding that accompanied welfare reform, while inadequate to meet growing demand, could have been used to build on New York City's historical commitment to quality, public child care: "They [the administration] didn't view it as an opportunity. Here we have all this additional child care money coming down from the federal and state governments, and the city didn't ask 'how can we build a really strong program?' Instead it was 'let's just get kids into whoever's house we can and get those parents into a work activity.'" Work enforcement, not child care, was the city's main priority. The use of informal care to meet growing need and demand for child care "was not by default but *by design*" (Interview 3; emphasis added).

CHAPTER 4

Resistance

Welfare Rights and Child Care Struggles, 1996–2010

> Each neoliberal-urban formation, New York City included, has its own unique
> vulnerabilities, zones of overextension, undefended flanks. Anti-neoliberal
> forces are consequently confronted by spatially differentiated political
> opportunity structures, just as they draw upon distinctive political capacities,
> cultures, and visions of their own. If neoliberalization is far from monolithic,
> the contemporary politics of contestation are also anything but unitary.
>
> **—Helga Leitner, Jamie Peck, and Eric Sheppard, 2007**

On a hot summer's day in June 1998, fifty welfare rights activists—some of them mothers with children in tow—marched into the lobby of the Human Resource Administration's headquarters in downtown Manhattan, hung up a sign declaring the space a day care center, and proceeded to pass out jump ropes and balls to the kids (Dulchin and Kasmir 2004, 5). The demonstration was organized by WEP Workers Together (WWT), a coalition of community groups dedicated to organizing the city's workfare workers. As the playing children effectively shut down the entrance to the building, the adults demanded a meeting with the HRA commissioner. They wanted to know why welfare mothers were being forced into workfare assignments before securing adequate child care, and they demanded that this practice stop (Dulchin and Kasmir 2004, 7–8).

The processes of neoliberalization detailed in the preceding chapter did not go uncontested: neoliberal restructuring at the intersection of welfare and child care in New York City generated fierce opposition.[1] Indeed, in the wake of welfare reform, struggles over child care sprang up in cities and states across the United States, ranging from small campaigns to defend poor mothers' right to provide care to their own children, to bigger and more well-resourced efforts to expand and improve subsidized child care programs and advance home child care providers' rights as workers (Reese 2011). These struggles exhibited place-specific characteristics, since, as Krinsky has argued, wherever neoliberal restructuring is tried, "it generates specific sorts of opposition depending upon the existing configuration of, and division of labor in, state and civil society groups in political-economic space" (Krinsky 2006, 159).

In New York, a range of progressive forces rejected the city's attempts to mediate the child care crisis through strategies of privatization. Welfare rights and child care activists, labor unions, and low-income community groups—alongside allies in child care advocacy associations, women's organizations, and community legal clinics—developed strategies of resistance that pushed the city to socialize more of the costs of and responsibilities for child care. This resistance evoked the rich tradition of poor and working-class women's struggle over welfare, child care, and the value of women's care work in New York, struggles that shaped the urban politics of social reproduction from below. In this chapter, I focus on five campaigns that took root in the ten-plus years following welfare reform, extending beyond the Giuliani years and into the administration of "CEO mayor" Michael Bloomberg.

As each of these campaigns illustrate, neoliberal forces in New York had their own "unique vulnerabilities, zones of overextension, undefended flanks" (Leitner, Peck, and Sheppard 2007, 315). Privatized solutions for the child care crisis opened space for contestation and resistance. While the city restructured the relationships between poor women, the state, and the market along neoliberal lines, progressive forces resisted the logic of "child care on the cheap" and sought to reshape this relationship on terms more favorable to welfare mothers and child care providers. Before exploring these campaigns in depth, and to help situate struggles at the intersection of welfare and child care, I first provide a brief overview of welfare rights organizing in 1990s New York.

Welfare Rights Organizing in Giuliani's New York

Welfare recipients and welfare rights groups had no shortage of grievances with New York City's workfare regime. As the New York Bar Association's Committee on Social Welfare Law put it, the city's welfare-to-work strategy was one of "diversion, misinformation, and discrimination," and the Giuliani administration "seemed to violate welfare law with impunity" (CSWL 2001, 328). However, while New York was once the center of militant welfare rights struggles, by the 1990s, according to organizers, "welfare organizing in the city had been largely anemic for ten years" (Dulchin and Kasmir 2004, 2).

In terms of its strength and effectiveness, resistance to welfare reform in New York was uneven, as it was across the country.[2] Most welfare rights activism was defensive in nature, what Mimi Abramovitz in her overview of post-TANF welfare activism has called "damage control" (2000, 142–52). While the city's welfare rights advocates and activists sought to limit the harm inflicted on the poor by a punitive welfare bureaucracy, city officials claimed that these efforts had little impact on the HRA's policies and practices. According to Jason Turner, the city's welfare rights movement "was ineffective . . . they [welfare rights groups] did very little that slowed us down" (Turner, personal communication, August 25, 2009).

Due to its centrality in New York's workfare regime, and the degree to which it threatened well-paid union jobs, the Work Experience Program became the primary target of welfare rights activism, bringing together antipoverty organizations and unions (Tait 2005). This activism focused on the harsh working conditions and various indignities experienced by welfare recipients placed in unpaid public-sector jobs (Dulchin and Kasmir 2006; Krinsky 2007a; Tait 2005). Some unions and community organizations made attempts to unionize WEP workers, but their efforts faced numerous obstacles, including lukewarm support from some elements of the city's labor movement—particularly the city's largest public employees' union, DC 37—and a series of court decisions that cemented the legal status of workfare workers as public assistance recipients, not city employees (Krinsky 2007a).[3] Welfare rights campaigners did, however, win a number of important changes to the WEP, including around health and safety and basic respect and dignity on the job, as well as the right to count time spent in school, internships, and vocational training toward a recipient's work requirement of thirty-five hours a week (Krinksy 2007a).

Beyond resistance to the WEP, welfare rights organizing produced a number of small but important victories. Antipoverty lawyers launched legal challenges at the administrative level, representing welfare recipients in the HRA's "fair hearings" procedures—the only formal mechanism by which clients can challenge the decisions of welfare bureaucrats (Interview 1). These challenges brought about important changes to the frontline practices of welfare caseworkers and to city and state laws and regulations. For instance, the HRA was forced to make some progressive changes to policies around eligibility determination, the appropriateness of work assignments, and the ease of access to welfare benefits and support services. Such victories struck blows against the rampant and illegal use of sanctions by welfare caseworkers and the various strategies used to divert families from the welfare rolls (Krinsky 2006; Krinsky 2007a).

While these were small victories, and the disciplinary apparatus of New York's workfare regime was largely left intact, welfare rights organizations pushed the city to address issues of access and equity it would have otherwise ignored (Krinsky 2006; Krinsky 2007a). In other words, welfare rights activism ensured that a punitive and inhumane workfare regime was made a little less punitive and slightly less inhumane. The gains made by activists and advocates organizing at the intersection of welfare and child care were more far-reaching.

The Child Care Activism of WEP Workers Together, 1996–1998

In 1996, three nonprofit community organizations came together to form a welfare rights coalition to organize WEP workers under the banner of WEP Workers Together (WWT).[4] The WEP required welfare recipients to "pay off" their welfare benefits by working for the city at poverty wages. Recipients were assigned to a variety of unskilled jobs, often in clerical or custodial services or in the city's parks department, regardless of their work experience, skills, or level of education. While working alongside unionized city employees, WEP workers were denied health and safety training, vacation and sick leave, and a paycheck. In addition, they were deprived of the right to form a union and collectively bargain (Krinsky 2007a). WWT set out to document these abuses and organize the nearly forty thousand WEP participants in their communities and at their job sites. At the time, it was the largest campaign to organize workfare workers in the country (Tait 2005).[5]

WWT initially focused on "work-related issues," such as wages, workers' lack of rights, and routine health and safety violations.[6] Child care was not an immediate priority, and the reasons for this are complex. First, the WEP initially drew welfare recipients from the state's Safety Net Assistance program, a program for single individuals and childless couples. Thus, from WWT's inception in 1996 to the peak of anti-WEP organizing in 1998, child care was not a concern for the majority of workfare participants (Interview 11).

Second, in contrast to the welfare rights organizing of the 1960s and 1970s, which saw women on welfare mobilize around a multilayered political identity—as welfare recipients, mothers, members of a racial group, and community members (Nadasen 2005)—for strategic reasons, WWT sought to organize workfare participants by focusing on their identity as "workers." This strategy was designed to advance the coalition's initial claim on the state, which was to have WEP participants reclassified as employees of the city under state law, opening the way for their unionization (Krinsky 2007a). Furthermore, according to organizers the identity of "worker," as opposed to "welfare recipient" or "welfare mother," was gender-neutral and more likely to foster solidarity between WEP workers and potential allies in the labor movement (Tait 2005).

Yet according to Krinsky, by the end of 1997, WWT's focus on "WEP workers' rights and identity *as workers* was giving way to, or at least coexisting with, a focus on WEP workers as *potential workers*, whose primary needs were education, training, and child care" (Krinsky 2007a, 17; emphasis in original). WWT's failure to successfully challenge WEP participants' misclassification under labor law necessitated this shift. With unionization off the cards, the identity of "potential worker" opened space to make claims on the state that took into consideration the needs of poor single mothers in WEP as gendered subjects—that is, as mothers with child care needs that had to be met in order for them to participate in welfare-to-work activities.

In addition, by early 1998 an increasing number of TANF recipients were being placed in WEP assignments, changing the balance between single mothers and childless adults in the program. Over the next year, WWT organizers gained a heightened awareness of the systemic violation of welfare mothers' child care rights, including the illegal use of sanctions to push mothers to rely on informal child care. Lacking stable child care arrangements, increasing numbers of WEP participants were failing to show up for their work assignments and as a result were being sanctioned by the HRA (Interview 11).

With these dynamics at play, WWT turned its attention to child care. In June 1998, the coalition organized a "guerrilla day care" center demonstration at HRA headquarters (Interview 11). As mentioned in the introduction to this chapter, close to fifty children and adults marched into the building on Water Street in downtown Manhattan, hung up a sign declaring the space a day care center, and jumped rope and played ball (Dulchin and Kasmir 2004, 5). According to organizers, the demonstration sent security guards and HRA staff "into a tizzy" and shut down the entrance to the building. After a period of negotiation with lower-level staff, Commissioner Lilliam Barrios-Paoli—Jason Turner's predecessor at HRA—agreed to meet with a WWT delegation at a later date (Interview 11).

At that meeting, WEP workers aired their child care–related grievances (Interview 11). Barrios-Paoli agreed to work with activists to compose a two-page child care fact sheet to be included in HRA call-in notices and to develop a child care checklist for welfare caseworkers. The commissioner also agreed to a small increase in the value of child care vouchers allotted to WEP participants (Interview 11). Responding to reporters after the meeting, a spokesperson for the commissioner said that the delegation's "ideas were valid and their suggestions very good." For their part, WWT organizers believed the commissioner seemed "genuinely committed to improving the system so that HRA can provide people with better child care options" (quoted in Brooke and Epstein 1997, 4).

However, by late 1998, Barrios-Paoli—who publicly criticized some of the more draconian elements of the city's workfare regime—had been replaced by Turner. With Giuliani's handpicked commissioner in place, many of WWT's child care grievances went unaddressed. While WWT was eventually successful in forcing the city to create a transitional jobs program that emphasized training and education instead of public-sector job placements (perhaps the coalition's most important victory), the guerrilla day care center was the only direct action that focused exclusively on the issue of child care. According to a lead organizer, WWT "didn't do that much around the issue of child care" as the coalition's focus "was on jobs." If this focus necessitated action on child care, then the issue would be incorporated into WWT's work (Interview 11). As a member-driven organization, WWT claimed to organize around those issues that most troubled its members, and, according to the organizer, "Child care just wasn't the issue that was raised the most . . . the issues that came up were worksite violations, health and safety concerns, and that people wanted a paycheck. The thing is, if you're at a job that doesn't pay, you might be concerned about child care, but your fight isn't to get better child care at an unpaid job but to get a paid job" (Interview 11).

In sum, in making claims on the state, WWT initially organized around a masculine construct of "work" and "worker" that precluded the child care needs of TANF participants as mothers. When the campaign's demand to have WEP participants reclassified as employees failed, WWT shifted its organizing to focus on the needs of WEP participants as "potential workers," including training and education. This shift opened the space to organize around the demands of welfare mothers as gendered subjects, including the need for adequate child care. However, throughout WWT's campaign, its members, the majority of whom were single adults without children, did not prioritize child care.

Yet with its direct action tactics, WWT made an important contribution to future struggles at the intersection of welfare and child care. Prior to the city's implementation of federal welfare reform, little attention had been given to the connection between child care and welfare rights. The "guerrilla day care center" was one of the first public demonstrations to center child care in welfare rights organizing and to turn the media's spotlight on the city's child care crisis and the inadequacy of the welfare bureaucracy in dealing with it. As child care advocates, welfare rights groups, and legal-aid lawyers ramped up their activism and advocacy efforts, child care would come to take a prominent place in struggles against the city's workfare regime.

Contesting "Choice" in Child Care and Welfare Rights Advocacy, 1996–2001

In contrast to the direct action tactics employed by WWT, child care and welfare rights advocates took a less confrontational and more sustained approach to defend poor mothers' welfare and child care rights. Organizations such as Child Care Inc. and the NOW Legal Defense and Education Fund and community legal clinic South Brooklyn Legal Services relied on outreach, popular education, and "know your rights" workshops to make welfare mothers aware of their rights under state and federal law. They represented welfare mothers in "fair hearings" procedures—where recipients could contest their caseworker's decisions—and produced research reports with the intent of publicly shaming the city into action on child care. In their advocacy work, these organizations invoked the administration's rhetoric of "parental choice" to claim that real choice in child care required public investment in affordable, quality care as well as an end to the policies and frontline practices that played a role in poor mothers' overreliance on informal care.

PATHWAYS TO SUCCESS

By 1998, the HRA was facing negative coverage in the media and sustained public criticism from child care advocates for its failure to provide welfare mothers with adequate child care. In response, in the fall of 1999 the HRA agreed to fund Child Care Inc. (CCI), along with four other child care resource and referral agencies, to provide on-site child care information and referral services at selected welfare offices (Interview 5). Under this project, a "child care councillor" spent one day a week at an HRA job center providing advice and support to welfare recipients. The nature of this support included making sure recipients were aware of the child care benefits to which they were entitled and informing recipients that they could not be lawfully sanctioned for failure to comply with work requirements due to lack of adequate child care. The councillor would also assist mothers in locating a child care provider of their choice, playing a role in which welfare caseworkers had proven to be negligent.

Over the length of this project, CCI's child care councillors served over four hundred women (CCI 2003). Belying the city's rhetoric of "parental choice," the project found that 90 percent of mothers who received child care assistance from CCI's on-site councillor opted for a regulated child care setting for their children (CCI 2003). These findings contradicted the Giuliani administration's line on child care and caused some embarrassment for the HRA's top brass (Interview 5). Yet in a move that further revealed the city's commitment to child care on the cheap, the HRA failed to renew CCI's contract, and the information and referral program was subsequently ended due to "lack of resources" (CCI 2003, 11). While CCI had connected with a few allies in the child care division of HRA—city staffers who were also concerned about poor mothers' reliance on informal child care—these voices were marginalized by the agency's senior administrators (Interview 12; Interview 5).

Not to be deterred, CCI decided to embark on a child care referral project of its own. The project, called Pathways to Success, had a dual function: first, to ensure that welfare mothers had access to regulated child care through outreach and a telephone support line, and second, a more expressly political function, to further demonstrate that poor single mothers' overreliance on informal care did not reflect their preferences—that is, was not simply a matter of "parental choice" (Interview 5). With no funding from the city, CCI secured financial support for the project from a liberal philanthropic foundation.

Pathways ran over two phases between 1996 and 1999 and provided child care counseling to close to three thousand welfare mothers (CCI 1999). Under the project, advocates conducted citywide outreach to welfare mothers in job centers, employment programs, and community agencies. They tracked the progress of around eighteen hundred women who called the Pathways child care phone line for assistance (CCI 1999).

The project confirmed what CCI and other agencies had found during their HRA-funded research: while 83 percent of TANF families placed their children in informal care, 85 percent of Pathways families opted for regulated settings. Furthermore, for mothers looking to access transitional child care, 75 percent were not aware of their eligibility or even the existence of TCC before calling Pathways. CCI concluded that HRA caseworkers were systematically failing to notify their clients about transitional child care benefits (CCI 1999).

As a respected child care advocacy group and one that occasionally relied on contracts with municipal agencies, CCI had to decide the most effective way of mobilizing its knowledge without jeopardizing its relationship with

the city (Interview 5). While the organization's tactics were less confrontational than WWT, they nonetheless had some impact. In an attempt to publicly shame the Giuliani administration, CCI issued a press release stating that
its research had conclusively demonstrated that informal child care arrangements did not work long-term for women transitioning into the labor market from public assistance. With the proper information and support to make
"good child care choices," CCI argued, welfare mothers could access "child
care that meets their child's developmental and education needs, and supports
their transition to employment" (CCI 1999, 3).

While the press release garnered some media interest, change was not immediately forthcoming. Yet representatives from CCI did win an audience
with HRA senior staff, who agreed to look into the procedures surrounding
the issuance of child care information and advice by the agency's caseworkers
(Interview 12). While this may seem like a small victory, the Giuliani administration's doors were typically closed to any advocacy or community group perceived to be critical of the mayor's policies, including CCI. Advocates believed
that the positive media attention given to Pathways, and ongoing coverage of
welfare mothers' child care crisis, pushed the administration to invite CCI to
the table (Interview 12).

CCI's work was complemented by the legal advocacy work of the New York
chapter of NOW. The feminist organization's Legal Defense and Education
Fund took up the cases of welfare mothers whose child care rights had been
violated by HRA, particularly the practice of illegally sanctioning mothers for
failure to work due to lack of adequate child care. Much to the chagrin of the
city's welfare bureaucracy, NOW-LDEF was successful in almost all of its cases
(Interview 12). As the organization's lead lawyer put it, "The city was counting
on people not to complain, but we did. If you had a representative, you could
take them [HRA] on over child care" (Interview 12). This legal advocacy, along
with popular education and outreach to welfare mothers, was sustained between 1998 and 2002 (Interview 12).

NOW-LDEF's work helped other organizations identify and act on child
care and welfare rights violations (Interview 2). For instance, South Brooklyn
Legal Services (SBLS), a community legal clinic with roots in the War on Poverty, was granted a two-year fellowship, funded by the National Association of
Public Law, to focus on the child care rights of TANF recipients. SBLS's lead
lawyer found that "there were all kinds of procedures that [HRA staff] weren't
following that they should have been" (Interview 2). SBLS built on the work of
NOW-LDEF and CCI, representing hundreds of welfare recipients at individual "fair hearings" procedures and conducting "know your rights" workshops

with women on welfare and low-income community organizations throughout the city (Interview 2).

This collective work had a significant impact on welfare mothers, repealing sanctions and allowing them the time they needed to find adequate child care arrangements. Fewer mothers were to be forced into relying on unsafe and poor-quality child care. More mothers could head to their workfare placements with some peace of mind. And the city's welfare bureaucracy was being held accountable for the most egregious violations of poor women's welfare rights (Interview 2). Yet despite hundreds of successful interventions by lawyers, the institutional culture of HRA resisted change, and the violations were seemingly systemic in nature.

REGULATING INFORMAL CHILD CARE

Frustrated with the intransigence of HRA, child care advocates and welfare rights lawyers made the decision to shift their focus to the state agencies responsible for child care and welfare (Interview 12). Armed with the findings of CCI's research reports as well as case law, NOW-LDEF convinced state officials to issue a Local Commissioner's Memorandum advising all New York county welfare administrators, including Jason Turner at HRA, of their responsibility to inform parents on public assistance that they could not be sanctioned due to lack of adequate child care. The state issued a second notice that apprised TANF recipients of their child care rights and options. In response to the memorandum, HRA reissued a policy directive informing welfare caseworkers of the availability of the notice and providing instructions for conveying child care information to TANF clients, including a written notice about their child care rights (Powell and Cahill 2000, 3).

However, as lawyers with NOW remarked, "While the issuance of the memorandum and the policy directive are significant in that they reiterate the city's pre-existing obligation to inform parents of their child care rights, it is important to point out that the city has a record of ignoring precisely these rights" (Powell and Cahill 2000, 8). Indeed, a 2001 follow-up study found that the city had all but ignored the directives and that many parents were still not given "adequate information about child care" and were "actually wrongly threatened with sanctions, i.e. a reduction or termination of their welfare benefits, if they could not work due to lack of child care" (Powell and Cahill 2001, 2). With the city still failing to live up to its obligations under law, child care and welfare rights advocates continued to lobby state policy makers and found an important ally in the Office of the State Deputy Comptroller, the veteran

Democratic Party politician Carl McCall. McCall had been one of the key voices warning of the escalation of the city's child care crisis in the years leading up to welfare reform (see McCall 1997). As an elected official, the state comptroller is responsible for auditing New York's local governments, hence McCall's interest in how state TANF monies were being spent by the city.

McCall had publicly opposed the use of TANF funds for informal child care, arguing that it was not developmentally appropriate and by nature lacked regulatory oversight (McCall 1997). In a series of reports, McCall criticized the city for its use of child care–related sanctions, its failure to expand regulated day care slots despite significant increases in state and federal child care funding, and its failure to reimburse home and center-based child care providers promptly—a common occurrence when parents used vouchers to pay for child care services (A. Hevesi 2002; McCall 2000). McCall's office also criticized the state child care bureaucracy for doing too little to regulate the health and safety of informal child care settings (A. Hevesi 2002).

The sustained criticism from advocates, state officials, and activists finally had a substantive impact on the city's child care policies. The Administration for Children's Services committed to a new regulatory regime for informal child care, implementing new health and safety regulations that required criminal background checks and checks of a child abuse and negligence registry for all informal providers caring for children outside the child's home. ACS staff were to monitor compliance by visiting informal providers within sixty days of the providers receiving voucher payments. In addition, staff were instructed to provide informal providers with information on health and safety, link interested providers to technical assistance and nutrition training, and offer providers assistance and advice on how to become licensed (ACS 2001). According to the ACS, the goal was to "assure that care provided through informal and license-exempt caregivers, and supported with public funds, provides a healthy and safe environment for children" (ACS 2001, 1).

Overall, child care advocates believed that the changes would have a positive impact on the quality, safety, and stability of informal child care (Interview 4). And in offering informal caregivers a pathway to becoming licensed family day care providers, the new regime would not only expand the supply of regulated child care in the city but also raise the incomes of an underpaid, largely female workforce. If one outcome of the city's policies at the intersection of welfare reform and child care was the deregulation of publicly funded child care services, advocates had successfully fought for and won some regulation and oversight of informal care and a route to professionalization for informal providers.

There were other signs of progress. By 2003, 77 percent of welfare recipients were using vouchers to purchase informal care, down from 84 percent in 2001 and a high of 89 percent in 2000. This meant thousands more of the city's poorest and most vulnerable children were now in regulated and, by most accounts, better-quality child care settings. Child care advocates and welfare rights groups believed this shift was a direct result of their ongoing efforts (Interview 4; Interview 5). According to a senior child care official in the HRA, the sustained advocacy and activism pushed the welfare bureaucracy to place greater emphasis on regulated care, informing caseworkers of its importance and ensuring compliance with state-issued memorandums (Interview 16).

Advocates reported that the HRA had indeed made "extensive efforts to increase the agency's responsiveness to child care concerns" (CCI 2003, 4). Child Care Inc. cited progress in the way the HRA operated in a number of areas, including improved parents' access to information regarding child care options, improved timeliness and consistency of payments to home-based child care providers, enhanced quality and safety of informal care, and, perhaps most importantly, increased and continuous child care training for welfare caseworkers (CCI 2003). While acknowledging this progress, CCI noted that "questions remain about how much consistent information and access HRA families have about their range of child care options ... families may continue to lack information about or access to other regulated child care options that meet their needs" (CCI 2003, 4). Thus, while advocates recognized and celebrated the progress that had been made, they recognized too the need to remain vigilant and continue to hold city agencies accountable.

FROM WELFARE RIGHTS TO ORGANIZING THE "POOR MOTHER'S NANNY"

Child care advocates and welfare rights activists had pushed for greater regulation of informal care and fought with some success to ensure that poor mothers had real choice in child care, as evidenced by the increasing number of mothers gaining access to both subsidies and regulated care. Yet as the welfare rolls continued their rapid decline, advocacy and activism at the intersection of welfare and child care began to shift. As one of the city's leading welfare rights lawyers recalls, "From 1998 to 2000 we were helping welfare recipients get access to child care benefits. But as time went on, we started getting calls from child care providers who weren't being paid ... many of these providers were barely indistinguishable from our clients on public assistance. They were very low-income women of color. By 2002, our work had almost completely shifted from recipients to providers" (Interview 2). South Brooklyn Legal Services (SBLS) and other welfare rights organizations increasingly began to serve home-based child care providers—primarily family day care providers—helping these women navigate municipal day care regulations and win back pay owed by negligent city agencies and assisting them with auditing and taxation issues.

According to some advocates, one reason for this shift was that as welfare reform moved from "political hot button" to "new normal," philanthropic funding for welfare rights casework began to dry up (Interview 1; Interview 2), and campaigns to defend the rights of poor mothers to stay at home and care for their own children found little political traction (Reese 2011, 20). Yet there was another dynamic at play: by 2000, the flow of public child care dollars to informal and family day care providers seemed irreversible. In New York and across the country, thousands of home-based child care providers were now receiving subsidies from the state for serving children from low-income families. Racial justice activists Rinku Sen and Gabriel Thompson called this kind of provider "the poor mother's nanny," noting that "few things distinguish her from her clientele—they live in the same neighborhood, they are the same color and they're all occupying the lower shelves of the economy" (2006, 20). Some of these women had recently transitioned from welfare to paid work as licensed family day care providers, while others were aunts or grandmothers, friends, or neighbors providing child care to help out kith and kin (Chaudry 2004; Jones 2014; Sen and Thompson 2006).

Labor and welfare rights activists argued that organizing this low-wage workforce to push for higher subsidy reimbursement rates, access to benefits, and increased public investment in child care would bring together poor mothers' need for affordable and quality care with home child care providers' desire for recognition, respect, and decent wages (Brooks 2005). As child care advocates pointed out, raising wages and standards in the home-based sector, including through training and professional development, would result in lower turnover, more stability in care arrangements, and better-quality care, benefiting providers, parents, and children (Whitebook 2001). This common interest, in addition to their shared social location and community ties, proved to be fertile ground for home child care organizing and building solidarity between care providers and poor single mothers.

Rather than lament the shift in public resources from New York's high-quality, center-based child care programs (and their unionized workforce) to the least-regulated, least-trained, and worst-paid sectors of the child care industry, low-income community organizations, child care advocates, and labor activists set about organizing the "poor mother's nanny" to challenge the devaluation of her work and fight for a better deal from the city and state. In this they sought to make the work of home child care visible, break providers' isolation, and build their political capacities and collective power.

Toward Quality Care and Decent Work in the Home Child Care Sector

By 2003, the pool of home-based providers caring for publicly subsidized children in New York City numbered around twenty-eight thousand—seven thousand licensed family day care providers and approximately twenty-one thousand license-exempt or "informal" providers.[7] Over a period of ten years, from 1993 to 2003, the number of family day cares in the city had more than doubled (McMillan 2002; Sen and Thompson 2006).[8] Almost all of this growth was concentrated in low-income neighborhoods, where the demand for child care unleashed by welfare reform was greatest (ACS 2005).

Unlike their unionized peers in the center-based programs funded and overseen by the city, home child care workers experience a high degree of precariousness in employment. Under state and federal labor law, home-based providers are classified as either independent contractors—that is as self-employed small business owners—or otherwise not in an employer-employee relationship, in the case of a small number of informal providers who provide care in a child's home (Chalfie, Blank, and Entmacher 2007, 7). Excluded from the legal definition of "employee," they are left out of basic labor and employment laws that offer protection to most other workers, including minimum wage, overtime, and employment insurance, and from the right to organize and collectively bargain.[9] Furthermore, owing to the low subsidy reimbursement rates set by the state, many providers had average hourly earnings below the minimum wage, and it was not unusual for providers to earn annual incomes that left them living below the poverty line (Sen and Thompson 2006; Whitebook 1999). Bureaucratic delays in reimbursement payments from city agencies and problems in the approval and payment of child care subsidies exacerbated providers' financial difficulties, leaving many unable to pay rent and other household bills on time (Interview 8). Home-based providers did not have access to sick days, health insurance, or a pension plan through their work (UFT 2005).

Unlike a center-based child care worker, a home-based provider's job tenure is directly dependent on one's relationships with the parents of children in their care. Whereas the city's center-based workers are paid an hourly wage, home child care providers are paid on a per child basis, and parents can withdraw a child from their care with little or no notice. For home child care providers, this means little to no job security and incomes that fluctuate depending on the number of children in their care and the duration of care (Black 2012). Finally, with parents often working nonstandard hours or varying schedules (or both), home-based providers have little control over their hours: some New York City providers report working as many as twelve to fifteen hours a day (Sen and Thompson 2006). In sum, by channeling public funds to home child care providers, the state had facilitated the expansion of a precarious, low-wage workforce while denying that the home was a workplace and denying that providers were public employees deserving of rights, benefits, decent wages and working conditions.

THE SATELLITE CHILD CARE PROGRAM, 2000–2005

The Satellite Child Care program was an innovative attempt to harness government funds to organize the "poor mother's nanny." The program was the brainchild of labor activists at the Consortium for Worker Education (CWE), a nonprofit education and training institute that is an arms-length body of the New York City Central Labor Council. Seed money for Satellite came in the form of a $5 million federal welfare-to-work grant, one of many competitive grants awarded to local governments by the U.S. Department of Labor for the purpose of promoting experimentation and discovering "best practices" in workfare programming. More often than not, these grants were used by local welfare agencies to demonstrate just how quickly and cheaply they could push welfare mothers into the labor market and thereby draw down TANF funds from state governments (Peck 2001).

While welfare reform abrogated poor mothers' rights to care full-time for their own children, caring for other women's children, including those of women on welfare, is a recognized work activity under TANF (Mink 2002, 108).[10] States and counties have long considered care work as both an acceptable and viable career option for poor mothers transitioning into employment, and, in the wake of welfare reform, many local governments encouraged welfare recipients to become paid child care providers or home health aides (Boris and Klein 2008; Chaudry 2004; Jones 2014). Over half of states encouraged former welfare recipients to become child care providers but did so "without [establishing] the necessary training or support that leads to quality care or decent child care jobs" (Whitebook 2001, 16–17). In contrast, Satellite sought to leverage state funds to subvert this model of welfare-to-work, providing poor women on public assistance with the education and training necessary to become qualified child care providers (Interview 8).

The CWE pitched Satellite as a "workfare" program that would provide welfare mothers with supports to enable their transition from public assistance to work as home child care providers. The consortium applied its significant union-backed lobbying power to convince New York State legislators to help fund the project and recognize Satellite Child Care as a distinct category of child care from center-based, family day care, and informal child care. Seeing its potential as a workfare initiative, the HRA and New York State's Office of Children and Family Services provided the CWE with technical assistance. Welfare recipients were recommended to the program by their caseworkers or through the consortium's community contacts. Despite these partnerships, the CWE remained the sole sponsor and manager of the program (Interview 8).

According to Satellite's founders, the program sought to address two fundamental problems that arose from welfare reform: the lack of good jobs for women leaving welfare and the shortage of affordable, quality child care for low-income working moms (Interview 8). To this end, Satellite established a comprehensive training and professional development regime for its participants. Trainees underwent an assessment process to determine their suitability for the program, including a background check and a two-week job-readiness course. In partnership with a child care resource and referral agency, participants were placed in a twelve-week internship in which 60 percent of their time was spent in supervised, hands-on work activity at a partnering day care agency and the rest devoted to studying early childhood education in a classroom setting. This extensive professional development counted toward trainees' welfare-to-work requirements under state law and was the equivalent of earning an associate's degree in early childhood education. After participants completed their training, Satellite set up family day cares in their homes, calling them "off-site classrooms," and they became affiliated with an existing family child care agency.

Satellite was designed to match the developmental aspects of center-based care and included structured programming, high-nutrition meal plans, and parental involvement. Although Satellite received funds from all three levels of government, providers were employees of the CWE, importantly, not independent contractors like their peers in home child care. Furthermore, as a labor council affiliate, the CWE ensured that Satellite providers were unionized and represented by District Council (DC) 1707 of AFSCME, the same union that represented the city's day care workers. As unionized employees they were covered by a collective agreement.

Once their family child care program was established, this new employment model meant that Satellite providers, although working in-home like family day care providers, were given assistance in site preparation, a start-up kit of safety and educational supplies, and received biweekly visits from qualified support staff to ensure that program requirements were being met. Yet as trained professionals, providers maintained a degree of autonomy in determining programming for children in their care, and they were encouraged to work toward further professional accreditation.

Despite an ambitious plan to train one thousand new family child care providers citywide, Satellite at its peak had just over 170 providers on its books, caring for a total of about fourteen hundred children (Interview 8). In terms of job security, the tenure of Satellite providers was tied to their job as a Satellite employee, and it was up to the CWE, not providers, to recruit children to the program. Crucially, if providers did not have the maximum number of children in their care for any length of time, they still remained full-time employees and were not subject to reduced pay. If a parent pulled a child from care, the CWE, not the individual provider, was responsible for filling the space. In addition, under their collective agreement, Satellite providers were covered by seniority provisions. A sympathetic employer, the CWE, along with the union, ensured that providers' overtime was recorded and paid, health and safety conditions met, and vacations covered.

Perhaps most importantly, the providers' starting salary was around $18,200 per year, and under their collective agreement they received cost of living allowances of 2 percent each year for three years and then a 3 percent increase in year five of the contract. Providers were paid approved overtime for hours worked beyond forty a week and could earn up to $25,000 a year, bringing them above the federal poverty line for a two-adult, two-child family. Providers received benefits, including health insurance, a pension, and vacation and sick leave, as well as tuition reimbursement for their professional development. They also received $1,500 in start-up materials like naptime cots, books, and toys (McMillan 2002). Satellite providers' wages, benefits, and working conditions were comparable to that of workers in the city's unionized day care centers and markedly better than that of a typical home-based child care provider.

THE DEMISE OF SATELLITE

Ultimately, Satellite ran up against political and economic constraints imposed by a city (and state) committed to a privatized, low-cost model of child care. In order for Satellite to be successful, the subsidy reimbursement rates paid by the city to the CWE, which in turn paid the salaries of the program's providers, had to be set at or near the rate paid to the city's day care centers. In effect, Satellite was to be home-based child care subsidized at the level of center-based care. Yet despite intense lobbying by Satellite's directors, this rate was never realized, and eventually alternative funding streams, such as legislative line items from the state, began to dry up. While the CWE fought to keep the program alive, incurring significant debts, the program shut down in 2005 due to lack of funds. Some Satellite providers went on to find employment in child care centers, while others set up independent home day cares, using the skills acquired through the program to earn livelihoods as accredited family day care providers.

In short, by linking quality care with improved pay and working conditions—and union representation—Satellite failed to meet the city's test of delivering child care on the cheap. Yet the program was only the first shot across the bow in a protracted struggle that pitted the city and state against a coalition of low-income community organizations and labor unions seeking to raise wages, working conditions, and quality standards in the city's home child care sector. Whereas Satellite sought to organize the "poor mother's nanny" on a small scale, other activists and advocates dreamed big. By 2002, community organizations such as the New York chapter of the Association of Community Organizations for Reform Now (ACORN) and Families United for Racial and Economic Equality (FUREE) were strategizing child care provider campaigns of their own (Interview 7; Interview 10). In time they would be joined by one of the city's most powerful and politically connected unions, the United Federation of Teachers.

The FUREE Child Care Campaign, 2004–2007

FUREE is a Brooklyn-based multiracial community organization made up almost exclusively of poor and working-class women of color (FUREE 2008). In its emphasis on direct action, community organizing, and grassroots leadership, and its recognition of the intersections of race, class, and gender justice, FUREE is grounded in the legacy and traditions of the welfare rights movement. And, like that movement, FUREE is committed to organizing low-income women, whether doing paid work in the formal economy or unpaid work in the household and community. As FUREE's mission statement puts it, "We seek to build power to change the system so that all people's work is valued and all people have the right and economic means to decide and live out our own destinies" (FUREE 2008).

FUREE was founded in the winter of 2000 when a group of fifteen welfare mothers came together to demand access to education and training in the WEP. With common grievances, the women organized a direct action campaign against the HRA and participated in New York's first anti-WEP coalition (FUREE 2008). Through this work, FUREE built a base among welfare mothers in downtown Brooklyn. In addition to women on welfare, the group's founding members included a number of family day care providers, some of whom had recently transitioned from public assistance to paid child care work (Interview 6).

In June 2001, FUREE held a leadership retreat where members engaged in intensive political education, strategized campaigns, and set the organization's agenda for the coming year. In small group discussions, members made connections between the interests of welfare mothers and home-based child care providers (Interview 6). On the one hand, women on public assistance expressed frustration with the lack of stable, quality child care in their neighborhoods. The shortage of decent child care was a barrier to complying with the HRA's work requirements, and a number of FUREE members had been sanctioned by their caseworkers for failure to find child care. On the other hand, FUREE members who were family day care providers complained that they were not being reimbursed by the city in time to pay their bills, if reimbursed at all. This had led a growing number of providers to refuse to accept child care vouchers, exacerbating the shortage of regulated child care in the low-income neighborhoods FUREE members called home (Interview 7).

While these dynamics might have become a source of tension between the two groups, child care providers and welfare mothers broke bread. Engaging in what organizers called "consciousness-raising," they shared stories and found common ground for collective struggle. As one family day care provider put it, "We came to realize that us [child care] providers are treated by the city just like women on welfare . . . not in a respectable way" (Interview 7). As one of the retreat's organizers observed, some of FUREE's home child care providers "had come off the welfare rolls, so they understood the needs of those members still on public assistance" (Interview 7).

Coming out of these discussions, FUREE decided to organize at the intersection of welfare and child care, launching a campaign that centered on economic justice for welfare recipients and home child care providers. In researching the home child care sector, FUREE quickly learned about other issues impacting providers' livelihoods and ability to "successfully do their jobs," including their lack of health insurance and sick days, as well as the presence of burdensome and confusing day care regulations (FUREE 2008). According to one organizer, "We came to realize how connected parents' and providers' issues were, because when providers are treated poorly, parents can't keep their jobs, go to school, or comply with workfare requirements" (Interview 7). FUREE's child care campaign would seek to bring together parents and providers "to fight for better working conditions for providers" and ensure "that all work is valued and respected equally" (FUREE 2008).

After moving in fits and starts, by 2004 FUREE's child care campaign had begun in earnest. The organization devoted a staff member, herself a former welfare recipient, to the campaign full-time. She was joined by a well-respected family child care provider and veteran community activist (Interview 7). In the initial stages of the campaign, FUREE-affiliated child care providers conducted outreach to friends, family, and acquaintances who also operated home day cares. In addition, FUREE members with children in home child care encouraged their providers to attend organizing meetings and get involved in the campaign. Without a common worksite, this community organizing approach was vital to breaking home-based child care providers' isolation and building a grassroots network of activist providers.

According to organizers, the common grievances of family day care providers, particularly the issue of late payments from the city, fueled the rapid growth of the campaign. While only three home child care providers attended the campaign's founding meeting in late 2004, within a few months FUREE had organized just over two hundred dues-paying providers (Interview 7). Before the launch of the campaign, FUREE's total membership stood at around three hundred, so family day care providers had quickly come to make up a significant part of the organization's membership base.

The child care campaign centered on two issues that FUREE considered vital to providers' survival: late reimbursement payments from the HRA and ACS, and the matter of the city's health and safety regulations and their enforcement. The latter issue took priority as city inspectors were threatening to close hundreds of family day cares throughout Brooklyn on the grounds that they were unsafe. While FUREE was steadfast in its support of quality child care, providers argued that the state's Office of Children and Family Services, working with the city's Fire and Health Departments, were unfairly applying complex and onerous safety regulations that disproportionately impacted family day cares in poor neighborhoods (Grace 2005). Most of these day cares were housed in older buildings, either in the brownstone row houses found in Brooklyn's oldest neighborhoods or in multistory public housing projects (Fahim 2005).

While there was confusion as to whether the regulations were new or just newly enforced, all family day cares were to now have two means of exit that were remote from each other and led to city streets. This disqualified a large number of family day care providers who lived in row houses where rear exits led only to a backyard. In public housing apartments, many built without fire escapes, officials were enforcing rules that forbade providers from using roof-tops connected to neighboring buildings as an alternate escape route (Grace 2005). Family day care advocates contended that the regulations were tailored more to home-based day cares upstate, which were typically located in single-family dwellings, and argued for changes that took into account the differences between housing stock upstate and in dense urban areas (Bleyer 2006).

According to one FUREE organizer, the closures threatened to displace "thousands of children who come from low-income households already living with a salary that is way below what is now minimum wage and cannot find other services with the same quality of care or better" (Interview 7). The aggressive inspection campaign had already left six hundred day care providers on the brink of being shut down, with little regard to the potential impact on providers and parents (Interview 7). Over a short period of time, city inspectors had issued more than one hundred violations and revoked the licenses of forty-one family day care providers (Bleyer 2006).[11] Given their low incomes, many providers could not afford to renovate their homes to bring them to code, and those who were tenants did not have the option.

While city officials defended the regulations and inspection regimen, closures on this scale stood to drastically reduce the supply of regulated child care in some of Brooklyn's poorest neighborhoods, just as the city was doubling down on efforts to push poor single mothers off the welfare rolls. In what appeared to be a case of city agencies working at cross purposes, the closures threatened the livelihoods of women who had transitioned from welfare to work as family day care providers as well as the women who relied on them for the care of their children (Interview 7). "I'll have to quit my job to be home," one mother told a reporter after hearing that her eighteen-month-old son's child care provider had received a violation. "They [city officials] say they want more people going to work, but they're making it harder," said another mother with a child at the same day care (quoted in Grace 2005). FUREE noted that city agencies had failed to consult providers regarding the regulations and saw the "whole mess" as indicative of how the city treated low-income women of color, further demonstrating the need for providers to organize and speak with a collective voice (Interview 7).

THE "STOP THE SHUTDOWNS" CAMPAIGN

In response to this crisis, FUREE devised a "Stop the Shutdowns" campaign with support from South Brooklyn Legal Services, allies on city council—including future mayor Bill de Blasio—and the city-contracted family child care networks to which some providers were affiliated. Organizers made a three-pronged argument. First, the regulations and inspection regimen not only threatened subsidized child care slots but also jeopardized child care quality as hundreds of providers stood to lose their licenses. Low-income children were already at risk of being placed in unregulated child care due to lack of subsidies; the mass closure of family day cares would only heighten the city's child care crisis (Fahim 2005).

Second, appealing to the logic of welfare reform, FUREE argued that the shutdowns threatened to undermine the very employment supports poor women needed to get off welfare, "as there will be no one to care for their children." Organizers pointed out that home child care was "an extremely flexible personalized type of day care that is an essential support for many low-income families to exit poverty" (FUREE 2004, 1). Ironically, this point was made all the more clear when seven thousand workers at the city's 350 subsidized day care centers, members of AFSCME Local 205, went out on strike in June 2004 demanding more pay and a contract. The strike forced the city to let mothers in welfare-to-work programs miss up to five days of work without any loss of benefits (Kaufman 2004).

Finally, FUREE made the point that the "home-grown economy of providers who reinvest money back into their communities" would be negatively impacted by the closures, possibly pushing family day care providers to rely on public assistance (FUREE 2004, 1). Again, this was counterproductive to the city's aims of curbing welfare dependency and promoting economic self-sufficiency among low-income women.

FUREE made four demands on the city and state: first, that providers be given access to easy-to-understand regulations concerning the safety of children in their care; second, that inspectors and providers be trained and educated about the new regulations; third, that the process of policy change be made transparent and public; and fourth, that a pool of money be made available as a one-time "facility improvement grant" to save family day cares from closing or going "off the books." Combined, these interventions would "protect the vital supply of child care in low-income communities, while continuing to work for the safety of children in home-based day care centers" (FUREE

2004, 2). It was an agenda that both child care providers and low-income parents could rally around.

In order to increase pressure on city hall, FUREE did intensive research to determine the actual number of child care slots at risk if the shutdowns proceeded as planned. According to this research, in three of Brooklyn's highest-needs neighborhoods—predominantly black communities with high rates of poverty and a low supply of regulated child care—anywhere from 51 percent to 91 percent of family day care spaces were at risk. A report detailing these findings was sent to every member of the city council and to the mayor's office (Interview 7).

FUREE issued a press release to publicize the report and met individually with councillors representing Brooklyn districts, all of whom proved to be sympathetic to the cause. Of particular help was Yvette Clarke, an African American councillor who, before entering politics, had worked as a child care specialist training family day care providers (Hicks 2006). Clarke coordinated city council opposition to the new regulations (Interview 7). In addition, FUREE directed its lobbying efforts at the chairs of the council's Committees on Health and Public Housing at city hall and at the city's New York State assembly members in Albany. The campaign made ample use of research by organizations like Child Care Inc., emphasizing that regulated child care in New York "was next to impossible to find" (FUREE n.d., 3). In doing so, FUREE hammered home the message that family day care providers, low-income families, and policy makers all had a common interest in stopping the shutdowns.

Reflecting the media's interest in the city's child care crisis, the campaign was covered by a number of newspapers. In addition to covering campaign rallies organized by FUREE outside the state Office of Family and Children Services, community newspapers in Brooklyn and the city's major dailies ran stories on providers who had been forced to close their day cares, leaving poor mothers and their children stranded (Grace 2005; Bleyer 2006). The *New York Times* ran an article featuring family day care provider and FUREE board member Sandra Robinson in which Robinson pleaded with the city and state, saying, "Everybody's [parents and providers] are literally in tears. Women who've had a license for twenty-five years in the same place, on the same floor, are now being shut down. There's no other choice but to change the policy" (quoted in Bleyer 2006).

At the height of the campaign, the *New York Daily News* ran a debate pitting the associate commissioner of the Health Department's Bureau of Day Care against Robinson and FUREE's director, Ilana Berger. While the associate commissioner argued that the regulations "balanced safety with the growing demand for quality child care in New York City" (Marcus 2006), Robinson and Berger called the rules "senseless," saying they did "nothing to improve quality" and "threatened the survival of 600 city daycares, where about 5,000 kids are served" (Robinson and Berger 2006). Contra the commissioner, Robinson and Berger argued that quality and safety were being jeopardized by the closures as families were being forced to use informal child care or "underground" day cares.

In the fall of 2006, FUREE held a tense press conference at the foot of Samuel's Day Care in the Flatbush section of Brooklyn. The day care was run by Sheila Samuel, a middle-aged African American woman and well-liked and respected member of the community (Malcolm 2006). City inspectors had told Samuel that her long-running day care would be forced to shut down because she lived on the sixth floor of her apartment building—one floor higher than the new regulations allowed (Malcolm 2006). A number of FUREE-affiliated home child care providers, sporting red "Stop the Shutdowns" T-shirts, stood behind a table where Samuel, Councillor Clarke, Sandra Robinson, and another family day care provider, Andrea Lugo, were seated.

Samuel told reporters that she had "cared for children in this facility—safely and with love—for 26 years" and wanted only to continue to serve her community. She extolled the virtues of family day care, saying, "The state's narrow definition of safety does not even begin to take into account the many factors that contribute to a child's safety in the community, and quality child care is one of the most important ways to keep children safe" (quoted in Witt 2006). Lugo, whose family day care had recently been closed by inspectors, broke down in tears, telling reporters she had slipped into depression since losing her business (Malcolm 2006). "There are over 60,000 children in New York who need child care," Lugo said angrily, "and we're getting shut down!" Finally, Sandra Robinson made a moving appeal: "In the time when there was the terrorist attack [September 11, 2001] . . . parents could not reach us by telephone, couldn't even get to us. But you know what, they walked and walked until they did. I remember that night so clearly. One of my parents worked in Upper Manhattan and she walked from Upper Manhattan to Bed-Stuy, Brooklyn to get to her children. And when she got there 1:30 in the morning, she lay down in my daycare with her kids until daylight when she could leave. We're not just a day care; we are part of the community" (quoted in Malcolm 2006).

The press conference received overwhelmingly positive coverage in two of New York's dailies and in the city's ethnic community newspapers (see Malcolm 2006; Shelby 2006; Witt 2006). FUREE had clearly conveyed the message that closures were negatively impacting providers, parents, and children;

that alternative child care arrangements were often unregulated and unsafe; and that the city and state were being unresponsive and insensitive to the needs of home child care providers, parents, and low-income communities of color in general. It seemed that in the court of public opinion, FUREE had gained the upper hand.

THE SHUTDOWNS STOPPED

Just weeks after the press conference, and with campaign momentum building, FUREE and its allies on city council sat down in negotiations with city and state bureaucrats to resolve the building and fire code issues. Soon after this meeting, regulatory changes were made to reflect the realities of the city's older housing stock, and family day care providers were guaranteed that future inspections would be carried out in a "respectful manner." FUREE also convinced the city to fund any "reasonable" repairs necessary to bring a day care providers' residence in line with new regulations and to help with relocation costs should providers be forced to move to stay in business (Interview 6). The victory spared hundreds of family day cares from closure and put the city on notice that home child care providers would now speak with a collective voice and demand inclusion in the policy-making process—"a seat at the table," as organizers put it. Hoping to build on its success, FUREE launched a campaign to raise subsidy reimbursement rates. Rates had been frozen since 1996, meaning that providers had gone ten years without a raise (Interview 6).

Yet while FUREE was winning battles in Brooklyn, two other organizations, ACORN and the United Federation of Teachers, had embarked on a citywide campaign to organize home child care providers.[12] Rather than bring providers into a grassroots community organization like FUREE, which relied almost exclusively on direct action militancy and community mobilization to win gains, ACORN and the United Federation of Teachers insisted that it was through a combination of community organizing strategies *and* unionization and collective bargaining that providers could best build their collective power.

ACORN and the UFT looked to home care organizing campaigns in places like California and Illinois for lessons. Like home child care providers, home health aides are a mostly female group of decentralized low-wage workers, disproportionately women of color, who provide home-based caregiving services (Boris and Klein 2008). Beginning in the 1980s, Service Employees International Union (SEIU) had pioneered a model of home care worker unionism that took into account the nontraditional nature of this work, home health workers' classification as independent contractors under the law, and their subsequent exclusion from key employment protections and labor rights, including the right to form a union and collectively bargain (Brooks 2005; Boris and Klein 2008). With home care workers paid through subsidies from the state, under programs administered by the state, the success of this model hinged on convincing policy makers to either recognize the state as an "employer of record," as in Illinois, or on the creation of a public authority with whom providers could bargain, as had happened in California (Boris and Klein 2008; Brooks 2005; Chalfie, Blank, and Entmacher 2007).[13]

Home health care unions linked demands for respect, dignity, and higher wages to improved conditions for service users, building political coalitions with stakeholders—namely senior citizens and disability activists—around the shared interest of greater public investment to improve access and quality (Boris and Klein 2008, 33). The political pressure mobilized by these coalitions was essential to home health care unions winning contracts and ensuring that state governments adequately funded home care services and fulfilled the terms of these contracts come budget time. As subsidized home-based child care exploded in the wake of welfare reform, SEIU, AFSCME, and a number of other unions believed that this innovative model of unionism could be adapted to the home child care sector (Boris and Klein 2008; Brooks 2005).

Illinois proved the testing ground. Illinois home child care providers began building their union in 1996, when some members of the pioneering home care local, SEIU 880, transitioned from home health into home child care work and requested union representation (Boris and Klein 2008, 38–39). Local 880 overcame the dispersal of home child care workers by obtaining lists of providers from the state, calling and visiting potential recruits, holding house meetings, and mobilizing existing provider associations. By 1999 their organizing efforts had paid dividends, with a legislated increase in the provider reimbursement rate (Boris and Klein 2008, 38). Then, in 2003, the state's newly elected governor—a Democrat backed by SEIU, by then the state's largest union—signed an executive order granting collective bargaining rights to home health care workers. Two years later, these rights were extended to home-based child care providers, requiring the state to engage in collective negotiations with SEIU over reimbursement rates, health insurance, training and professional development, and payment procedures (Blank, Campbell, and Entmacher 2010).

By 2005, SEIU and AFSCME were waging simultaneous home child care organizing campaigns in a number states, some of which had led to executive orders facilitating the unionization of providers (Chalfie, Blank, and Entmacher 2007).[14] In response to the deep recession of the early 2000s, state governments had passed austerity budgets, making severe cuts to child care programs, among other social services. A number of states set payment for subsidized child care at two-thirds of private costs, down from the 75 percent recommended by the federal Office of Child Care (Reese 2010). This added to providers' economic hardship as hourly earnings dropped even farther below the minimum wage, and against this backdrop AFSCME and SEIU found a workforce "ripe for mobilization" (Reese 2010, 233).

In New York, FUREE had demonstrated that despite the absence of a common worksite, the city's home child care providers could be organized and mobilized to defend their interests and those of the families they served. Yet FUREE recognized its limits as a relatively small and under-resourced community group, heavily reliant on foundation money for its survival. While the small Brooklyn-based organization could engage in community organizing and direct action, unlike a union they had neither the resources to represent providers in collective bargaining nor the political clout to lobby the state (Interview 7). ACORN and the UFT, on the other hand, were powerful actors in city and state politics, and the UFT in particular was a major contributor, both in terms of dollars and in volunteer union labor, to city and state Democrats. If home child care providers were going to secure the right to unionize and collectively bargain, they would need a strong voice in Albany.

The UFT-ACORN Campaign, 2005–2010

Before falling victim to an orchestrated assault by right-wing forces, ACORN was a national organization of membership-based, low-income community groups (Tait 2005).[15] Although its roots were in welfare rights struggles in the South, ACORN had a long-established presence in New York City, dating back to squatters' rights campaigns in the early 1980s (Atlas 2009). Throughout the 1980s and early 1990s, ACORN's New York chapter waged campaigns around gentrification, homelessness, and the city's housing crisis, and by the mid-1990s this expanded to include welfare reform and the Work Experience Program (Atlas and Dreier 2013). Like the Consortium for Workers Education, South Brooklyn Legal Services, and FUREE, by the early 2000s ACORN had begun strategizing around child care. According to a lead organizer: "In 2002, a few child care providers, all members of ACORN, came in and told our staff organizer that they loved being child care providers but that the working conditions were so awful they were actually considering quitting. They talked about never knowing when they would get paid by the city, about being ha-rassed by inspectors, and feeling like they had no one to turn to for support" (Interview 9). As with FUREE, ACORN understood these grievances as fertile soil in which an organizing campaign could take root. Through its borough chapters, ACORN canvassed home child care providers across the city, gaug-ing their receptiveness to collective action (Interview 9). A community meet-ing soon followed in which providers from all corners of the city aired their grievances and voiced their determination to build a home child care provid-ers' association to represent their interests (Interview 9).

Yet in the months that followed, this group of around two hundred pro-viders found it hard to build momentum and experienced limited success in their lobbying efforts. As one organizer tells it, "It became very clear that our campaign did not get far because we did not have the kind of political pull we needed in order to really create change from the city to state level" (Inter-view 9). ACORN concluded that in order to make significant gains, providers would have to "scale up" their campaign to the state level.

At this point, ACORN organizers reached out to the UFT. The two orga-nizations had a healthy working relationship, having partnered together on a number of campaigns, including one to thwart the Giuliani administration's efforts to privatize the city's public schools. This particular campaign built sol-idarity between the UFT's disproportionately white membership and commu-nities of color in low-income neighborhoods (Atlas and Drier 2013).[16] ACORN was convinced that the 150,000 member–strong UFT had the political and or-ganizational clout necessary to make the home child care provider campaign a success.

Organizers from the UFT and ACORN agreed that the campaign should be framed using the language of professionalism in public education; it would be a campaign to earn respect for many low-income children's "first teachers." When the organizing drive went public, the UFT declared that it sought to represent home-based providers "because of their important yet undervalued role in the education system" (Interview 9; see also Greenhouse 2005b). This frame worked in two ways. First, teacher unionism had been built on the idea that through collective bargaining and political action, teachers could secure both decent work and a quality education system, in recognition that teachers' working conditions are the same conditions under which students learn. The UFT had a history of organizing women of color in low-wage jobs as part of its broader educational mission (see Juravich 2015). In the late 1960s the union had successfully organized four thousand paraprofessionals, who were pri-marily the mothers of schoolchildren, working in the city's public schools. The

campaign framed paraprofessionals as "pedagogical assistants" and unionization as a route not only to better wages but also to teacher accreditation and
professionalization (Juravich 2015).[17] Organizing home child care providers was in keeping with the UFT's "big tent" approach to teacher unionism
(Amlung 2010). Second, referring to providers as low-income children's "first
teachers" clearly located providers in the public sector, that is, as workers providing a vital public service and deserving of the same rights and protections
provided to other state employees, including the right to organize and be represented by a union.

With the UFT-ACORN partnership in place, organizing recommenced in
the spring of 2005. The UFT leveraged its political capital to acquire a list of
subsidized home child care providers from the Administration for Children's
Services. For its part, ACORN assembled a team of twenty full-time organizers to once again survey providers and gauge support for unionization (Interview 10).

The campaign overcame the hurdle of a dispersed workforce by organizing
on a geographic basis and through providers' informal social networks. As had
FUREE, ACORN encouraged its members with children in home child care
to alert their providers about the campaign. But with the list acquired from
the ACS, organizers could also engage in a massive door-knocking and can-
vassing effort focused in those neighborhoods with a high number of providers. Organizers signed up both unlicensed, "informal" providers and licensed
family day care providers. "We knew that with 28,000 providers we had to
do a serious grassroots effort," said one of the campaign's lead organizers, "so
that meant knocking on doors rain or shine" (Interview 13). Remarkably, in
just three months, organizers collected 6,000 signed union cards and held a
founding meeting with over 250 providers in attendance (Interview 9).

The campaign did face a number of other obstacles. Licensed providers
feared that organizing would upset the city-contracted family child care networks with which some of them were affiliated. These networks facilitated enrollment in family day cares by linking parents looking for child care to providers with open slots, in addition to assisting with taxation, paperwork, and
payment issues in return for an administrative fee.[18] While network-affiliated
providers recognized that a union would give them the power to address
any number of grievances—including the high administrative fees that took
money out of their already too-low pay—they worried that networks would
refuse to place children with pro-union providers. Then there was the pros-
pect of a protracted struggle with the state to secure either legislation or an ex-

ecutive order that defined providers as employees of the state for the purposes of collective bargaining, to say nothing of securing a first contract; organizers wondered if providers would "stick it out" (Interview 10). Finally, there were cultural barriers: the campaign brought together African American and Latina women, and more than 40 percent of the nascent union spoke Spanish exclusively (Interview 10).

But perhaps the most difficult challenge, according to organizers, "was getting providers to believe that change was possible. That is, if providers came together and organized, they could really change the way their work was viewed and compensated" (Interview 10). To this end, the UFT-ACORN coalition held meetings in the city's five boroughs in which hundreds of providers participated (with simultaneous English-Spanish translation). A group of around fifty "member-leaders" ran the meetings and worked to convince their peers that, like the teachers represented by the UFT, "they too were educators who deserved to be treated with respect and dignity" (Interview 10). By demanding public investment in training and professional development, they could collectively enhance the quality of care they provided, benefiting themselves and the families and communities they served. Organizers used these meetings to do intensive leadership development, allay providers' fears, and build their confidence, while talking through issues of power and respect (Interview 9).

The meetings were essential to breaking providers' isolation and building their capacities for collective action. As one rank-and-file leader explained: "When reaching out to other providers, we would say, 'I am a provider like you. Here are the problems I'm having. Are you having these problems too?' So our strategy was simple: tell our story and hear their story. In listening to others' stories we immediately validated them as *professionals*. Part of the problem with being a provider is you are isolated, and when you are disrespected it impacts your life and how you view yourself. When we reached out to other providers to hear about their lives, about their profession, it totally validated them" (Interview 13).

This last point was crucial. Compared to the city's unionized child care workers, the home child care workforce was invisible and politically weak. Yet the welfare state location of their labor had opened the legal and discursive space to make claims on the state as *public employees*—that is, as children's "first teachers" and professionals, not "babysitters" as family child care providers are often labeled. To be successful, organizers believed, the campaign would have to convince state legislators that investment in home child care—

in wages and benefits, training, and professional development—was an investment in improving child care quality, enhancing the "school readiness" of low-income children and helping to close "the achievement gap" (UFT 2005).

After months of grassroots organizing and outreach, in the fall of 2005 thirteen hundred home child care providers rallied on the steps of city hall (Interview 10). The speakers' list at the rally featured UFT president Randi Weingarten and New York ACORN's executive director Bertha Lewis, alongside faith leaders and supportive city council members and state legislators. From the steps of city hall, providers demanded that the city set up a mechanism to resolve disputes over payments, alleged health and safety violations, and license renewals (Allen 2005). It was a clear show of strength, putting the city and state on notice that the UFT-ACORN coalition was capable of mobilizing home child care providers en masse and generating "street heat" in the campaign for union recognition.

Providers exercised this newfound strength to secure some important victories, including back pay totalling $138,000—owed to thirty-five providers by the HRA and ACS—as well as a city-funded pilot program, called Provider's Choice, which reimbursed licensed family child care providers for out-of-pocket expenses for supplies and learning materials. The UFT-ACORN coalition also demanded and won meetings with the ACS and the city's Department of Health in which they discussed ongoing problems with communication, payment delays and pay stub issues, and various regulatory burdens. One important outcome of these meetings was a cut in the wait time for reimbursement checks, from 120 to 30 days, if a provider agreed to use of direct deposit (UFT 2005).

These victories gave home child care providers greater belief that, as the old labor anthem goes, "there is power in a union." As one of the campaign's key strategists put it, "Even before we won the right to represent providers as a union, we were trying to function as a union" (Interview 9). If providers failed to make progress in negotiations with the city, this person said, "we would rev up our strategy . . . do a rally or press conference or attend a city council hearing. Anything to stay visible and in their faces to let them know we were not going anywhere until they made the changes and corrected the problem" (Interview 13).

Yet despite building power at the local level, the biggest obstacle to unionization remained providers' problematic employment status, a matter of state, not municipal, politics. To win the right to union representation and collective bargaining, the UFT-ACORN coalition leveraged its formidable political power in Albany by broadening to include AFSCME (which had established an agreement with the UFT for organizing jurisdictions outside of the city), New York State's progressive Working Families Party, influential church ministers, and members of the state Black and Latino Legislative Caucus. This downstate-upstate coalition used its political capital to lobby state legislators, urging them to look to states, such as Illinois and Oregon, in which home child care providers had been granted rights to union representation and "the sky did not fall" (Interview 9). Fortunately for providers, the political winds were shifting in the right direction. A gubernatorial election was on the horizon, and the Democratic Party candidate, the union-backed Elliot Spitzer, was polling well ahead of his Republican challenger.

There was also a shift in the broader public discourse on child care that favored providers' cause. By the mid-2000s, the popularization of research into the benefits of early childhood education and care had convinced a growing number of policy makers, even some conservatives, that public investment in quality child care was good for children, good for families, and good for the economy. Economic research had helped recast the debate around early childhood education and care in terms of "investments" in "human capital," strengthening the future workforce and boosting productivity and economic growth (see Kirp 2007). Harnessed to the neoliberal politics of urban competitiveness, this so-called business case for child care had informed the decision of Giuliani's successor, Michael Bloomberg, to commit local tax dollars to expanding the state's underfunded pre-kindergarten program (Goldstein 2016). While the resulting pre-K slots were half-day, restricted to four-year-olds, and served only the city's poorest children—and the mayor showed little interest in raising the wages and working conditions of any public-sector workers, teachers included—organizers believed that the mayor's acknowledgement of the importance of early childhood education and care constituted a political opening for the UFT-ACORN coalition and indicated a gradual progressive shift in the politics of child care.

FOR JUSTICE AND RESPECT

In March 2006, the coalition's lobbying efforts paid off. In a massive victory for providers, the Republican-controlled state senate passed a bill establishing the state as subsidized home child care providers' employer of record for the purposes of collective bargaining.[19] The bill afforded home child care providers the same statutory right provided to public employees to organize and be represented by a union, and to collectively negotiate terms of employment with the state. The Democrat-controlled state assembly followed soon after.

According to the bill's sponsor, unionization would give home child care providers a collective voice and representation in the state's child care assistance program, help ensure quality care, facilitate higher standards for the children and families served, and improve the delivery of services (Gregory 2008, 287). In its emphasis on unionization as a means to improve child care quality, the bill reflected the issue frames employed by UFT and ACORN.

The victory was relatively short-lived. Despite a boisterous rally of hundreds of home child care providers outside of his Midtown Manhattan office, outgoing Republican governor George Pataki vetoed the bill in June 2006 (Witt 2006). In his veto letter to the senate, Pataki called the bill an "extreme expansion of the definition of public employee" under state labor law and argued that providers "are in no way State employees, as the State has no direct relationship with these providers" (quoted in Gregory 2007, 288). For decades, state governments had employed such arguments to deny responsibility for paying home care workers the minimum wage (Boris and Klein 2015). Furthermore, echoing conservative arguments against the unionization of home health care, Pataki cast home child care as a zero-sum game, with unionized providers taking scarce child care dollars out of the hands of parents and putting them into union coffers, leading to less availability of child care to both subsidized and non-subsidized families (see Gregory 2008, 288).

Not surprisingly, Mayor Bloomberg joined Pataki in his opposition to unionization. Since entering office in 2002, Bloomberg had presided over the rapid expansion of nonunion charter schools in the city's public education system in the name of "school choice" and closed or consolidated at least twenty city-funded, unionized day cares, citing "budget constraints" (Hilliard 2011). His administration had also refused to bargain with Local 205, leaving the eight thousand workers who staffed the city's 350 subsidized child care centers without a contract or raise for five years (Greenhouse 2005a).

Bloomberg argued that unionization of home child care providers could cost the city up to $100 million a year in increased wages and benefits (Greenhouse 2007). While the mayor may have acknowledged the importance of child care, as evidenced in his commitment—albeit weak—to pre-kindergarten, he remained fiercely antiunion and committed to delivering key city services on the cheap.

The mayor was backed by allies in civil society. The Manhattan Institute asserted that unionization would "increase day care costs for everybody" and—perhaps the rub for the think tank—also "increase the power of the states' most powerful unions" (quoted in Greenhouse 2007). For its part, the state's most influential business lobby, the Business Council of New York, argued that the state already had more public employees per capita than most others and that unionization of home child care perpetuated a political culture "that serves the interests of those who get paid to provide public services, more often than it does the people who are the ostensible beneficiaries of such services" (quoted in Gregory 2008, 290). From Bloomberg to big business, opponents of unionization sought to pit poor mothers who relied on subsidized child care against the low-wage women workers who provided it.

In response to these attacks, UFT president Randi Weingarten stuck to script, noting that unionization would improve training for home child care providers, raising standards for both providers and children. "I have a vision of educational unionism from birth through university," declared Weingarten, "Here you have child care providers who are not just custodians of kids, but they can play a pivotal role in teaching kids" (quoted in Greenhouse 2007). UFT's sister union for teachers upstate, New York State United Teachers, made a similar argument, pointing out that "research demonstrates that quality early childhood education results in greater achievement throughout one's educational experiences" and that "investment in the quality and stability of early childcare workers correlates with better social and academic outcomes for children" (quoted in Gregory 2008, 292). By increasing reimbursement rates and training to improve quality, unionization would help close the achievement gap between children from the highest- and lowest-income families.

In the op-ed pages of the *New York Amsterdam News*, the city's leading black newspaper, Weingarten and Bertha Lewis urged state lawmakers "to do the right thing and override the veto" and reminded readers that home child care providers, mostly black and Latina women, were among the lowest-paid workers in the state. "With the gap between rich and poor in our city and nation growing wider every year," Weingarten and Lewis declared, "bold steps are necessary to give working families a shot at the middle class" (Weingarten and Lewis 2006, 13).

UFT and ACORN's arguments carried the day, and in June the state senate voted overwhelmingly to override Pataki's veto. However, to the frustration of organizers, the timing of gubernatorial elections blocked a vote by the state assembly, and the union had to wait to work with the soon-to-be-elected Elliot Spitzer. Spitzer had made sympathetic overtures to home-based child care providers during his campaign, and as a liberal Democrat he drew support from the progressive base of unions, ministers, the Working Families Party, and poor and working-class communities of color that made up the UFT-ACORN coalition.

As expected, soon after taking office in 2007 Governor Spitzer issued an executive order classifying home child care providers as state employees for the purpose of collective bargaining. The order authorized state agencies to meet and confer with providers' representatives in order to reach a contract that might "address the stability, funding and operation of child care programs; expansion of quality child care; and improvement of working conditions, including subsidies, benefits or payment, for child care providers."[20] In the order's introduction, the governor stated that home child care providers "perform an essential service for working parents and guardians in this state, by creating a safe, enjoyable and educational home-like environment for their children" and should be empowered to make decisions on issues that impact their services since they "receive compensation and benefits that are not commensurate with the value of the work they perform." The order established "a framework for child-care providers to secure representation [that] can help improve the environment in which they work, their benefits, and the funding they receive" (New York State Executive Chamber 2007).

While awaiting the executive order, UFT and ACORN had kept busy, organizing rallies and going door-to-door to solicit card signatures from providers. With the order in place, in May 2007 the UFT submitted 12,000 signed authorization cards to the State Employment Relations Board. In the ensuing October election, 8,382 providers voted to join the UFT Family Child Care Providers Chapter, with only 96 providers against.[21] The vote gave formal authorization for the UFT to act as a bargaining representative for New York City's 28,000 home child care providers. It was the largest successful union organizing drive the city had seen since 45,000 teachers joined the UFT in 1960 (Greenhouse 2007).[22]

FROM CRISIS TO CONTRACT

The financial crisis of 2007–8 put enormous fiscal pressures on cities and states, ushering in a decade of austerity. Rather than create jobs through public investment and the expansion of social programs, or end a foreclosure crisis disproportionately felt by single mothers and their children, the Obama administration bailed out Wall Street. While the stimulus package did provide some relief to cities and states, as Boris and Klein (2015, 219) note, "The relief was too little to more than forestall furloughs and layoffs of public employees or cuts in programs in the face of intransigent Republican opposition to raising taxes." Overall, the administration's response to the crisis represented continuity with, rather than a departure from, neoliberalism.

As the banks recovered, unemployment continued to rise, and state revenues continued to fall. In response, state governments unleashed a wave of austerity measures, including the systematic dumping of debts and deficits to local governments, "a hallmark of austerity urbanism, U.S. style" (Peck 2015, 21). As Jamie Peck has argued, in the course of a few years the financial crisis was transformed into a fiscal crisis of the state, which was then transformed into an urban crisis, as austerity was becoming "the new urban condition in many parts of the United States" (Peck 2015, 22). In cities across the United States, the post-crisis "recovery" led to a consolidation of elite class power through urban governance and an intensification of neoliberalization, including the privatization of core city services, cutbacks to social services and welfare benefits, and attacks on municipal workers and their unions (Harvey 2015; Peck 2015). Facing a hard-nosed opponent in Mayor Bloomberg, New York's public-sector unions were unable to negotiate contracts for several years, leaving city workers without an increase in pay or benefits (see Milkman and Luce 2018).

Against this backdrop, the UFT Family Child Care Providers Chapter spent two years in tough first contract negotiations with the state, while in the city, citing debt and decreases in state and federal aid, the Bloomberg administration's push for deep spending cuts was tempered only by opposition from Democrats on the city council. When New York State adjusted subsidy reimbursement rates to account for the increased costs of providing child care, Bloomberg cried poverty, and the Administration for Children's Services, which is responsible for paying the rates, refused to respect the adjustment, in violation of state regulations, making the city's five boroughs the only counties in the entire state in which home child care providers did not immediately receive a raise (Landau 2009).

Providers responded to this affront by holding weekly rallies outside of city hall, calling for "justice and respect." A consistent supporter of the providers' cause, New York City public advocate and future mayor Bill de Blasio, chastised the mayor for his inaction (Landau 2009). Finally, some eighteen months after the city's home child care providers had voted to unionize, the Bloomberg administration agreed to pay the new rates and make $80 million in retroactive payments. UFT Providers Chapter chair and longtime family day care provider Tammie Miller called the decision "a victory not only for providers, but also for all working families in New York City who depend upon providers' vital services" (quoted in Landau 2009).

In January 2010, the city's home child care providers voted overwhelmingly to ratify their first contract (Landau 2010). The contract took important steps toward mitigating the precariousness of home child care work, improving care quality, and increasing public investment in child care overall. First, it locked in a new standard for determining the rate (per child) that providers were paid by the state. While this was a modest gain compared to the rate increase nego-tiated—pre-economic crisis—by SEIU in Illinois, it reflected the difficult bar-gaining climate for public-sector workers. The state did, however, guarantee health insurance for all providers to be phased in over a period of four years, a significant victory, especially for those not covered by state health insurance or Medicaid.

The contract outlined the development of a new grievance procedure in consultation with the city and state. The procedure can be used to resolve pay-ment and contract disputes as well as licensure and inspection issues, protect-ing providers from unfair treatment at the hands of city and state agencies. Relatedly, the union negotiated for regular meetings with the various agen-cies that regulate home child care, including the ACS, the city's Department of Health, and the New York State Office of Child and Family Services. Through these meetings, home child care providers would have a voice in shaping the rules and regulations governing their work.

In terms of child care quality, the contract provided $3 million in quality improvement grants to help licensed providers pay for supplies and upgrades to their facilities—overhead costs that were previously shouldered solely by providers. The contract also incentivized quality, providing funds for training and professional development to facilitate the transition of informal provid-ers into licensed family day care providers, effectively expanding the number of regulated child care spaces in the city and reversing the trend toward in-formalization. Using union funds as well as monies secured in the providers' contract, by 2012 the UFT had held over sixteen thousand training sessions for providers, including ten hours in health, safety, and child development for more than five thousand informal providers and workshops to help more than four thousand informal providers meet the professional development require-ments set by the state to become a registered family child care provider (Mul-grew 2012).

Finally, all provider training was to be conducted by the UFT in union-sponsored "Teacher Centers." Given the dispersed nature of home child care work and high turnover in the sector, particularly among informal caregivers, this provision put the union in contact with new and existing providers on a regular basis. Along with annual provider recognition ceremonies, a Provider Appreciation Day (proclaimed by the governor), and monthly meetings and professional development workshops, the provision reflected the union's com-mitment to fostering member participation, solidarity, and a culture of rank-and-file activism.

The campaign to organize home child care providers broke the isolation of a highly gendered and racialized low-wage workforce. As the "poor mothers' nanny" mobilized for change, moving from the "private" sphere of the home into city and state politics, they established a collective voice demanding dignity and respect as children's "first teachers." Through rallies, press conferences, and sustained lobbying they forced the state to recognize its invisible workforce and accord home child care work the social recognition it deserved. Home child care providers now had an organized political presence in city and state politics and a solid contract on which to build in future rounds of collective bargaining. Speaking about their first contract, Tammie Miller said, "There was a time when providers were disrespected by the city and state of New York. Those days are over" (quoted in Landau 2010).

CHILD CARE WORKERS VERSUS THE ONE PERCENT

The struggles of New York's home child care providers were part of a progressive shift in the urban politics of social reproduction. Under Giuliani and Bloomberg, the neoliberal restructuring of New York's urban welfare regime had eroded the legacies of the city's social democracy, devolved costs of social reproduction back onto poor and working-class households and communities, and intensified gendered and racialized class inequalities in urban space. As the majority of public-sector program users, workers, and union members, women—disproportionately women of color—bore the brunt of this restructuring.

Yet in the wake of the economic crisis, a vision of a different kind of city began to emerge along with the makings of a political coalition to bring that vision into existence. On May 11, 2011, several thousand child care workers rallied outside city hall to protest Mayor Bloomberg's executive budget (Landau 2011). The budget proposed a $51 million cut to subsidized child care, which amounted to the loss of 16,500 subsidies for low-income working families. It was the fourth year in a row that Bloomberg had attempted to scale back child care services in the city. With workers chanting "We are one!" the rally saw UFT's home child care providers standing side-by-side with their union sisters and brothers from Local 205, child care workers and support staff employed in city day care centers. They were joined by parents, teachers, city council allies, and advocates from the Day Care Council of New York, who together with the child care unions formed the Emergency Coalition to Save Child Care (Hill 2011).

Months before, workers in Wisconsin had risen up en masse against antiunion legislation and cuts to public services in what became known as the "Wisconsin Uprising" (Manski and Manski 2018). Months later, only blocks from where child care workers and their allies were now assembled, thousands of young people would descend upon Zuccotti Park to occupy Wall Street, the epicenter of the global financial crisis, and decry corporate greed and rising inequality. And the following year, hundreds of the city's fast-food workers, backed by SEIU and New York Communities for Change (formerly ACORN), would walk off the job to demand $15 an hour and union rights, sparking a nationwide wave of job actions by low-wage workers and launching the movement that would become the Fight for 15.

Speaking to the crowd at city hall, New York AFL-CIO president Denis Hughes said, "Child care is about the future of our city. We need to make choices to build the city we want to live in" (quoted in Hill 2011). A longtime ally of child care workers, Councilman Charles Barron, pointed out that the city had a $3.1 billion budget surplus, yet Bloomberg was cutting child care services "to predominantly black and Latino low-income communities" (quoted in Hill 2011). Before the crowd set off to march on Wall Street, making connections between the financial crisis and a billionaire mayor pushing austerity, UFT president Michael Mulgrew took to the microphone. With UFT Family Child Care Providers chapter chair Tammie Miller by his side, Mulgrew denounced the mayor's cuts and his notion of "shared sacrifice" since, as Mulgrew declared, "the only people asked to sacrifice are the middle class, workers and the poor. Enough is enough!" (quoted in Frazier 2011).

CONCLUSION

Child Care against the Neoliberal City

> Cities are the sites of both the most acute articulation of
> neoliberalism and of its most acute opposition.
> —Jason Hackworth, 2007

> The perspective of social reproduction is essential not only to
> understanding the historical origins of the present conjuncture but
> to answering the burning strategic questions of our time.
> —Salar Mohandesi and Emma Teitelman, 2017

In the early 1990s, New York City became one of the most aggressive jurisdictions in the nation in reducing the welfare rolls and putting poor people "to work" for their benefits. Against the backdrop of federal welfare reform, thousands of poor single mothers were pushed off welfare and into workfare and the low-wage labor market. As I have argued, the answer to the question of how poor mothers' child care needs would be met—by whom, under what conditions, and to what effect—was fiercely contested. Over a span of fifteen years, the answer was the subject of political and social struggles pitting child care advocates, welfare rights organizers, legal aid lawyers, low-income community groups, activist mothers, and public-sector unions against successive mayoral administrations committed to the neoliberal logic of child care on the cheap.

How New York City responded to this question was of great consequence in the national politics of welfare reform, and in the years leading up to President Clinton's ending of "welfare as we know it," welfare's critics and defenders turned their eyes to New York. The city's welfare caseload was bigger than that of every state in the nation bar California, and the Giuliani administration rolled out its welfare-to-work program a year prior to the passage of the federal welfare reform, pioneering the placement of welfare recipients in public-sector workfare jobs. But New York was also the symbolic home of the national welfare rights movement and remained a center of antipoverty activism and welfare rights advocacy. In the right's war on welfare, there was perhaps no battleground more important than New York City.

The question of who would care for the children was not a new one. The location of child care, the conditions of those who provide it, and the value accorded this work was the subject of a long history of struggle in the city. As the epicenter of welfare rights, thousands of poor African American and Puerto Rican New Yorkers, primarily single mothers, had mobilized to demand state support for the work of raising and caring for their children. The militancy of this movement meant that for a short time, from the late 1960s to the mid-1970s, many of the city's poor single mothers could stay home to care for their children and live at levels not worse than low-wage workers.

The question had been answered in the 1930s, when unemployed workers took to the city's streets en masse during the Great Depression. As part of the New Deal, the La Guardia administration established public day nurseries with federal aid, creating jobs for unemployed teachers and providing care for children whose parents were out looking for work. When women entered the war industries in the late 1940s, the question was answered with the expansion of these New Deal day cares. And when the state government attempted to shut down the city's nascent child care system at war's end, poor and working-class women, socialists and communists among them, resisted, and New York City became the first local government in the nation to fund and provide child care services.

When these services expanded in the 1960s, as part of the federal government's War on Poverty and response to uprisings of the urban poor, the workers on whose labor these services rested formed a union and went out on strike. New York's unionized day care workers and support staff, members of Local 205 Day Care Employees, would set the bar for wages and working conditions in the child care sector for years to come. Feminists and child care advocates who entered the city's bureaucracy during this decade worked in tandem with Local 205 to push for innovations in child care, including round-the-clock services to accommodate the schedules of the increasing number of women working irregular and nonstandard hours.

In the early 1970s, the parents, community organizers, and trade unionists who made up New York City's child care movement ambitiously pushed for universal, high-quality, municipally funded day care in the wake of President Nixon's veto of universal child care legislation. When the city's fiscal crisis hit, this movement took to the streets to defend child care services against austerity. While cuts led to the erosion of standards in the city's publicly funded day cares, "the best legacy" New York had of the 1960s survived and continued to serve thousands of the city's low-income families and provide decent union jobs for women working in child care. In the 1980s, as the Reagan administration waged its war on the poor and urban liberalism, cutting federal aid to cities and orchestrating the privatization of municipal services from above, New York City—under pressure from the day care workers' union, parents, and child care advocates—held fast to its role in the delivery, funding, and regulation of child care.

So, by the early 1990s, feminists, welfare rights organizers, child care advocates, day care workers, and progressive policy makers had an answer to the question of who might care for the children of poor women pushed into workfare and the bottom of the labor market. The answer was the nation's most comprehensive publicly funded, center-based child care system, a system diminished by successive rounds of neoliberal restructuring but one that nonetheless remained a source of quality, affordable child care for the city's low-income families. It was a system staffed by unionized workers, women who had helped build New York's child care exceptionalism, making the city something of an urban outlier in a nation in which child care is largely left to the market and child care providers are woefully underpaid.

But that system was not the answer the Giuliani or Bloomberg administrations chose to give. Since the city's neoliberal turn, New York had experimented with new ways to get public service work done cheaply: contracting out services to the private sector, encouraging volunteering, getting welfare recipients to do public-sector work previously done by unionized city workers, and offloading costs of and responsibilities for caregiving to families and communities. This restructuring exacerbated class, gender, and racial inequalities. When social spending was cut and welfare services privatized, poor and working-class women took up the slack at home and in the community, and it was disproportionately women whose union jobs—in home care, child care, community health care, and other social services—were on the line. For women of color, these jobs had been one of the few sources of decent work in a labor market rife with sexism and racial discrimination.

Yet for the city's neoliberal think tanks, corporate and financial elite, and conservative policy makers, the continued existence of a publicly funded, center-based child care system staffed by a unionized workforce was evidence that the neoliberal restructuring of New York's urban social democracy had not gone far enough. Some politicians put the case for restructuring in the most dramatic of terms, as if the city's very survival depended on the fulfillment of the neoliberal counterrevolution begun in 1975. As Newt Gingrich said of New York in 1992, its "bankrupt welfare statism" and "rapacious unionism" were "contributing to the slow-motion suicide of the world's once greatest city" (Gingrich 1992).

So, in response to the escalation of the city's child care crisis, the Giuliani administration channeled welfare mothers into reliance on an expanding pool of home-based child care providers for the care of their children, and the policy was left intact when Giuliani's successor, Michael Bloomberg, entered the mayor's office. Excluded from basic labor protections, without a union to advance their interests, and doing public care work in private homes at a fraction of the cost of center-based care, these women provided a much-needed service on the cheap. Meanwhile, a number of unionized city day cares were closed, and members of Local 205 Day Care Employees went years without a contract or a raise.

That poor women on welfare did not necessarily prefer home child care was no obstacle to the city's privatized remedies for the crisis. While neoliberal ideology criticizes "big government," neoliberalization always involves "coercive, disciplinary forms of state intervention in order to impose market rule upon all aspects of social life" (Brenner and Theodore 2002, 2). Despite welfare recipients' legislated right to choose among a variety of child care options, New York's welfare bureaucracy systematically ignored this right and pushed welfare mothers—often illegally, through threat of sanction—to rely on informal care arrangements and, to a lesser extent, family day care. In this way, the city engaged in a form of "market-making," expanding a low-wage labor market in child care through the voucherization of services and via a workfare state that foreclosed poor women's child care choices. As welfare reform reduced the social problem of poverty to a matter of personal responsibility, the social problem of a child care crisis—manifest in the lack of quality, affordable child care *and* the crisis of low-wage, precarious care work—once addressed, albeit inadequately, through the public provision of child care by unionized workers, was individualized and recast as the product of poor women's rational, market-based choices.

The idea that there was no alternative—that expanding the city's unionized, center-based child care system and making it more responsive to the needs of working mothers was too costly or unworkable—was false. While New York City's status as the nation's child care leader had been under assault since the neoliberal turn of the mid-1970s, in the years following welfare reform, dozens of cities, including another with a progressive child care legacy, San Francisco, experimented with publicly financed, flexible-hour, center-based child care (S. Kershaw 2000). Even Chattanooga, Tennessee—not known for being an innovator in social policy—established twenty-four-hour child care centers for low-income working mothers. As the executive director of one such center put it, "Who knew Chattanooga would be ahead of New York in anything?" (quoted in S. Kershaw 2000). And while federal and state funds were never adequate to meet the increasing need and demand for child care services, New York nevertheless retreated from its historical commitment to spending local tax dollars on child care. While the Giuliani and Bloomberg administrations gave tax breaks to developers and the superrich and oversaw a significant expansion of the city's police force, poor mothers struggled to find stable, quality child care arrangements, and women working as child care providers struggled to earn a decent living.

Consequently, I have argued that the city's response to the child care crisis, although occurring against the backdrop of federal welfare reform, is best understood as one part of a broader project of urban neoliberalization targeting the institutional legacies of past rounds of popular struggle over social reproduction. During the Giuliani and Bloomberg years, the city contracted out services to private providers in home health care, homeless services, and employment training, raised tuition in the CUNY system, attempted to privatize the city's public hospitals, and, especially under Bloomberg, marketized public education through the aggressive expansion of nonunion charter schools. What was public was to be privatized; what was delivered by unionized, public-sector workers was to be delivered by nonunion labor; what were costs of and responsibilities for social reproduction borne by the state were to be offloaded to poor, working-class, and single-parent households.

Yet at the intersection of welfare reform and child care, social movements rejected this project and the logic of child care on the cheap. If New York City was the site of the most acute articulation of neoliberal welfare and child care policy, it was also the site of its most acute opposition. Through a variety of resistance strategies, child care advocates, welfare rights groups, community organizations, activist mothers, and unions pushed the state to socialize more of the costs of and responsibilities for caregiving. Collectively, they aimed to mediate the child care crisis on terms more favorable to welfare mothers and the home child care providers who cared for their children.

What this dialectic of restructuring and resistance suggests is that state-driven efforts at mediating social-reproductive crisis tendencies—in this case, as manifest in the privatized response to an escalating child care crisis—can be partial, inadequate, and even paradoxical, giving rise to contradictions and opening space for social movements to contest the terms of mediation and secure more progressive forms of social reproduction. Indeed, it was around the very contradictions unleashed by neoliberal strategies, policies, and practices that progressive forces found the political space to organize, mobilize, and win victories in New York.

While early attempts to demand changes to the city's child care policies—such as WEP Workers Together's guerrilla day care center—had some impact, it was not until child care advocates and welfare rights activists began to fight the city on its own terms that campaigners saw results. Child care advocates in particular employed the discourse of "choice" to demand that the city's welfare bureaucracy adhere to state and federal regulations designed to protect welfare mothers' child care rights. Choice discourse facilitates the articulation of neoliberal principles "within a rhetorical framework that conveys a sense of political neutrality and individualizes responsibility for social inequalities" (P. Kershaw 2004, 1). In their organizing around choice, child care advocates revealed that this discourse was not politically neutral but grounded in a strategy to limit poor women's child care choices by undermining unionized child care services, individualizing responsibility for care, and externalizing costs onto home child care providers in low-income communities, thereby exacerbating classed, gendered, and racialized inequalities in urban space.

As welfare rights activists and child care advocates got word of the systemic violations of welfare recipients' child care rights, they mobilized to ensure that poor mothers had real choice in child care. Child care advocates successfully pressured the city into giving them access to welfare offices to provide poor mothers with child care information and advice, something caseworkers had failed to do. Advocates' presence in the city's job centers curtailed caseworkers' use and abuse of child care–related sanctions. And advocacy organizations produced studies showing that when given a range of child care options, the majority of welfare mothers preferred regulated, center-based, developmentally appropriate care for their children, not unstable and poor-quality informal arrangements. As a result of these efforts, fewer and fewer of the city's welfare mothers came to rely on informal child care.

Welfare reform was also accompanied by federal welfare-to-work grants designed to fund workfare schemes that pushed poor women into low-wage jobs—including in care work—with minimal education, training, or skills development. In the case of Satellite, child care advocates and labor activists used such a grant to develop a new form of child care, which provided quality care for children and quality care work for women transitioning off public assistance. Satellite trained welfare mothers as early childhood educators, subsidizing their college education and setting them up as unionized family day care providers covered by a collective agreement, thus mitigating the precariousness that characterizes home-based care work. While eventually starved of funding, Satellite challenged the devaluation of women's care work and offered an alternative, progressive model of welfare-to-work that addressed the social reproductive needs of poor and working-class women, whether in their role as mothers desperate for quality, affordable child care or as paid care providers.

Finally, by channeling public dollars to informal and family day care providers, successive mayoral administrations expanded the ranks of the publicly subsidized home child care workforce. Many "private-pay" providers came to receive state subsidies for the care of children of poor mothers entering the labor market. While these providers emerged as a quasi-public-sector workforce performing the care work of a neoliberalizing welfare state, it was the welfare state location of their work that opened the legal and discursive space to organize, form a union, and make claims on the state as public employees providing an essential service and deserving of better wages and working conditions, access to training and professional development, and a voice in child care policy. This mobilization had its seeds in the activism and advocacy of low-income community organizations in which poor women of color—some home child care providers, others poor women on welfare—strategized around their shared grievances with the city's welfare and child care bureaucracies. They came to recognize their common cause in stable, affordable child care, provided by women paid a decent wage. By improving compensation and securing benefits, the UFT Family Child Care Providers Chapter developed a more stable and better-trained home child care workforce, which in turn has enabled providers to better support children and their families. From an isolated and invisible workforce, home child care providers emerged as a political force in wake of welfare reform, demanding greater socialization of the costs of and responsibilities for child care and ultimately more socially just solutions to the city's child care crisis.

Together, these progressive forces—child care advocates, activist mothers, welfare rights organizations, community groups, legal aid lawyers, and unions—provided a different answer to the question of who will care for the children. In the tradition of the city's welfare rights movement and its unionized day care workers, home child care providers and their allies fought to revalue poor and working-class women's social reproductive labor. They took to the streets to demand recognition and respect, to be treated as child care professionals—as children's "first teachers"—and to say to policy makers that they refused to be a "cheap" solution to a crisis of politicians' own making. What

their struggles suggest is that even in the age of the urban neoliberalization—
an age in which privatization, deregulation, and welfare state retrenchment
appear to be near-hegemonic processes—poor and working-class women and
their allies maintain the capacity to shape welfare regimes and the politics of
social reproduction from below.

POSTSCRIPT

From Setbacks to Fightbacks

In the decade following welfare reform, home child care providers in a number of states followed their sisters in New York into unions like SEIU, AFSCME, and the American Federation of Teachers. Disproportionately African American, Latina, and immigrant women, home-based child care providers, together with home health aides, used the welfare state location of their work to collectively organize, form coalitions with the beneficiaries of their services, and demand public investment in care (Boris and Klein 2008, 40). Whether in New Jersey, Rhode Island, or Washington State, these campaigns looked much like the one waged by the UFT-ACORN coalition in New York, with intensive door-to-door, neighborhood-to-neighborhood organizing; rallies and demonstrations outside city and state agencies with oversight of child care; and the scaling up of campaigns from the local to the state level to win union recognition, rights, and eventually collective agreements.

Yet the 2008 economic crisis provided an opportunity for right-wing forces to undermine not only the welfare state but also, as Boris and Klein put it, "the union movement that had become intertwined with it" (Boris and Klein 2015, 220). In the wake of the crisis, state governments moved to dismantle public assistance programs, tighten eligibility requirements, and use tax cuts for the wealthy to drain government coffers and justify the privatization of social services. In addition to targeting service users, they attacked public-sector workers and their unions. Six states have passed right-to-work laws since 2012, including traditional union strongholds like Wisconsin and Michigan (Maisano 2018).[1] And in the precursor to its decision in *Janus v. AFSCME*, in July 2014 the Supreme Court ruled that publicly funded home-based care workers who enjoy the benefits of collective bargaining but are not themselves union members can no longer be required to pay mandatory union fees, known as "fairshare fees" or "agency fees."

The decision in *Harris v. Quinn* effectively transformed state-funded home health care and home child care into "right-to-work" shops. Writing for the majority, Justice Samuel Alito created a new category of worker, the "partial public employee," distorting the status of state-funded home care workers and "denying women working in the home the same rights as other workers." The plaintiff in the case, Illinois-based home care worker Pamela Harris, was backed by an array of conservative billionaires and the right-wing foundations they fund. As Boris and Klein write: "Bridging the boundaries between home and state, public and private, work and welfare, care worker unionism not only injected much needed energy into the labor movement but also boosted the welfare state itself. Anti-labor conservatives find this outcome intolerable" (Boris and Klein 2014).

Not surprisingly, given the history of conservative attempts to roll back the gains of progressive movements, this latest assault on the welfare state and public-sector unions spoke a racist and sexist language (Mohandesi and Teitelman 2017). Regurgitating the racist and sexist logics that informed welfare reform, right-wing forces have labeled public employees—including home child care providers, home health care aides, teachers and nurses—the "new welfare queens" (Boris and Klein 2015, 226; see also Cohn 2010; Jones 2014). Having declared and largely won the war on welfare—and subsequently eliminated a poor woman's right to provide care for her own children—conservatives intensified their war on women doing care work in the public sector.

Yet a decade of neoliberal austerity has produced uneven geographies of restructuring and resistance, of setbacks and fightback. While in some states home child care and home health care unions—public-sector unions more generally—have been devastated by social spending cuts and privatization on the one hand, and legislative and judicial assaults on their collective bargaining rights on the other, in others unions and the public services they protect have proven more resilient. And in a number of cities these unions have forged coalitions with low-wage workers in fast food and private-sector home care, child care, and hospital workers, in the Fight for 15 (Zillman 2015).

As Collins and Mayer (2010) point out, many of the jobs found by women moving from welfare into paid work are in the low-wage service sector and particularly in areas such as child care, home health care, and food services—jobs that actually substitute for unpaid labor formerly performed in the home. Thus, while welfare rights activism has dwindled, far from marking an end to poor, working-class women's struggles over the value of their social reproductive labor, in the wake of welfare reform these struggles are shifting terrain.

Emerging urban coalitions of progressive forces have paved the way for left-leaning mayors in a number of cities, including New York (M. Goldberg 2014). In 2013, former city councillor and public advocate Bill de Blasio was elected mayor of New York. In a campaign energized by Occupy, fast-food strikes, and the struggle to end the racist police practice of "stop-and-frisk" and backed by municipal unions and progressive community organizations, including New York Communities for Change, de Blasio told a "tale of two cities" and vowed aggressive action to tackle inequality. In the words of veteran journalist Juan González, de Blasio's victory "heralded the advent of the most progressive New York City government in generations" and "the reclaiming of Gotham" by left-wing forces after two decades of neoliberal rule (González 2017, 2).

When it comes to affordable housing and homelessness, gentrification, and development, de Blasio's progressive credentials have been called into question (Chang 2019). Yet his administration has made some important interventions in social reproduction to ease burdens on individuals, households, and communities. The city has rolled out a Free Lunch for All program, making lunch at New York public schools free of charge for all 1.1 million students, it settled expired municipal union contracts, giving three hundred thousand low- and moderate-income workers wage increases, and introduced paid family leave for twenty thousand city workers whose contracts were not covered by collective bargaining (Kurshid 2017). The creation of the city's Paid Care Division, charged with raising employment standards in the care sector, informing care workers of their rights, and generally strengthening and supporting the city's paid care workforce, is also a welcome development.

With a fierce critic of Giuliani's workfare regime at its helm, the Human Resources Administration has effectively phased out the Work Experience Program, easing mandatory work requirements and allowing college enrollment and training to count as welfare-to-work activities (Chen 2014). Yet the 2018 case of Jazmine Headley, a young African American mother who was violently arrested in an HRA office, her one-year-old son pried from her arms by the police after a dispute over whether she was allowed to sit on the waiting area floor (there were no seats available), suggests that reforms have not gone far enough. Headley had gone to the office "to find out why the city had abruptly stopped paying for him [her one-year-old] to go to day care while she worked cleaning offices" (Southall and Stewart 2018). Alongside de Blasio's mixed record on police reform, the Headley case illustrates that a racialized "double regulation of the poor" (Wacquant 2009a) remains a central function of city government, even under a progressive mayor.

But de Blasio had won the praise of child care advocates and the UFT for his signature initiative, the expansion of pre-kindergarten. Before 2014, the city had approximately thirty-six thousand half-day and nineteen thousand full-day pre-kindergarten spaces (Stivers 2016). Through the mayor's signature Pre-K for All policy, the city has made pre-kindergarten for four-year-olds universal, effectively extending the kindergarten through grade twelve school system with an additional year of free, academically rigorous public education and child care. In a city in which child care remains the single greatest expense among low-income families, surpassing both food and housing, Pre-K for All has put an estimated $1.4 billion back into the wallets of New Yorkers who no longer have to pay for child care (González 2017). To the praise of parents and child care advocates alike, the mayor has promised to extend free, full-day, high-quality early childhood education to every three-year-old by 2020 (Stivers 2016). While far from perfect, these policies mark a radical transformation of child care in the city, turning it into a universal public good.

Beyond New York, myriad struggles have emerged in urban America in which poor and working-class women's activism is central, including grassroots community movements for housing, health care, and food security, campaigns for domestic worker bills of rights, efforts to defend workers in for-profit nursing homes, hospitals, and child care centers, struggles for safe neighborhoods free from police violence, and the fight for sanctuary cities in which undocumented migrants can access essential social services without fear (see Mohandesi and Teitelman 2017). In 2018–19, a wave of teachers' strikes in Republican-controlled states saw thousands of underpaid and overworked educators—close to 80 percent of whom were women—hit the streets, occupy state capitols, and demand and win public investment in education (Bhattacharya 2018). And in December 2018, Chicago saw the first charter school strike in U.S. history, followed in 2019 by a successful citywide teachers' strike, both led by the Chicago Teachers Union.

As Jamie Peck has argued, "Austerity is, by its very nature, a form of redistributive politics in spatial, scalar, and social terms." In the wake of the economic crisis, cities have been not only "beachheads and staging grounds" for fiscal revanchism but also for "progressive forms of counter-politics" (Peck 2015, 20). While the struggles listed above may appear disparate in form, the lens of feminist political economy allows us to recognize what they have in common: they are struggles on the terrain of social reproduction. And while struggles over social reproduction are at the heart of struggles to build socially just cities, one must hope that they are laying the foundations for a more progressive America.

NOTES

INTRODUCTION

1. Home-based child care providers are classified as either independent contractors—that is, self-employed business owners—or, in the case of a small number of providers who provide care in a child's home, otherwise not in an employer-employee relationship under federal labor laws (Blank, Chalfie, and Entmacher 2007).

2. As of 1998, this was the maximum hourly rate New York City paid to family day care providers caring for children under one and a half years of age (New York State Office of Family Services 1996). Child care subsidies and the reimbursement paid to providers are largely funded by states through a federal block grant and administered by city or county government. In New York, the state government's Office of Children and Family Services sets the pay levels (reimbursement rates) of home-based publicly subsidized child care providers.

3. Nationally, in the mid-to-late 1990s, family child care providers who were subject to licensing or other forms of regulation earned between $8,500 and $10,000 per year after expenses (Whitebook 1999). According to the Center for the Child Care Workforce, the median wage for family child care providers in 1998 was $3.37 (Whitebook 1999, 148). According to a 2005 survey, over 50 percent of New York City home-based child care providers earned poverty-level wages and averaged around $19,000 a year (Greenhouse 2007).

4. The term "private-pay" is used to denote child care providers who receive full payment from parents as opposed to full or partial payment, in the form of a child care subsidy, from the state.

5. Research employing an urban lens does not feature in three of the most recent collections of FPE scholarship (Bezanson and Luxton 2006; Braedley and Luxton 2010; and Rai and Waylen 2014). And while there is renewed feminist engagement with the city and urban space (e.g., Peake and Rieker 2013), little of this work employs a materialist or political economy perspective. For its part, feminist scholarship on the welfare state has overwhelmingly reflected the "methodological nationalism" of the mainstream scholarship with which it is in dialogue.

6. For a notable exception, see Parker 2017.

7. Andreotti, Mingione and Polizzi have developed the concept of "local welfare sys-

tems" to capture the "dynamic arrangements in which specific local socioeconomic and cultural conditions give rise to different mixes of formal and informal actors, public or not, involved in the provision of welfare resources." They argue that municipalities are the most suitable proxy for the study of local welfare systems: "Every city . . . has in fact its own specific history, in which specific features have emerged in terms of socioeconomic organizations, socio-demographic structure, organization of the 'civil society' and of political/institutional traditions that contribute towards the shaping of different local welfare systems and of the 'vision' that they express in welfare policies" (Andreotti, Mingione, and Polizzi 2012, 1925, 1934).

8. Women, disproportionately women of color and immigrant women, make up 94 percent of the child care workforce. Black women are 13 percent of all workers but 15 percent of all child care workers. Latinas are 15 percent of all workers but 21 percent of all child care workers. Fifteen percent of white (non-Hispanic) child care workers are living in poverty, compared to 23 percent of black workers and 22 percent of Latinas (Vogtman 2017).

9. As Vogtman notes, this data likely overestimates child care worker pay and underestimates financial need as it fails to capture significant segments of the child care workforce, namely those who provide informal care in their homes (typically called "family, friend, and neighbor care") and women who work in private homes as nannies or au pairs (Vogtman 2017, 8).

10. Turnover and limited training are two determinants of quality in child care. A 2006 federal study gave a "high quality" rating to only 10 percent of the nation's child care programs (see NICHD 2006).

11. The Child Care and Development Block Grant (CCDBG), also called the Child Care and Development Fund (CCDF), is the primary source of federal funding for child care subsidies for low-income families and funds to improve child care quality. The CCDBG was enacted in 1990 and was amended and reauthorized by the Personal Responsibility and Work Opportunity Reconciliation Act of 1996. States are authorized to transfer up to 30 percent of their TANF funds to the CCDF program, and almost all states transfer some of their TANF resources to child care expenditures (Gornick, Howes, and Braslow 2012).

12. Only 16 percent of the 13.4 million children eligible for federal child care assistance received it in 2013, the most recent year for which data are available, and twenty-two states had waiting lists or had frozen intake for child care assistance (National Women's Law Center 2018). While TANF recipients are eligible for child care assistance under federal law, they are not entitled under state regulations. As of 2016, thirty-five states provided a child care guarantee for TANF families, while twenty-seven states continued to guarantee child care for families leaving TANF for up to one year (Lynch 2016).

13. Nationwide and in New York City, home-based child care is the most common form of care for infants and toddlers from low-income families (Hurley 2016). Research (see Adams et al. 2006; Hurley 2016; P. Smith 2007; Tuominen 2003) shows that low-income families may prefer home-based child care for a host of reasons: it is typically more affordable than center-based care, it is more conveniently located, and home-based care programs have more flexible hours of operation than centers, accommodating parents with nonstandard work schedules. Parents may also prefer home-based

care because it resembles a family setting or appears warmer and more nurturing than center-based care, or because they prefer a provider who shares their language, culture, and child-rearing beliefs—many home child care networks consist of providers of a particular ethnic identity. Yet parent selection of child care arrangements is also shaped by public policy. Chaudry's 2004 study followed forty-two low-income mothers in New York City over three years and found that scarce subsidies, complicated bureaucracies, inflexible work schedules, and limited choices forced mothers to patch together care arrangements that were often unstable, inconvenient, and of limited quality. For a similar study of single mothers with histories of welfare receipt in Cleveland, Milwaukee, and Philadelphia, see Knox et al. 2003. On how contextual constraints impact low-income parents' child care choices, see also Chaudry, Sandstrom, and Giesen 2012; Chaudry et al. 2011. On how welfare caseworkers use child care subsidies as a disciplinary tool in caseworker-client interactions, shaping poor single mothers' selection of child care arrangements, see Houser et al. 2014. For research on child care choice and low-income families in other liberal welfare regimes, see Baker and Tippin 1999. On neoliberalism, "choice," and child care, see P. Kershaw 2004; McKinley 2010; Teghtsoonian 1996.

14. Ninety-five percent of home-based child care providers are women. Sixty-three percent of licensed home-based child care providers are white, 16 percent are African American, and 16 percent are Hispanic. Fifty-one percent of unlicensed home-based providers are white, 21 percent are African American, and 23 percent are Hispanic (Whitebook, McLean, and Austin 2016, 8).

15. According to the Center for the Study of Child Care Employment, in the United States the median hourly wage for self-employed home child care providers is $10.35 (Whitebook et al. 2018, 6).

16. New York is one of a minority of states in which welfare is still administered by local rather than state agencies. The city is responsible for administering welfare and for paying for approximately half of welfare's local net cost of the federal contribution (CSWL 2001).

17. In 1998, the racial composition of the city's TANF caseload was 5 percent white, 33 percent black, and 59 percent Hispanic (DeParle 1998).

18. While there is no shortage of excellent studies of the neoliberalization of New York City (e.g., Moody 2007; Brash 2011; Busa 2017; Phillips-Fein 2017), nor is there a shortage of studies of the city's workfare program (e.g., C. Goldberg 2001; Krinksy 2007a; Krinksy 2007b), these studies tend to neglect restructuring and resistance around the social organization of care. Beyond its broader contribution to feminist political economy, this book seeks to fill this particular gap in the scholarship on neoliberal New York.

CHAPTER 1. SOCIAL REPRODUCTION AND THE CITY

1. For international political economy, see, for example, Bakker and Silvey 2008; Rai and Waylen 2014; A. Roberts 2016. For critical geography, see, for example, Meehan and Strauss 2015; Mitchell, Marston and Katz 2004. For welfare state studies, see, for example, Porter 2003; Bezanson 2006; Vosko 2006. For feminist debates around intersectionality, see, for example, Brenner 2014; McNally 2017. For histories of the feminist political economy tradition, see Luxton 2006, Vosko 2002a and Rai and Waylen 2014. For an

introduction to social reproduction theory, as taken up by scholars and activists both within and outside of the feminist political economy tradition, see Bhattacharya 2017.

2. The concept of a "welfare regime," as opposed to the narrower "welfare state," refers to the relationships among states, markets, and families in the provision of welfare (Esping-Andersen 1990).

3. In *Social Reproduction: The Political Economy of the Labor Market*, Picchio refers to the state's role in mediating the contradictions and conflicts between capital accumulation and social reproduction as that of "regulator"—that is, the state plays a substantial role in establishing the conditions under which social reproduction takes place by regulating capital and the labor market and providing supports for social reproduction through social transfers and services. For Picchio, the family/household's function can be understood as that of an "alternator," in adjusting to demands as women's labor within and outside the household takes up the space for reduced state spending and labor market insecurity. As Picchio makes clear, however, this alternator role is politically, socially, and culturally given and not an automatic mechanism that adjusts to external conditions (Picchio 1992, 85–88).

4. As Luxton notes, early FPE scholarship tended to equate social reproduction with women's unpaid work in the household (Luxton 2006, 36). The more expansive understanding of social reproduction employed here moves beyond the central focus on women's work in the home that tends to blur its relationship to the complementary work (also often done by women for pay) done in the market or in services, such as education, provided by the state.

5. As Mahon points out, feminist analyses of the welfare state have privileged the national scale as a level of analysis, "not the least because post-war welfare regimes, and more broadly gender regimes, came to be consolidated at the national scale" (Mahon 2006, 458). In this, feminist welfare state scholarship has reflected the methodological nationalism of mainstream scholarship with which it is in dialogue (see, for example, Esping-Andersen 1990).

6. Most comparative feminist welfare state scholarship does not account for subnational variation. See, for instance, O'Connor, Orloff, and Shaver's classic study of gender relations and social policy across advanced *national* welfare regimes (O'Connor, Orloff, and Shaver 1999).

7. See, for instance, Prentice's and Michel's studies of women and child care politics in Canada and the United States, respectively (Prentice 1989; Michel 1999). In both cases, the women's movement's push for universal child care had its genesis in struggles to save publicly funded municipal day care centers in the immediate post–World War II period.

8. See also Abramovitz's brief history of poor and working-class women's activism in the United States (Abramovitz 2000).

9. The crisis was manifest in a sustained global recession, declining rates of profit across advanced capitalist countries, and high unemployment combined with high inflation, or "stagflation" (see Harvey 2005; Dumenil and Levy 2004, and Larner 2000).

10. Following Roberts, I understand "financialization" as a general "expression of shifts that have taken place within relations of production globally, which have made it increasingly profitable for many firms to accumulate via financial channels" (A. Roberts

2016, 130). The term also captures the expansion and deepening of financial relations into more and more spaces of everyday life.

CHAPTER 2. FROM URBAN SOCIAL DEMOCRACY
TO NEOLIBERALIZING CITY

1. On New York City's fiscal crisis, see Tabb 1982, Freeman 2000, Harvey 2005 (44–48), and Phillips-Fein 2017.

2. As Kornbluh has argued, local case studies are essential to the study of twentieth-century American politics because "much political power was exercised, and fought, at the local level" (Kornbluh 2007, 197). While the development of New York's welfare state is intimately tied to politics at the national scale, the aim here is to elucidate the unique history of the city's welfare regime and especially popular struggles over the social organization of care. As such, I highlight federal policies and politics only when particularly relevant to the local New York City context.

3. For an account of the role of popular struggles in the rise of the New Deal welfare state, see Piven and Cloward 1977 (chapter 2).

4. The committee also laid the groundwork for a partnership between city, state, and nonprofit child care sponsoring boards that continues to this day (ACS 2005).

5. As Piven and Cloward make clear in *Regulating the Poor* (1971), these arrangements were the product of a compromise by the FDR administration with southern Democrats who feared welfare would jeopardize the supply of cheap black labor relied on by white farmers and wealthy white households. As a result, in order to accommodate local labor requirements and the demands of powerful southern politicians, the new legislation gave a great deal of discretion to state legislatures and local officials in program design and administration.

6. As early as the late 1950s, poor women on welfare had started coming together in local, community-based groups around the country, attempting to address violations of their civil rights, low benefit levels, and negative portrayals of welfare recipients in the media (Nadasen 2010, 103). Federal funding through the War on Poverty provided these organizations with the resources needed to expand their organizing and develop political influence (Nadasen 2005; Nadasen 2010; Kornbluh 2007).

7. As both Nadasen (2005) and Silvia Federici (2006) have argued, welfare rights activists articulated a working-class black feminism distinct from the politics of the mainstream and predominantly white liberal middle-class women's movement, which rejected domesticity as oppressive and emphasized equality of opportunity in the labor market and equal rights at work.

8. The national office of the National Welfare Rights Organization produced a guide for local welfare rights chapters on how to organize comprehensive community-controlled child care programs and demanded universal child care (Nadasen 2010, 115–16).

9. Political elites responded to this strike wave with the passage of the Taylor Law in 1967, which banned strikes by public employees in New York and set stiff penalties for striking, including jail time for leaders.

10. The community control movement had its origins in struggles for racial justice and the Johnson administration's War on Poverty. The Economic Opportunity Act of 1964, a central piece of the Great Society, stated that federally funded programs would be "developed, conducted, and administered with the maximum feasible participation of the residents of the areas and members of the groups served." It called for community action programs to mobilize resources that could be used in a direct attack on the roots of poverty and racial injustice (M. Katz 2008).

11. The city's day care movement also sought to build on its local success by organizing a child care coalition at the state level. In 1973, the Day Care Council of New York, the organization representing the city's nonprofit child care agencies, spearheaded the first statewide association of child care advocates and child care development councils in the country (Day Care Council of New York 2012). New York's day care movement continued to lead the nation in innovative organizing and advocacy work, establishing a strong political presence in the state capital of Albany to match its work in New York City.

12. On the causes of New York's fiscal crisis, see Harvey 2005 (44–48), Freeman 2000 (256–87), Tabb 1982, and Phillips-Fein 2017.

13. Federal funds paid 75 percent of the city's day care costs, mainly under Title 20 of the Social Security Act. The city and New York State shared the remaining 25 percent.

14. In what became known as the New Federalism, policy authority was increasingly devolved to states and redesigned along market models (see M. Katz 2008).

15. In Reagan's first two years in office alone, means-tested programs were cut by 54 percent, housing assistance by 47 percent, and job training by 81 percent (Danziger 1983).

16. Federal aid to state and local governments declined in real dollars for the first time in two decades (Boris and Klein 2015, 152).

17. This shift entailed a change to Title 20 of the Social Security Act of 1935, which provides for funding for social services through the Social Services Block Grant (SSBG). Beginning under Reagan, states had more discretion in the use of SSBG funds, determining what services were provided, who was eligible to receive them, and how funds were used.

18. This was down from six years of age under the previous major welfare reform legislation, the Work Incentive Program (WIN), passed in 1969 (Naples 1991).

19. The legislation had four main components: expanded funding for Head Start; a new entitlement program that increased child care assistance for families deemed "at-risk" of welfare receipt, At-Risk Child Care; an expansion of the Earned Income Tax Credit designed to help low-income families with their child care costs; and the block grant (Michel 2004).

20. Child care vouchers were concomitant with the Reagan and Bush administrations' broader emphasis on decentralization, deregulation, and privatization. Voucherization was increasingly tied to federal funding in a range of programs such as education and housing, reflecting the broader neoliberal shift toward private responsibility for social reproduction.

CHAPTER 3. RESTRUCTURING

1. The Giuliani administration found an ally in state government in Republican governor George Pataki. Pataki was elected on a platform of restoring the state's competitiveness, attracting investment and creating jobs through a mix of tax cuts and austerity. According to Duggan, any resistance to a neoliberal policy agenda in New York was "largely swept from many state level institutions as downsizing and privatization, along with tax cutting and 'welfare' shrinkage became policy priorities" (Duggan 2012, 31). Pataki was a firm supporter of welfare reform, and the state's welfare reform bill ratified nearly all of Giuliani's locally initiated reforms (Krinsky 2007b).

2. Under Giuliani's watch, there were a series of police shootings of unarmed black men. In the cases of Amadou Diallo and Patrick Dorismond, these shootings were fatal. See "Rudy Giuliani's Racial Myths," *New York Times*, July 11, 2016.

3. This included the contracting-out of fleet management in the Parks and Recreation Department and custodial work at public schools; franchising private ferries; divesting radio and television stations; crafting a public-private partnership for new school construction; and privatizing the day-to-day production and management of Central Park (Cooke 2008).

4. The office of public advocate is a citywide elected position in New York City, and the officeholder is first in line to succeed the mayor. The office serves as a direct link between the electorate and city government, and the officeholder acts as an ombud for New Yorkers by providing oversight for city agencies, investigating citizens' complaints about city services, and making proposals to address perceived shortcomings or failures of those services.

5. The Begin Employment Gain Independence Now (BEGIN) program under the HRA's Office of Employment Services administered NYC-WAY for AFDC recipients.

6. Twenty-two of fifty states exempted single parents from work-related activities if they cared for a child under the age of twelve months. Vermont was the most liberal of jurisdictions, exempting recipients caring for a child under the age of twenty-four months. New York City found itself in the company of traditionally conservative states, such as Alabama, Arkansas, and Florida, and the workfare pioneer Wisconsin (see Urban Institute 1999).

7. Exemptions information from Urban Institute 1999 (106–9). There are exceptions to the rule. Idaho and Iowa, for example, where black and Hispanic families make up a low percentage of the caseload, maintain no work exemptions for single parents caring for a child of any age.

8. Information presented in this section is drawn from Powell and Cahill 2000 (8–9). New York City's TANF regime dates from 1998, when the state welfare reform act was passed.

9. These findings were corroborated in interviews with welfare rights caseworkers in two legal clinics (Interview 1; Interview 2).

CHAPTER 4. RESISTANCE

1. On resistance to the city's workfare regime in general, see Krinsky 2006; Krinsky 2007a; Krinsky 2007b; C. Goldberg 2001; Tait 2005; Krinsky and Reese 2006; Dulchin and Kasmir 2004.

2. For excellent overviews of welfare rights organizing in the wake of TANF, see Reese 2011, Abramovitz 2000, and Krinsky and Reese 2006.

3. District Council 37 of AFSCME was the most likely candidate to organize WEP workers, yet for much of Giuliani's time in office the union was mired in a corruption scandal and under undemocratic and ineffective leadership. The master contract negotiated between the union and the city in 1995 had side agreements that, as Krinsky points out, "tacitly, if not explicitly, accepted WEP by giving unionized employees substantial pay differentials if they supervised WEP workers" (Krinsky 2007a, 83).

4. WEP Workers Together was founded jointly by the Urban Justice Center, a city-wide legal advocacy project; the Fifth Avenue Committee, a Brooklyn-based low-income housing developer with a community-organizing and social justice mission; and Community Voices Heard, a membership-based organization with a focus on welfare rights (Dulchin and Kasmir 2004).

5. This organizing intensified as participation in the WEP peaked around 1998 and then receded as the city became less reliant on public-sector job placements to reduce its welfare rolls and more focused on strategies of diversion. For an extensive analysis and discussion of this campaign, see Krinsky 2007a and C. Goldberg 2001.

6. WEP workers were classified as trainees, not employees, under federal law. Therefore, they were neither covered by the National Labor Relations Act nor permitted to form a union or bargain collectively (Dulchin and Kasmir 2004, 3).

7. As of 2006, there were 52,000 home child care providers statewide in New York and 1.8 million in the United States, including an estimated 804,000 providers who were relatives of the children in their care, another 650,000 providers who cared for unrelated children in the provider's own home, and about 298,000 nonrelatives who provided care in the child's home (Sen and Thompson 2006; Chalfie, Blank, and Entmacher 2007).

8. In contrast, over roughly the same period, care in formal child care centers had grown by just 7 percent (McMillan 2002).

9. Self-employed persons or businesses are "competitors" and therefore subject to state and federal antitrust laws that prohibit them from "combining" and agreeing on matters such as rates (Chalfie, Blank, and Entmacher 2007).

10. The PRWORA recognizes "the provision of child care services to an individual who is participating in a community service program" as a defined work activity (H.R. 3734 29).

11. Family day care advocates suspected that the city's health and safety blitz was in response to the recent death of a seven-month-old boy in a Queen's day care center. The boy died after two unsupervised children piled toys into his crib, suffocating him (Fahim 2005).

12. ACORN had tried and failed to organize providers in 2002–3 but returned to organizing after forming a partnership with UFT. This produced some tension between

ACORN and FUREE as the latter had stuck with the campaign and won important gains (Interview 6).

13. In Chicago, SEIU had built a union of home care workers, Local 880. The local began as part of the United Labor Unions, a project of ACORN, and was a workforce counterpart to the neighborhood organizing of ACORN (Boris and Klein 2015, 149). Local 880 had grown from just seven members in 1983 to over sixty-eight thousand members by 2008. The union had successfully lobbied the state legislature to win rate increases, a grievance procedure, and improvements in payment procedures for home health care workers (Chalfie, Blank, and Entmacher 2007, 7).

14. In addition to Illinois, by 2005 SEIU and AFSCME were organizing home-based child care providers in Iowa, Michigan, New Jersey, Oregon, Washington, Wisconsin, California, Massachusetts, and Rhode Island. In Illinois, Washington, Oregon and New Jersey, these campaigns had secured executive orders facilitating unionization of home child care providers (Chalfie, Blank, and Entmacher 2007).

15. In 2010, the New York City chapter of ACORN transformed into New York Communities for Change.

16. Building solidarity between UFT members and low-income communities of color was significant, given the history of tension between the union and the city's Latino and African American communities dating back to the 1960s, struggles for community control, and the Ocean Hill–Brownsville dispute that led to the teachers' strike of 1968 (Juravich 2015).

17. According to Juravich, the Elementary and Secondary Education Act of 1965 provided millions of dollars of new funding to local education agencies to combat poverty in schools. Local school boards used these funds to hire thousands of people, primarily the mothers of schoolchildren, to work in neighborhood schools (Juravich 2015). Administrators and activists hoped that paraprofessional programs would improve instruction and discipline by bringing local knowledge into classrooms, enhance communication and cooperation between schools and communities by acting as conduits between parents and teachers, and create careers for low-income women through opportunities for teacher training.

18. By the early 2000s, there were around ninety family child care networks operating in New York City, fifty-five of them with city contracts (McMillan 2002).

19. The legislation did not, however, classify home child care providers as public employees for purposes of pensions or health care (Gregory 2008).

20. In keeping with New York State's Taylor Law, which prohibits public employees' right to strike, the executive order stated that nothing in the order permitted "the child care providers collectively to engage in any strike or work action to secure any right or privilege from the State." The executive order did not render home child care providers state officers or employees and did not imply that there existed "any employer-employee relationship between the child care operator and the State . . . for any purpose, including but not limited to any public retirement system, membership in any public health insurance program, unemployment insurance, workers' compensation, disability coverage, New York Civil Service Law, or indemnification under New York Public Officers Law." In addition, the order stated that it in no way interfered "with the existing relationship be-

tween consumers and the child care providers, including the existing rights of parents or guardians to choose their own provider, or to terminate that provider's services at any time" (quoted in Gregory 2008, 293–94).

21. Under New York State labor law, if a majority of the workers who vote are in favor of unionization, the vote is binding on all members of the bargaining unit.

22. Seventy-five hundred home child care providers in New York City's suburban counties and upstate New York voted to join the Civil Service Employees Association of AFSCME (Greenhouse 2007).

POSTSCRIPT

1. In the U.S. context, right-to-work laws are a type of statute under which the union shop is prohibited, as are maintenance of membership, preferential hiring, or any other clauses requiring union membership. The purpose of such laws is to make it more difficult for unions to collect revenues, and thereby to weaken the labor movement.

REFERENCES

INTERVIEWS

Interview 1. In-person interview. Staff Lawyer, Welfare Law Center. New York City, June 17, 2009.

Interview 2. In-person interview. Staff lawyer, South Brooklyn Legal Services. New York City, July 13, 2009.

Interview 3. Phone interview. Senior staff, Office of the Public Advocate. New York City, July 13, 2009.

Interview 4. In-person interview. Child care advocate. New York City, July 24, 2009.

Interview 5. In-person interview. Child care advocate. New York City, July 24, 2009.

Interview 6. In-person interview. Organizer, Families United for Racial and Economic Equality. New York City, August 3, 2009.

Interview 7. In-person interview. Child care organizer, Families United for Racial and Economic Equality. New York City, August 3, 2009.

Interview 8. Phone interview. Organizer, Consortium for Worker Education. September 17, 2009.

Interview 9. In-person interview. Organizer, ACORN. New York City, November 6, 2009.

Interview 10. Phone interview. Organizer, ACORN. November 9, 2009.

Interview 11. Phone interview. Organizer, WEP Workers Together. January 12, 2010.

Interview 12. Phone interview. Staff lawyer, NOW Legal Defense and Education Fund. January 19, 2010.

Interview 13. Phone interview. Family child care provider and organizer, United Federation of Teachers. January 23, 2010.

Interview 14. Phone interview. Child care activist, Day Care Forum. March 9, 2011.

Interview 15. Phone interview. Jason Turner, commissioner at the New York City Human Resources Administration, 1998–2001. August 25, 2009.

Interview 16. Phone interview. Senior staff, Human Resources Administration. January 21, 2010.

Interview 17. Phone interview. Ajay Chaudry, deputy commissioner for early childhood development at the New York City Administration for Children's Services, 2004–2006. December 5, 2010.

Interview 18. In-person interview. Lawrence M. Mead, professor of politics and public policy at New York University. June 12, 2009.

PUBLISHED SOURCES

Abramovitz, Mimi. 1996. *Regulating the Lives of Women: Social Welfare Policy from Colonial Times to the Present*. Boston: South End Press.

———. 2000. *Under Attack, Fighting Back: Women and Welfare in the United States*. New York: Monthly Review Press.

———. 2002. "Learning from the History of Poor and Working-Class Women's Activism." In *Lost Ground: Welfare Reform, Poverty, and Beyond*, edited by Randy Albeda and Ann Withorn, 163–78. Cambridge, Mass.: South End Press.

———. 2006. "Welfare Reform in the United States: Race, Class, and Gender Matters." *Critical Social Policy* 26, no. 2:336–64.

———. 2010. "Women, Social Reproduction and the Neo-Liberal Assault on the US Welfare State." In *The Legal Tender of Gender: Law, Welfare, and the Regulation of Women's Poverty*, edited by Shelley A. M. Gavigan and Dorothy E. Chunn, 15–46. Oxford, UK: Hart Publishing.

———. 2012. "The Feminization of Austerity." *New Labor Forum* 21, no. 1 (winter 2012): 30–39.

———. 2017. "From the Welfare State to the Carceral State: Whither Social Reproduction?" In *Democracy and the Welfare State: The Two Wests in the Age of Austerity*, edited by Alice Kessler-Harris and Maurizio Vaudagna, 195–226. New York: Columbia University Press.

ACS (Administration for Children's Services). 2001. *Counting to 10: New Directions in Child Care and Head Start*. New York: New York City Administration for Children's Services.

———. 2005. *Rethinking Child Care: An Integrated Plan for Early Childhood Development in New York City*. New York: New York City Administration for Children's Services.

Adams, Gina, and Monica Rohacek. 2002. *Child Care and Welfare Reform*. Washington, D.C.: Brookings Institution.

Adams, Gina, Pamela Holcomb, Kathleen Snyder, Robin Koralek, Jeffrey Capizzano. 2006. *Child Care Subsidies for TANF Families: The Nexus of Systems and Policies*. Washington, D.C.: Urban Institute.

Aguirre, Adalberto, Jr., Volker Eick, and Ellen Reese. 2006. "Introduction: Neoliberal Globalization, Urban Privatization, and Resistance." *Social Justice* 33, no. 3:1–5.

Allard, Scott W. 2009. *Out of Reach: Place, Poverty, and the New American Welfare State*. New Haven, Conn.: Yale University Press.

Allawhala, Ahmed, Julie-Anne Boudreau, and Roger Keil. 2010. "Neo-Liberal Governance: Entrepreneurial Municipal Regimes in Canada." In *Canadian Cities in Transition: New Directions in the Twenty-First Century*, edited by Trudi Bunting, Pierre Filion, and Ryan Walker, 210–24. New York: Oxford University Press.

Allen, Zita. 2005. "Unions Race to Win over Childcare Workers." *New York Amsterdam News*, November 24, 2005.

Amlung, Susan. 2010. "Not for Teachers Only—Part 1." *New York Teacher*, April 1, 2010.

Andreotti, Alberta, Enzo Mingione, and Emanuele Polizzi. 2012. "Local Welfare Systems: A Challenge for Social Cohesion." *Urban Studies* 49, no. 9:1925–40.

Arat-Koç, Sedef. 2006. "Whose Social Reproduction? Transnational Motherhood and Challenges to Feminist Political Economy." In *Social Reproduction: Feminist Political Economy Challenges Neoliberalism*, edited by Kate Bezanson and Meg Luxton, 75–92. Montreal: McGill-Queen's University Press.

Armstrong, Pat, and Hugh Armstrong. 2004. "Thinking It Through: Women, Work and Caring in the New Millennium." In *Caring For/Caring About: Women, Home Care, and Unpaid Caregiving*, edited by Karen R. Grant, Carol Amartunga, Pat Armstrong, Madeline Boscoe, Ann Pederson, and Kay Willson, 5–44. Toronto: University of Toronto Press.

Arruzza, Cinzia, Tithi Bhattacharya, and Nancy Fraser. 2019. *Feminism for the 99 Percent: A Manifesto*. New York: Verso.

Atlas, John, and Peter Dreier. 2013. "The De Blasio Victory: Jon Kest's Legacy." *Nation*, December 2, 2013. https://www.thenation.com/article/de-blasio-victory-jon-kests-legacy.

Baker, Maureen, and David Tippin. 1999. *Poverty, Social Assistance, and the Employability of Single Mothers: Restructuring Welfare States*. Toronto: University of Toronto Press.

Bakker, Isabella. 2007. "Social Reproduction and the Constitution of a Gendered Political Economy." *New Political Economy* 12, no. 4:541–56.

Bakker, Isabella, and Rachel Silvey. 2008. *Beyond States and Markets: The Challenges of Social Reproduction*. New York: Routledge.

Bashevkin, Sylvia. 2002. *Welfare Hot Buttons: Women, Work, and Social Policy Reform*. Toronto: University of Toronto Press.

Berg, Bruce F. 2007. *New York City Politics: Governing Gotham*. New Brunswick, N.J.: Rutgers University Press.

Besharov, Douglas J., and Peter Germanis. 2005. "Achieving 'Full Engagement.'" In *Managing Welfare Reform in New York City*, edited by E. S. Savas, 146–70. Lanham, Md.: Rowman and Littlefield.

Besharov, Douglas J., and Nazanin Samari. 2001. "Child Care after Welfare Reform." In *The New World of Welfare*, edited by Rebecca Blank and Ron Haskins, 461–89. Washington D.C.: Brookings Institution Press.

———. 2005. "The Wisconsin Miracle: Creating a Responsive Market for Child Care." *Fraser Forum*, May 2005, 9–11.

Bezanson, Kate. 2006. *Gender, the State, and Social Reproduction: Household Insecurity in Neo-Liberal Times*. Toronto: University of Toronto Press.

———. 2015. "Return of the Nightwatchman State? Federalism, Social Reproduction, and Social Policy in Conservative Canada." In *Precarious Worlds: Contested Geographies of Social Reproduction*, edited by Katie Meehan and Kendra Strauss, 25–44. Athens: University of Georgia Press.

Bezanson, Kate, and Meg Luxton. 2006. "Social Reproduction and Feminist Political Economy." In *Social Reproduction: Feminist Political Economy Challenges Neoliberalism*, edited by Kate Bezanson and Meg Luxton, 3–10. Montreal: McGill-Queen's University Press.

Bhattacharya, Tithi, ed. 2017. *Social Reproduction Theory: Remapping Class, Recentering Oppression*. London: Pluto Press.

———. 2018. "Women Are Leading the Wave of Strikes in America. Here's Why." *Guardian*, April 10, 2018.

Black, Simon. 2012. "Mitigating Precarious Employment in New York City's Home-Based Child Care Sector." *Labor, Capital, and Society* 45, no. 1:96–121.

Blank, Helen, Deborah Chalfie, and Joan Entmacher. 2007. *Getting Organized: Unionizing Home-Based Child Care Providers*. Washington D.C.: National Women's Law Center.

Blank, Helen, Nancy Duff Campbell, and Joan Entmacher. 2010. *Getting Organized: Unionizing Home-Based Child Care Providers, 2010 Update*. Washington, D.C.: National Women's Law Center.

———. 2014. *Getting Organized: Unionizing Home-Based Child Care Providers, 2013 Update*. Washington, D.C.: National Women's Law Center.

Bleyer, Jennifer. 2006. "At Day Care Centers, the Bogeyman Looms." *New York Times*, December 10, 2006.

Block, Fred L., Richard A. Cloward, Barbara Ehrenreich, and Frances Fox Piven. 1987. *The Mean Season: The Attack on the Welfare State*. New York: Pantheon Books.

Boris, Eileen. 2012. "Home as Work." In *Labor Rising: The Past and Future of Working People in America*, edited by Daniel Katz and Richard A. Greenwald, 145–56. New York: New Press.

———. 1995. "The Racialized Gendered State: Constructions of Citizenship in the United States." *Social Politics* 2, no. 2:160–80.

Boris, Eileen, and Jennifer Klein. 2008. "Labor on the Home Front: Unionizing Home-Based Care Workers." *New Labor Forum* 17, no. 2 (summer 2008): 32–41.

———. 2014. "Reducing Labor to Love." *Nation*, July 2, 2014. https://www.thenation.com/article/after-harris-v-quinn-state-our-unions.

———. 2015. *Caring for America: Home Health Care Workers in the Shadow of the Welfare State*. New York: Oxford University Press.

Boudreau, Julie Ann, Roger Keil, and Douglas Young. 2009. *Changing Toronto: Governing Urban Neoliberalism*. Toronto: University of Toronto Press.

Braedley, Susan, and Meg Luxton. 2010. *Neoliberalism and Everyday Life*. Montreal: McGill-Queen's University Press.

Brash, Julian. 2011. *Bloomberg's New York: Class and Governance in the Luxury City*. Athens: University of Georgia Press.

Brenner, Johanna. 2014. "Caring in the City." *Jacobin*, October 3, 2014. https://jacobinmag.com/2014/10/caring-in-the-city.

Brenner, Neil, Peter Marcuse, and Margit Mayer. 2012. *Cities for People, Not for Profit: Critical Urban Theory and the Right to the City.* New York: Routledge.

Brenner, Neil, Jamie Peck, and Nik Theodore. 2010. "Variegated Neoliberalization: Geographies, Modalities, Pathways." *Global Networks* 10, no. 2:1–41.

Brenner, Neil, and Nik Theodore. 2002. "Cities and the Geographies of 'Actually Existing Neoliberalism.'" *Antipode* 34:349–79.

Briggs, Laura. 2017. *How All Politics Became Reproductive Politics: From Welfare Reform to Foreclosure to Trump.* Oakland: University of California Press.

Brooke, Richie, and Robin Epstein. 1997. "Day Carelessness." *City Limits*, 22, no. 7:12–14.

Brooks, Fred P. 2005. "New Turf for Organizing: Family Child Care Providers." *Labor Studies Journal* 29, no. 4:45–64.

Brozan, Nadine. 1979. "The City's Day-Care System: Resilient in Difficult Times." *New York Times*, March 13, 1979.

Busa, Alessandro. 2017. *The Creative Destruction of New York City: Engineering the City for the Elite.* New York: Oxford University Press.

Cameron, Barbara. 2006. "Social Reproduction and Canadian Federalism." In *Social Reproduction: Feminist Political Economy Challenges Neoliberalism*, edited by Kate Bezanson and Meg Luxton, 45–74. Montreal: McGill-Queen's University Press.

Capizzano, Jeffrey, and Gina Adams. 2003. "Children in Low-Income Families Are Less Likely to Be in Center-Based Child Care." *Snapshots of America's Families 3* (Urban Institute), no. 16. https://www.urban.org/sites/default/files/publication/57566/310923 -Children-in-Low-Income-Families-Are-Less-Likely-to-Be-in-Center-Based-Child -Care.PDF.

Carney Smith, Jessie. 1996. *Notable Black American Women.* Detroit: Gale Research.

Casey, Timothy, and Laurie Maldonado. 2012. *Worst Off: Single Parents in the United States.* New York: Legal Momentum.

Castells, Manuel. 1977. *The Urban Question: A Marxist Approach.* London: Edward Arnold.

CBC (Citizens Budget Commission). 1994. *Poverty and Public Spending Related to Poverty in New York City.* New York: Citizens Budget Commission.

——. 1997. *The State of Municipal Services in the 1990s: Social Service in New York City.* New York: Citizens Budget Commission.

CCI (Child Care Inc.). 1990. *CCI Primer 1990.* New York: Child Care, Inc.

——. 1994. *CCI Primer 1994.* New York: Child Care, Inc.

——. 1996. *CCI Primer 1996.* New York: Child Care, Inc.

——. 1998. *CCI Primer 1998.* New York: Child Care, Inc.

——. 1999. *CCI Primer 1999.* New York: Child Care, Inc.

——. 2003. *CCI Primer 2003.* New York: Child Care, Inc.

——. 2004. *CCI Primer 2004.* New York: Child Care, Inc.

Center for the Child Care Workforce. 1998. *State Initiative to Train TANF Recipients for Child Care Employment.* Washington D.C.: Center for the Child Care Workforce.

Chalfie, Deborah, Helen Blank, and Joan Entmacher. 2007. *Getting Organized: Unionizing Home-Based Child Care Providers.* Washington, D.C.: National Women's Law Center.

Chang, Clio. 2019. "If New Yorkers Won't Back Bill de Blasio, Nobody Else Will." *Guardian*, May 16, 2019.

Chaudry, Ajay. 2004. *Putting Children First: How Low-Wage Working Mothers Manage Child Care*. New York: Russell Sage Foundation.

Chaudry, Ajay, Juan Manuel Pedroza, Heather Sandstrom, Anna Danziger, Michel Grosz, Molly Scott, and Sarah Ting. 2011. *Child Care Choices of Low-Income Working Families*. Washington, D.C.: Urban Institute.

Chaudry, Ajay, Heather Sandstrom, and Lindsay Giesen. 2012. *How Contextual Constraints Affect Low-Income Working Parents' Child Care Choices*. Washington D.C.: Urban Institute.

Chen, Michelle. 2014. "Can New York City's Welfare System Be Saved?" *Nation*, May 29, 2014. https://www.thenation.com/article/can-new-york-citys-welfare-system-be -saved.

———. 2017. "How to Fix American's Child Care Crisis." *Nation*, September 19, 2017. https://www.thenation.com/article/how-to-fix-americas-childcare-crisis.

Chira, Susan. 1994. "Broad Study Says Home-Based Day Care, Even if by Relatives, Often Fails Children." *New York Times*, April 8, 1994.

Clark, James. 2005. "Overcoming Opposition and Giving Work Experience to Welfare Applicants." In *Managing Welfare Reform in New York City*, edited by E. S. Savas, 171–209. Oxford, UK: Rowman and Littlefield.

Clines, Frances. 1969. "Day-Care Union Accepts New Pact." *New York Times*, September 20, 1969.

Cohn, Jonathan. 2010. "Why Public Employees Are the New Welfare Queens." *New Republic*, August 8, 2010. https://newrepublic.com/article/76884/why-your-fireman -has-better-pension-you.

Cole, Williams. 2006. "Against the Giuliani Legacy." *Brooklyn Rail*, May 9, 2006. http:// www.brooklynrail.org/2006/05/local/against-the-giuliani-legacy.

Collins, Jane L., and Victoria Mayer. 2010. *Both Hands Tied: Welfare Reform and the Race to the Bottom in the Low-Wage Labor Market*. Chicago: University of Chicago Press.

Collins, Sheila D., and Gertrude Goldberg. 2004. "Aid to Families with Dependent Children." In *Poverty in the United States: An Encyclopedia of History, Politics, and Policy*, edited by Gwendolyn Mink and Alice O'Connor, 76–84. Oxford, UK: ABC-CLIO.

Cooke, Oliver D. 2008. *Rethinking Municipal Privatization*. New York: Routledge.

Cooper, David, Mary Gable, and Algernon Austin. 2012. *The Public-Sector Jobs Crisis: Women and African Americans Hit Hardest by Job Losses in State and Local Governments*. Briefing Paper 339. Economic Policy Institute, May 2, 2012. http://www.epi .org/publication/bp339-public-sector-jobs-crisis.

Covery, Bryce. 2014. "We're Arresting Poor Mothers for Our Own Failures." *Nation*, July 22, 2014. http://www.thenation.com/blog/180753/were-arresting-poor-mothers-our -own-failures.

CSA (Council of School Supervisors and Administrators). 2012. "CSA: A Brief History." http://www.csa-nyc.org/ about/csa-history.

CSWL (Committee on Social Welfare Law of the New York City Bar Association). 2001.

"Welfare Reform in New York City: The Measure of Success." *Record* (New York City Bar Association) 56, no. 3:322–57.

Danzinger, Sheldon. 1983. "Budget Cuts as Welfare Reform." *American Economic Review* 73, no. 2:65.

Davis, Angela. 1980. "Child Care or Workfare?" *New Perspectives Quarterly* 7 (winter 1980): 19–22.

Davis, Dana-Ain, Ana Aparicio, Audrey Jacobs, Akemi Kochiyama, Andrea Queeley, Beverly Yuen Thompson, and Leith Mullings. 2002. *The Impact of Welfare Reform on Two Communities in New York City*. New York: Scholar Practitioner Program, Department of Anthropology, Graduate Center at the City University of New York.

Day Care Council of New York. 2012. "About the Day Care Council of New York." http://www.dccnyinc.org/view/page/about_us.

DeParle, Jason. 1998. "Shrinking Welfare Rolls Leave Record High Share of Minorities." *New York Times*, July 28, 1998.

———. 2012. "Welfare Limits Left Poor Adrift as Recession Hits." *New York Times*, April 8, 2012.

District Council 1707. 2012. "About Us." http://www.dc1707.net/.

Dreier, Peter. 2011. "Reagan's Real Legacy." *Nation*, February 4, 2011. https://www.thenation.com/article/reagans-real-legacy.

Duggan, Lisa. 2012. *The Twilight of Equality? Neoliberalism, Cultural Politics, and the Attack on Democracy*. Boston: Beacon Press.

Duffy, Mignon. 2011. *Making Care Count: A Century of Gender, Race, and Paid Care Work*. New Brunswick, N.J.: Rutgers University Press.

Dulchin, Benjamin, and Sharryn Kasmir. 2004. "Organizing and Identity in the New York City Workfare Program." *Regional Labor Review* 7, no. 1 (fall 2004): 1–7.

Dumenil, Gerard, and Dominique Levy. 2004. *Capital Resurgent: Roots of the Neoliberal Revolution*. London: Cambridge University Press.

Ehrenreich, Barbara, and Frances Fox Piven. 2006. "The Truth about Welfare Reform." In *Telling the Truth: 2006 Socialist Register*, edited by Leo Panitch and Colin Leys, 75–92. London: Merlin Press.

England, Paula, and Nancy Folbre. 1999. "The Cost of Caring." *Annals of the American Academy of Political and Social Science* 561:39–51.

Esping-Andersen, Gosta. 1990. *The Three Worlds of Welfare Capitalism*. Cambridge, UK: Polity Press.

Fahim, Kareem. 2005. "Enforcement of Fire Codes Threatens Day Care Sites." *New York Times*, May 22, 2005.

Federici, Silvia. 2006. "The Restructuring of Social Reproduction in the United States in the 1970s." *Commoner: A Web Journal for Other Values* 11 (spring 2006): 74–88.

———. 2012. *Revolution at Point Zero: Housework, Reproduction, and Feminist Struggle*. Oakland: PM Press.

Feigelson, Naomi. 1973. "Put Them All Together, They Spell Day Care." *Village Voice*, June 21, 41–42.

Ferguson, Sue. n.d. "Social Reproduction: What's the Big Idea?" Pluto Press blog. https://www.plutobooks.com/blog/social-reproduction-theory-ferguson.

Ferguson, Sue, Genevieve LeBaron, Angela Dimitrakaki, and Sara R. Farris, eds. 2016. "Symposium on Social Reproduction." *Historical Materialism* 24, no. 2:25–163.

Firestine, Netsy, and Nicola Dones. 2007. "Unions Fight for Work and Family Policies—Not for Women Only." In *The Sex of Class: Women Transforming American Labor*, edited by Dorothy Sue Cobble, 140–54. Ithaca, N.Y.: Cornell University Press.

Folbre, Nancy. 2006. "Measuring Care: Gender, Empowerment, and the Care Economy." *Journal of Human Development and Capabilities* 7, no. 2:183–99.

Folbre, Nancy, ed. 2012. *For Love and Money: Care Provision in the United States*. New York: Russell Sage Foundation.

Fording, Richard C. 2001. "The Political Response to Black Insurgency: A Critical Test of Competing Theories of the State." *American Political Science Review* 95, no. 1:115–30.

Forry, Nicole, Kathryn Trout, Laura Rothenberg, Heather Sandstrom, and Colleen Vesley. 2013. *Child Care Decision-Making Literature Review*. OPRE Brief 2013–45. Washington, D.C.: Office of Planning, Research and Evaluation, Administration for Children and Families, U.S. Department of Health and Human Services.

Fousekis, Natalie M. 2011. *Demanding Child Care: Women's Activism and the Politics of Welfare, 1940–1971*. Chicago: University of Illinois Press.

Fraser, Nancy. 2016. "Contradictions of Capital and Care." *New Left Review* 100:99–117.

Frazier, Craig D. 2011. "Unions March on Wall Street." *New York Amsterdam News*, May 19–May 25, 2011.

Freeman, Joshua. 2000. *Working-Class New York: Life and Labor Since World War II*. New York: New Press.

———. 2014. "If You Can Make It Here." *Jacobin* 15/16:24–28.

———. 2015. "Organizing New York." *Jacobin*. May 7, 2015. https://www.jacobinmag.com/2015/05/victor-gotbaum-dc-37-public-unions.

Fudge, Judy, and Brenda Cossman. 2002. Introduction to *Privatization, Law, and the Challenge to Feminism*, edited by Judy Fudge and Brenda Cossman, 3–40. Toronto: University of Toronto Press.

Fuller, Bruce, Sharon Lynn Kagan, Susanna Loeb, Yueh-Wen Chang. 2004. "Child Care Quality: Centers and Home Settings that Serve Poor Families." *Early Childhood Research Quarterly* 19:505–27.

FUREE (Families United for Racial and Economic Equality). 2008. *Who Are We*. Brooklyn: FUREE.

———. 2004. *Stop the Shutdowns!* Brooklyn: FUREE.

———. n.d. *FUREE Stop the Shutdowns Campaign Fact Sheet*. Brooklyn: FUREE.

Gilmore, Ruth Wilson. 2007. *Golden Gulag: Prisons, Surplus, Crisis, and Opposition in Globalizing California*. Berkeley: University of California Press.

Gingrich, Newt. 1992. "Letter to the Editor." *New York Times*, March 30, 1992.

Giuliani, Rudolph W. 1998. "Replacing Welfare with Work: Mayor's WINS Address." Archives of Rudolph W. Giuliani, July 26, 1998. http://www.nyc.gov/html/records/rwg/html/98b/me980726.html.

Glenn, Evelyn Nakano. 2010. *Forced to Care: Coercion and Caregiving in America*. Cambridge, Mass.: Harvard University Press.

Goldberg, Chad Allan. 2001. "Welfare Recipients or Workers? Contesting the Workfare State in New York City." *Sociological Theory* 19, no. 2:187–218.

Goldberg, Michelle. 2014. "The Rise of the Progressive City." *Nation*, April 2, 2014. https://www.thenation.com/article/rise-progressive-city.

Goldstein, Dana. 2016. "Bill de Blasio's Pre-K Crusade." *Atlantic*, September 7, 2016. http://www.theatlantic.com/education/archive/2016/09/bill-de-blasios-prek -crusade/498830.

González, Juan. 2017. *Reclaiming Gotham: Bill de Blasio and the Movement to End America's Tale of Two Cities*. New York: New Press.

Gordon, Linda. 1994. *Pitied but Not Entitled: Single Mothers and the History of Welfare*. Cambridge, Mass.: Harvard University Press.

Gornick, Janet, Candace Howes, and Laura Braslow. 2012. "The Care Policy Landscape." In *For Love and Money: Care Provision in the United States*, edited by Nancy Folbre, 112–39. New York: Russell Sage Foundation.

Grace, Melissa. 2005. "Ex-Day Care Provider's Woe." *New York Daily News*, June 23, 2005.

Greenhouse, Steven. 2005a. "After 4 Years, Day Care Workers Await Raise and Contract." *New York Times*, January 18, 2005.

———. 2005b. "Care Providers Need a Union, 3 Groups Say." *New York Times*, July 15, 2005.

———. 2007. "Child Care Workers in New York City Vote to Unionize." *New York Times*, October 24, 2007.

Greer, Scott, Heather Elliot, and Rebecca Oliver. 2015. "Differences that Matter: Overcoming Methodological Nationalism in Comparative Social Policy Research." *Journal of Comparative Policy Analysis: Research and Practice* 17, no. 4:408–29.

Gregory, David L. 2008. "Labor Organizing by Executive Order: Governor Spitzer and the Unionization of Home-Based Child Day-Care Providers." *Fordham Urban Law Journal* 35:277–305.

Grindal, Todd. 2015. "Who Cares for the Caregivers? What Unionization Could Mean for the Future of Publicly Funded Childcare." *HuffPost*, July 29, 2015. https://www .huffingtonpost.com/todd-grindal/who-cares-for-the-caregiv_2_b_7887526.html.

Grindal, Todd, Martin R. West, John B. Willet, and Hirokazu Yoshikawa. 2015. "The Impact of Home-Based Child Care Provider Unionization on the Cost, Type, and Availability of Subsidized Child Care in Illinois." *Journal of Policy Analysis and Management* 34, no. 4:853–80.

Hackworth, Jason. 2007. *The Neoliberal City: Governance, Ideology, and Development in American Urbanism*. Ithaca, N.Y.: Cornell University Press.

Harvey, David. 1989. "From Managerialism to Urban Entrepenurialism." *Geografiska Annaler: Series B, Human Geography* 71, no. 1:3–17.

———. 2005. *A Brief History of Neoliberalism*. New York: Oxford University Press.

———. 2007. "Neoliberalism and the City." *Studies in Social Justice* 1, no. 1:2–13.

———. 2012. *Rebel Cities: From the Right to the City to the Urban Revolution.* New York: Verso.

Hayden, Dolores. 1982. *The Grand Domestic Revolution: A History of Feminist Design for Homes, Neighborhoods, and Cities.* Boston: MIT Press.

Hester, Helen. 2018. "Care under Capitalism: The Crisis of 'Women's Work.'" *IPRR Progressive Review* 24, no. 4:344–52.

Hevesi, Alan G. 2002. *Office of Children and Family Services: Life Safety and Fiscal Issues Related to Legally Exempt Child Care.* Albany: New York State Office of the State Comptroller.

Hevesi, Dennis. 1995. "Plan for Cuts in Day Care Stirs Anxiety." *New York Times,* January 18, 1995.

Heynen, Nik. 2009. "Revolutionary Cooks in the Hungry Ghetto: The Black Panther Party's Biopolitics of Scale from Below." In *Leviathan Undone? Towards a Political Economy of Scale,* edited by Roger Keil and Rianne Mahon, 265–80. Vancouver: University of British Columbia Press.

Hicks, Jonathan. 2006. "In Her Mother's Footsteps, and Now in Shirley Chisholm's, Too." *New York Times,* September 14, 2006.

Hill, Selena. 2011. "Thousands Rally against Child Care Cuts." *New York Amsterdam News,* May 19–May 25, 2011.

Hill Collins, Patricia. 2000. "Gender, Black Feminism, and Black Political Economy." *Annals of the American Academy of Political and Social Science* 568:41–53.

Hilliard, Thomas. 2011. *Subsidizing Care, Supporting Work.* New York: Center for an Urban Future.

Houser, Linda, Sanford Schram, Joe Soss, and Richard Fording. 2014. "From Work Support to Work Motivator: Child Care Subsidies and Caseworker Discretion in the Post-Welfare Reform Era." *Journal of Women, Politics, and Policy* 35, no. 2:174–93.

Howes, Candace, Carrie Leana, and Kristin Smith. 2012. "Paid Care Work." In *For Love and Money: Care Provision in the United States,* edited by Nancy Folbre, 65–91. New York: Russell Sage Foundation.

Hurley, Kendra. 2016. *Bringing It All Home: Problems and Possibilities Facing New York City's Family Child Care.* New York: Center for New York City Affairs.

———. 2018. *New York's Tale of Two Child Care Cities.* New York: Center for New York City Affairs.

IBO (Independent Budget Office). 1997. *The Fiscal Impact of the New Federal Welfare Law on New York City.* New York: Independent Budget Office.

———. 2002. *City's Reliance on State and Federal Funds for Child Care Grows.* New York: Independent Budget Office. http://www.ibo.nyc.ny.us/.

International Labour Organization. 2018. *Care Work and Care Jobs for the Future of Decent Work.* Geneva: International Labour Organization.

Jackson, Larry R., and William A. Johnson. 1973. *Protest by the Poor: The Welfare Rights Movement in New York City.* New York: Rand Institute.

Jenson, Jane, and Mariette Sineau. 2001. *Who Cares? Women's Work, Child Care, and Welfare State Redesign.* Toronto: University of Toronto Press.

Jones, Anika Y. 2014. "From Welfare Queens to Day-Care Queens." *Anthropology Now* 6, no. 3:37–44.

Juravich, Nick. 2015. "Paraprofessional Educators and Labor-Community Coalitions, Past and Present." *LaborOnline* (Labor and Working-Class History Association), February 24, 2015. https://www.lawcha.org/2015/02/24/paraprofessional-educators-and -labor-community-coalitions-past-and-present.

Katz, Cindi. 2001. "Vagabond Capitalism and the Necessity of Social Reproduction." *Antipode* 33:709–28.

Katz, Michael B. 1986. *In the Shadow of the Poorhouse: A Social History of Welfare in America.* New York: Basic Books.

———. 2008. *The Price of Citizenship: Redefining the American Welfare State.* Philadelphia: University of Pennsylvania Press.

———. 2012. *Why Don't American Cities Burn?* Philadelphia: University of Pennsylvania Press.

———. 2013. *The Undeserving Poor: American's Enduring Confrontation with Poverty.* New York: Oxford University Press.

Kaufman, Leslie. 2004. "Women Who Leave Welfare Find Few Day Care Options." *New York Times,* May 10, 2004.

Kershaw, Paul. 2004. *"Choice" Discourse in BC Child Care: Distancing Policy from Research.* Occasional Paper 19. Toronto: Childcare Resource and Research Unit, University of Toronto. http://pdfs.semanticscholar.org/.

Kershaw, Sarah 2000. "Day Care at Night? New York Lags Behind." *New York Times,* April 2, 2000.

Kihss, Peter. 1976a. "New York City to Halt Aid for 49 Day-Care Centers." *New York Times,* May 28, 1976.

———. 1976b. "$37 Million Waste Found in Day Care." *New York Times,* October 7, 1976.

Kirp, David L. 2007. *The Sandbox Investment: The Preschool Movement and Kids-First Politics.* Cambridge, Mass.: Harvard University Press.

Klemserud, Judy. 1975. "March and Rally Celebrate First International Women's Day March." *New York Times,* March 29, 1975.

Kneebone, Elizabeth. 2017. "The Changing Geography of US Poverty." Testimony before the House Ways and Means Committee, Subcommittee on Human Resources, February 15, 2017. Brookings Institution. https://www.brookings.edu/testimonies/the -changing-geography-of-us-poverty.

Knox, Virginia, Andrew London, Ellen K. Scott, and Susan Blank. 2003. *Welfare Reform, Work, and Child Care: The Role of Informal Care in the Lives of Low-Income Women and Children.* New York: MDRC.

Kolben, Nancy. 1997. Child Care Inc. Memo to New York City on 1997 Budget. Document in possession of author.

Kornbluh, Felicia. 2007. *The Battle for Welfare Rights: Politics and Poverty in Modern America.* Philadelphia: University of Pennsylvania Press.

Krinsky, John. 2006. "The Dialectics of Privatization and Advocacy in New York City's Workfare State." *Social Justice* 33, no. 3:158–74.

———. 2007a. *Free Labor: Workfare and the Contested Language of Neoliberalism*. Chicago: University of Chicago Press.

———. 2007b. "The Urban Politics of Workfare: New York City's Welfare Reforms and the Dimensions of Welfare Policy Making." *Urban Affairs Review* 42, no. 6:771–98.

———. 2011. "Neoliberal Times: Intersecting Temporalities and the Neoliberalization of New York City's Public-Sector Labor Relations." *Social Science History* 35, no. 3:381–422.

Krinsky, John, and Ellen Reese. 2006. "Forging and Sustaining Labor-Community Coalitions: The Workfare Justice Movement in Three Cities." *Sociological Forum* 21, no. 4:623–58.

Kurshid, Samar. 2017. "De Blasio's Record on Poverty and Inequality." *Gotham Gazette*, November 1, 2017.

Lacks, Rosyln. 1971. "Only the Poor Can Afford Day Care." *Village Voice*, December 16, 1971, 11.

Landau, Micah. 2009. "City Agrees to Long Overdue Raise for Child Care Providers." United Federation of Teachers, May 10, 2009. http://www.uft.org/provider-news/city -agrees-long-overdue-raise-child-care-providers.

———. 2010. "Providers Overwhelmingly Ratify First Contract." United Federation of Teachers, February 4, 2010. https://web.archive.org/web/20110116044628/http:// www.uft.org/news-stories/providers-overwhelmingly-ratify-first-contract.

———. 2011. "Child Care Workers Protest City Funding Cut." United Federation of Teachers, May 26, 2011. http://www.uft.org/news-stories/child-care-workers-protest -city-funding-cut.

Larner, Wendy. 2000. "Neoliberalism: Policy, Ideology, Governmentality." *Studies in Political Economy* 63:5–25.

Laslett, Barbara, and Johanna Brenner. 1989. "Gender and Social Reproduction: Historical Perspectives." *Annual Review of Sociology* 15:381–404.

Layzer, Jean, and Barbara D. Goodson. 2006. "The 'Quality' of Early Care and Education Settings: Definitional and Measurement Issues." *Evaluation Review* 30, no. 5:556–76.

Legal Momentum. 2014. "The TANF Misery Index Climbed to a Record National High in 2012." Legal Momentum. http://www.legalmomentum.org/resources/tanf-misery -index-2014-update.

Leitner, Helga, Jamie Peck, and Eric Sheppard. 2007. *Contesting Neoliberalism: Urban Frontiers*. New York: Guilford Press.

Levenstein, Lisa. 2009. *A Movement without Marches: African American Women and the Politics of Poverty in Postwar Philadelphia*. Chapel Hill: University of North Carolina Press.

Levy, Denise Urias, and Sonya Michel. 2002. "More Can Be Less: Child Care and Welfare Reform in the United States." In *Child Care Policy at the Crossroads: Gender and Welfare State Restructuring*, edited by Sonya Michel and Rianne Mahon, 239–66. London, UK: Routledge.

Lewis, Jane. 1992. "Gender and the Development of Welfare Regimes." *Journal of European Social Policy* 2, no. 3:159–73.

Lipman, Pauline. 2011. *The New Political Economy of Urban Education: Neoliberalism, Race, and the Right to the City*. London: Routledge.

Love, Barbara. 2006. *Feminists Who Changed America*. Chicago: University of Illinois Press.

Lurie, Irene, and Mary Bryna Sanger. 1991. "The Family Support Act: Defining the Social Contract in New York." *Social Service Review* 65, no. 1:43–67.

Luxton, Meg. 2006. "Feminist Political Economy in Canada and the Politics of Social Reproduction." In *Social Reproduction: Feminist Political Economy Challenges Neoliberalism*, edited by Kate Bezanson and Meg Luxton, 11–44. Toronto: McGill-Queens University Press.

———. 2014. "Marxist Feminism and Anticapitalism: Reclaiming Our History, Reanimating Our Politics." *Studies in Political Economy* 94:137–60.

Lynch, Karen E. 2016. *Trends in Child Care Spending from the CCDF and TANF*. Congressional Research Service. https://fas.org/sgp/crs/misc/R44528.pdf.

Mac Donald, Heather. 2014. "Stephen Banks, Reporting for Duty." *City Journal*, April 18, 2014. http://www.city-journal.org/2014/eon0418hm.html.

Madden, David, and Peter Marcuse. 2016. *In Defense of Housing*. New York: Verso.

Magnet, Myron. 2004. "Gotham, GOP Poster Child." *City Journal*, August 24, 2004. http://www.city-journal.org/html/eon_08_24_04mm.html.

Mahon, Rianne. 2005. "Rescaling Social Reproduction: Childcare in Toronto/Canada and Stockholm/Sweden." *International Journal of Urban and Regional Research* 29, no. 2:341–57.

———. 2006. "Introduction: Gender and the Politics of Scale." *Social Politics* 13, no. 4:457–61.

———. 2009. "Of Scalar Hierarchies and Welfare Redesign: Child Care in Three Canadian Cities." In *Leviathan Undone? Towards a Political Economy of Scale*, edited by Roger Keil and Rianne Mahon, 209–30. Vancouver: University of British Columbia Press.

Mahon, Rianne, and Laura Macdonald. 2010. "Anti-Poverty Politics in Toronto and Mexico City." *Geoforum* 41:209–17.

Maisano, Chris. 2018. "Labor's Choice after Janus." *Jacobin*, June 27, 2018. https://jacobinmag.com/2018/06/labors-choice-after-janus.

Maitland, Leslie. 1975. "28 Day-Care Centers in City Face Closing." *New York Times*, November 14, 1975.

Malcolm, Noreen. 2006. "Home-Based Providers Demand Change." *New York Amsterdam News*, September 7, 2006.

Manksi, Ben, and Sarah Manski. 2018. "It Started in Wisconsin." *Jacobin*, March 1, 2018. https://jacobinmag.com/2018/03/wisconsin-uprising-janus-supreme-court-unions.

Marable, Manning. 2007. *Race, Reform and Rebellion: The Second Reconstruction and Beyond in Black America, 1945–2006*. 3rd ed. Jackson: University of Mississippi Press.

Marcus, Elliot. 2006. "Tighten Home Day Care Enforcement?" *New York Daily News*, August 5, 2006.

Marston, Sally. 2000. "The Social Construction of Scale." *Progress in Human Geography* 24:219–32.

Martin, Nina. 2010. "The Crisis of Social Reproduction among Migrant Workers: Interrogating the Role of Migrant Civil Society." *Antipode* 42: 127–51.

Mayer, Margit. 2007. "Contesting the Neoliberalization of Urban Governance." In *Contesting Neoliberalism: Urban Frontiers*, edited by Helga Leitner, Jamie Peck, and Eric S. Sheppard, 90–115. New York: Guilford Press.

[McCall, H. Carl]. 1997. *Child Care Services in New York City*. New York: Office of the State Deputy Comptroller.

———. 2000. *A Status Report of Selected Aspects of the Implementation of Welfare Reform in New York City*. Albany: State of New York Office of the State Comptroller, Division of Management Audit and State Financial Services.

McDowell, Linda. 1999. *Gender, Identity and Place: Understanding Feminist Geographies*. London: Polity Press.

McDowell, Linda, Kevin Ward, Collette Fagan, Diane Perrons, and Kath Ray. 2006. "Connecting Time and Space: The Significance of Transformations in Women's Work in the City." *International Journal of Urban and Regional Research* 30, no. 1:141–58.

McKinley, Renee. 2010. "Child Care by Choice or by Default? Examining the Experiences of Unregulated Home-Based Child Care for Women in Paid Work and Training." MA thesis, Brock University.

McMillan, Tracie. 2002. "Market Babies." *City Limits*, December 15, 2002. http://city limits.org/2002/12/15/market-babies.

Mead, Lawrence M. 2004. *Government Matters: Welfare Reform in Wisconsin*. Princeton, N.J.: Princeton University Press.

Meehan, Katie, and Kendra Strauss, eds. 2015. *Precarious Worlds: Contested Geographies of Social Reproduction*. Athens: University of Georgia Press.

Meyer, David S. and Debra C. Minkoff. 2004. "Conceptualizing Political Opportunity." *Social Forces* 82, no. 4:1457–92.

Meyers, M. K. 1990. "The ABCs of Child Care in a Mixed Economy." *Social Service Review*, December 1990, 559–79.

Michel, Sonya. 1999. *Children's Interests/Mothers' Rights: The Shaping of America's Child Care Policy*. New Haven, Conn.: Yale University Press.

———. 2004. "Child Care." In *Poverty in the United States: An Encyclopaedia of History, Politics, and Policy*, edited by Gwendolyn Mink and Alice O'Connor, 149–55. Santa Barbara, Calif.: ABC-CLIO.

Michel, Sonya, and Rianne Mahon, eds. 2002. *Child Care Policy at the Crossroads: Gender and Welfare State Restructuring*. New York: Routledge.

Milkman, Ruth, and Stephanie Luce. 2018. *The State of the Unions 2017: A Profile of Organized Labor in New York City, New York State, and the United States*. New York: Joseph S. Murphy Institute for Worker Education and Labor Studies.

Mink, Gwendolyn. 2002. *Welfare's End*. Rev. ed. Ithaca, N.Y.: Cornell University Press.

Mitchell, Katharyne, Sallie A. Marston, and Cindi Katz, eds. 2004. *Life's Work: Geographies of Social Reproduction*. Malden, Mass.: Blackwell.

Shaefer, H. Luke, and Kathryn Edin. 2018. "Welfare Reform and the Families It Left Behind." *Pathways* (Stanford Center on Poverty and Inequality), Winter 2018, 22–27.

Shelby, Joyce. 2006. "Day Care Crackdown." *New York Daily News*, August 31, 2006.

Sheppard, Nathaniel, Jr. 1976a. "7,200 Families Are Taken off Day Care in Toughening of the Rule on Income." *New York Times*, April 1, 1976.

———. 1976b. "Changes Are Expected in the City's Day-Care System." *New York Times*, April 3, 1976.

Sites, William. 2003. *Remaking New York: Primitive Globalization and the Politics of Urban Community*. Minneapolis: University of Minnesota Press.

Smith, Neil. 1998. "Giuliani Time: The Revanchist 1990s." *Social Text* 57:1–20.

Smith, Peggie R. 2007. "Welfare, Child Care, and the People Who Care: Union Representation of Family Child Care Providers." *University of Kansas Law Review* 55:321–64.

———. 2008. "The Publicization of Home-Based Care Work in State Labor Law." *Minnesota Law Review* 92:1390–1423.

Soffer, Jonathan. 2012. *Ed Koch and the Rebuilding of New York City*. New York: Columbia University Press.

Soss, Joe, Richard C. Fording, and Sanford F. Schram. 2011. *Disciplining the Poor: Neoliberal Paternalism and the Persistent Power of Race*. Chicago: University of Chicago Press.

Southall, Ashley, and Nikita Stewart. 2018. "They Grabbed Her Baby and Arrested Her at a Welfare Office. Now She's Speaking Out." *New York Times*, December 16, 2018.

Spain, Daphne. 2001. *How Women Saved the City*. Minneapolis: University of Minnesota Press.

Stack, Carol. 1975. *All Our Kin: Strategies for Survival in a Black Community*. New York: Basic Books.

Stivers, Mike. 2016. "The Promise of Universal Pre-K." *Jacobin*, September 8, 2016. https://www.jacobinmag.com/2016/09/universal-pre-k-de-blasio-new-york.

Stohr, Kate. 2002. "Day Care in New York". *Gotham Gazette*. December 2, 2002. http://www.gothamgazette.com/iotw/daycare.

Strauss, Kendra, and Feng Xu. 2018. "At the Intersection of Urban and Care Policy: The Invisibility of Eldercare Workers in the Global City." *Critical Sociology* 44, nos. 7–8:1163–78.

Swarns, Rachel. 1998. "Mothers Poised for Workfare Face Acute Lack of Day Care." *New York Times*, April 14, 1998.

Tabb, William A. 1982. *The Long Default: New York City and the Urban Fiscal Crisis*. New York: Monthly Review Press.

Tait, Vanessa. 2005. *Poor Workers' Unions: Rebuilding Labor from Below*. Boston: South End Press.

Teghtsoonian, Katherine. 1996. "Promises, Promises: 'Choices for Women' in Canadian and American Child Care Policy Debates." *Feminist Studies* 22, no. 1:119–46.

Treaster, Joseph. 1994. "Giuliani Considers a Tuition-Voucher Plan for Day Care." *New York Times*, February 26, 1994.

Tuominen, Mary. 2003. *We Are Not Babysitters: Family Child Care Providers Redefine Work and Care.* New Brunswick, N.J.: Rutgers University Press.

———. 2008. "The Right and Responsibility to Care: Oppositional Consciousness among Family Child Care Providers of Color." *Journal of Women, Politics and Policy* 29, no. 2:147–79.

Turner, Jason. 2005. "Reflections of the Commissioner." In *Managing Welfare Reform in New York City*, edited by E.S. Savas, 146–70. Lanham, Md.: Rowman and Littlefield.

UFT (United Federation of Teachers). 2005. "UFT Providers in New York." *UFT Providers Chapter Newsletter*, August 5, 2005, 10.

URBACT. 2019. "The Dilemma of Fighting Poverty Urban Poverty." http://urbact.eu /dilemma-fighting-urban-poverty.

Urban Institute. 1999. *Welfare Rules Databook 1996–1999: Work-Related Exemptions When Caring for a Child under X Months, 1996–1999.* http://anfdata.urban.org/wrd /tables.cfm.

———. 2002. *Work and Welfare Reform in New York City during the Giuliani Administration: A Study of Program Implementation.* Washington, D.C.: Urban Institute.

Vitale, Alex S. 2008. *City of Disorder: How the Quality of Life Campaign Transformed New York Politics.* New York: New York University Press.

Vogel, Carl, and Neil deMause. 1998. "Jason's Brain Trust." *City Limits*, December 1, 1998. https://citylimits.org/1998/12/01/jasons-brain-trust.

Vogel, Lise. 2013. *Marxism and the Oppression of Women: Towards a Unitary Theory.* New ed. Chicago: Haymarket Books.

Vogtman, Julie. 2017. *Undervalued: A Brief History of Women's Care Work and Child Care Policy in the United States.* Washington, D.C.: National Women's Law Center.

Vosko, Leah F. 2002a. "The Pasts (and Futures) of Feminist Political Economy in Canada: Reviving the Debate." *Studies in Political Economy* 68:55–83.

———. 2002b. "Mandatory Marriage or Obligatory Wage Work: Social Assistance and Single Mothers in Wisconsin and Ontario." In *Women's Work Is Never Done: Comparative Studies in Care-Giving, Employment, and Social Policy Reform*, edited by Sylvia Bashevkin, 165–200. London: Routledge.

———. 2006. "Crisis Tendencies in Social Reproduction: The Case of Ontario's Early Years Plan." In *Social Reproduction: Feminist Political Economy Challenges Neoliberalism*, edited by Meg Luxton and Kate Bezanson, 145–172. Montreal: McGill–Queen's University Press.

Wacquant, Loic. 2009a. *Prisons of Poverty.* Minneapolis: University of Minnesota Press.

———. 2009b. *Punishing the Poor: The Neoliberal Government of Social Insecurity.* Durham, N.C.: Duke University Press.

Warner, Mildred E., and Raymond H. J. M. Gradus. 2011. "The Consequences of Implementing a Child Care Voucher Scheme: Evidence from Australia, the Netherlands and the USA." *Social Policy and Administration* 45, no. 5:569–92.

Watkins-Hayes, Celeste. 2009. *The New Welfare Bureaucrats: Entanglements of Race, Class, and Policy Reform.* Chicago: University of Chicago Press.

Weikart, Lynne A. 2001. "The Giuliani Administration and the New Public Management in New York City." *Urban Affairs Review* 36:359–81.

Weingarten, Randi, and Bertha Lews. 2006. "Let Day Care Workers Organize." *New York Amsterdam News*, June 15, 2006.

Weisman, Steven R. 1975. "State Freezes $23-Million in City Day-Care Payments." *New York Times*, February 21, 1975.

Wekerle, Gerda. 1984. "A Woman's Place Is in the City." *Antipode* 16, no. 3:11–19.

Wekerle, Gerda, and Linda Peake. 1996. "New Social Movements and Women's Urban Activism." In *City Lives and City Forms: Critical Research and Canadian Urbanism*, edited by Jon Caulfield and Linda Peake, 263–81. Toronto: University of Toronto Press.

Whitebook, Marcy. 1999. "Child Care Workers: High Demand, Low Wages." *Annals of the American Academy of Political and Social Science* 563:146–61.

———. 2001. *Working for Worthy Wages: The Child Care Compensation Movement, 1970–2001*. Berkeley: Center for the Study of Child Care Employment.

Whitebook, Marcy, Deborah Philips, and Carollee Howes. 2014. *Worthy Work, STILL Unlivable Wages: The Early Childhood Workforce 25 Years after the National Child Care Staffing Study*. Berkeley: Center for the Study of Child Care Employment.

Whitebook, Marcy, Caitlin McLean, and Lea J. E. Austin. 2016. *The Early Childhood Workforce Index 2016*. Berkeley: Center for the Study of Child Care Employment. https://cscce.berkeley.edu/early-childhood-workforce-2016-index.

Whitebook, Marcy, Caitlin McLean, Lea J. E. Austin, and Bethany Edwards. 2018. *Early Childhood Workforce Index 2018*. Berkeley: Center for the Study of Child Care Employment. https://cscce.berkeley.edu/early-childhood-workforce-2018-index.

Whitt, Toni. 2006. "Workers Push Pataki for Unions in Day Care." *New York Times*, May 25, 2006.

Williams, Rhonda Y. 2004. *The Politics of Public Housing: Black Women's Struggles against Urban Inequality*. New York: Oxford University Press.

Witt, Stephen. 2006. "Crackdown Could Force Closure of Home-Based Day Care Centers." *Courier Life Publications*, October 10, 2006.

Zillman, Claire. 2015. "Child Care Workers Join Fast-Food Workers' Fight for $15 an Hour." *Fortune*, March 31, 2015. http://fortune.com/2015/03/30/child-care-workers-pay.

INDEX

Abramovitz, Mimi, 31, 120
activities, care work, 23–24
Administration for Children's Services (ACS),
  106, 113, 128, 146, 148, 154. *See also* Agency
  for Child Development (ACD)
advanced political economies, 8, 9, 23, 29, 32, 41
African Americans, 72; activism and campaigns, 27–28, 48, 51–52, 53–54, 158; community solidarity, 145, 177n16; employment
  opportunities, 32, 70–71, 86; exclusion from
  welfare programs, 31, 52–53; labor organizing, 58, 147, 165; urban social problems and,
  39–40; welfare caseloads and, 96, 175n7
AFSCME (American Federation of State,
  County, and Municipal Employees): District Council 37, 120, 176n3; District Council
  1707, 58, 68, 133; home child care organizing,
  143–44, 148, 177n14, 178n22
AFSCME Day Care (Local 205), 64, 67, 80, 113,
  150, 160; formation of, 58–59; organizing
  activities, 68–69, 139, 155, 158
Agency for Child Development (ACD),
  69, 106; commitment to quality care, 67,
  99–100; fiscal crisis and, 65–67; founding
  and reforms, 60; tensions with the CCCDC,
  61–62, 63; vouchers issued by, 74, 78, 89, 101.
  See also Administration for Children's Services (ACS)
Aid to Dependent Children (ADC), 52–53
Aid to Families with Dependent Children
  (AFDC), 11, 14, 17, 72, 91, 115; Child Care
  program, 75–76. *See also* Temporary Assistance to Needy Families (TANF)

American Federation of State, County and
  Municipal Employees (AFSCME). *See*
  AFSCME
American Federation of Teachers, 59, 165
Andreotti, Alberta, 169n7
antipoverty programs, 55, 72, 86. *See also* Great
  Society; War on Poverty
Arat-Koç, Sedef, 19
Association of Community Organizations for
  Reform Now (ACORN), 135, 156, 177n13,
  177n15; campaign history, 144; UFT partner-
  ship, 142, 145–49, 150, 151–52, 165, 176n12
austerity measures, 36, 40, 65, 84, 168; to child
  care services, 65–67, 144, 158; financial crisis
  (2008) and, 152–53; municipal unions and,
  69; to social services, 33, 44–45, 46–47

Bakker, Isabella, 35
Barrios-Paoli, Lilliam, 122–23
Barron, Charles, 156
Beame, Abe, 65, 83
Berge, Ilana, 140–41
Blasio, Bill de, 114, 139, 153, 167–68
Bloomberg administration, 45, 112, 119, 153,
  160, 161; antiunionism, 150–51; divestment
  from child care, 113–14, 116; investment in
  pre-kindergarten, 149; protest against bud-
  get cuts, 155, 156
Blum, Barbara, 104
Boris, Eileen, 72, 152, 165–66
Brenner, Johanna, 19, 27, 28
Brenner, Neil, 6, 29, 42
Briggs, Laura, 72, 79–80

GEOGRAPHIES OF JUSTICE AND SOCIAL TRANSFORMATION

Mohandesi, Salar, and Emma Teitelman. 2017. "Without Reserves." In *Social Reproduction Theory: Remapping Class, Recentering Oppression*, edited by Tithi Bhattacharya, 68–93. London: Pluto Press.

Moody, Kim. 2007. *From Welfare State to Real Estate: Regime Change in New York City, 1974 to the Present*. New York: New Press.

Morgen, Sandra, Joan Acker, and Jill Weigt. 2010. *Stretched Thin: Poor Families, Welfare Work, and Welfare Reform*. Ithaca, N.Y.: Cornell University Press.

Mulgrew, Michael. 2012. *Testimony on Informal Family Child Care*. New York: United Federation of Teachers.

Murch, Donna. 2016. "Paying for Punishment: The New Debtors' Prison." *Boston Review*, August 1, 2016. http://bostonreview.net/editors-picks-us/donna-murch-paying-punishment.

Nadasen, Premilla. 2005. *Welfare Warriors: The Welfare Rights Movement in the United States*. New York: Routledge.

———. 2010. "Mothers at Work: The Welfare Rights Movement and Welfare Reform in the 1960s." In *The Legal Tender of Gender: Historical and Contemporary Perspectives on Welfare Law, State Policies and the Regulation of Women's Poverty*, edited by Shelley Gavigan and Dorothy E. Chunn, 103–22. Oxford, UK: Hart Publishing.

Nadasen, Premilla, Jennifer Mittelstadt, and Marisa Chappell. 2009. *Welfare in the United States: A History with Documents 1935–1996*. New York: Routledge.

Naples, Nancy A. 1991. "A Socialist Feminist Analysis of the Family Support Act of 1988." *Affilia* 6:23–38.

———. 1998. *Grassroots Warriors: Activist Mothering, Community Work, and the War on Poverty*. New York: Routledge.

National Women's Law Center. 2018. *Child Care and Early Learning: Child Care Is Fundamental to America's Children, Families, and Economy* (fact sheet). Washington, D.C.: National Women's Law Center.

Ness, Immanuel. 2009. "Organizing Home Health-Care Workers: A New York City Case Study." *Working USA* 3, no. 4:59–95.

New York City Temporary Task Force on Child Care Funding. 1996. *Final Report*. New York: Agency for Child Development.

New York State Executive Chamber (Governor Eliot Spitzer). 2007. "Executive Order No. 12: Representation of Child Care Providers." May 8, 2007. https://web.archive.org/web/20090412231948/http://www.ny.gov/governor/executive_orders/exeorders/12.html.

New York State Office of Children and Family Services. 1996. "Child Care: Revised Market Rates." Administrative directive, January 16, 1996. https://ocfs.ny.gov/main/policies/external/1996/ADMs/96-ADM-03%20Child%20Care—Revised%20Market%20Rates.pdf.

New York State Office of the Governor. 1997. "Governor Pataki Announces Historic Welfare Reforms." Press release, June 29, 1997. http://www.state.ny.us/.

New York Times. 1969. "Day-Care Workers Reject Mediation," August 30, 1969.

———. 1975. "Day-Care Default," March 1, 1975.

———. 1976a. "New Federal Rules Will Reduce Eligibility for Day-Care in City," March 22, 1976.

———. 1976b. "New Rules Sought on Day-Care Plan," May 5, 1976.

———. 1976c. "Day Care Cuts Protested." May 6, 1976.

———. 1977. "New York Human Resources Aid Criticizes Carey's Day-Care Plan." February 17, 1977.

———. 1982. "U.S. Cuts Limiting Day Care for Poor." May 16, 1982.

———. 1993. "Death and Day Care." February 24, 1993.

———. 1996. "Workfare's Missing Link." October 21, 1996.

NICHD (National Institute of Child Health and Human Development). 2006. *The NICHD Study of Early Child Care and Youth Development: Findings for Children up to Age 4.5 Years*. Washington, D.C.: U.S. Department of Health and Human Services.

Nyary, Sasha. 2004a. "Child Care for Welfare Recipients." *Gotham Gazette*, April 29, 2004.

———. 2004b. "Daycare Workers." *Gotham Gazette*, July 7, 2004.

O'Connor, Alice. 2008. "The Privatized City: The Manhattan Institute, the Urban Crisis, and the Conservative Counterrevolution in New York." *Journal of Urban History* 34, no. 2:333–53.

O'Connor, James. 1973. *The Fiscal Crisis of the State*. New York: Transaction Publishers.

O'Connor, Julia, Ann Shola Orloff, and Sheila Shaver. *States, Markets, Families: Gender, Liberalism, and Social Policy in Australia, Canada, Great Britain, and the United States*. New York: Cambridge University Press.

OECD (Organisation for Economic Co-operation and Development). 2011. *Doing Better for Families*. Paris: OECD.

OPA (Office of the Public Advocate). 1998. *Welfare and Child Care: What about the Children?* New York City: Public Advocate for the City of New York.

Orloff, Ann Shola. 2006. "From Maternalism to 'Employment for All': State Policies to Promote Women's Employment Across the Affluent Democracies." In *The State after Statism: New State Activities in the Age of Liberalization*, edited by J. D. Levy, 230–68. Cambridge, Mass.: Harvard University Press.

Panican, Alexandru, and Hakan Johansson. 2016. *Combating Poverty in Local Welfare Systems*. London: Palgrave Macmillan.

Parker, Brenda. 2011. "Material Matters: Gender and the City." *Geography Compass* 5, no. 7:433–47.

———. 2017. *Masculinities and Markets: Raced and Gendered Urban Politics in Milwaukee*. Athens: University of Georgia Press.

Paterson, Stephanie. 2014. "Deinstitutionalizing Pregnancy and Birth: Alternative Childbirth and the New Scalar Politics of Reproduction." In *Fertile Ground: Exploring Reproduction in Canada*, edited by Stephanie Paterson, Francesca Scala, and Marlene K. Sokolon, 178–204. Montreal: McGill-Queen's University Press.

Paulsell, Diane, Toni Porter, and Gretchen Kirby. 2010. *Supporting Quality in Home-Based Child Care*. Princeton: Mathematica Policy Research.

Peake, Linda, and Martina Reiker. 2013. *Rethinking Feminist Interventions into the Urban.* London: Routledge.

Peck, Jamie. 2001. *Workfare States.* New York: Guilford Press.

———. 2003. "The Rise of the Workfare State." *Kurswechsel* 3:75–87.

———. 2015. *Austerity Urbanism: The Neoliberal Crisis of American Cities.* City Series 1. New York: Rosa Luxemburg Stiftung New York Office.

Peck, Jamie, Neil Brenner, and Nik Theodore. 2018. "Actually Existing Neoliberalism." In *The SAGE Handbook of Neoliberalism*, edited by Damien Cahill, Melinda Cooper, Martijn Konings, and David Primrose, 3–15. London: SAGE Publications.

Peck, Jamie, and Adam Tickell. 2002. "Neoliberalising Space." *Antipode* 34:380–404.

Phillips-Fein, Kim. 2013. "The Legacy of the 1970s Fiscal Crisis." *Nation*, April 16, 2013. http://www.thenation.com/article/legacy-1970s-fiscal-crisis.

———. 2017. *Fear City: New York's Fiscal Crisis and the Rise of Austerity Politics.* New York: Metropolitan Books.

Picchio, Antonella. 1992. *Social Reproduction: The Political Economy of the Labor Market.* New York: Cambridge University Press.

Piven, Frances Fox. 2011. *Who's Afraid of Frances Fox Piven? The Essential Writings of the Professor Glenn Beck Loves to Hate.* New York: New Press.

Piven, Frances Fox, and Richard A. Cloward. 1971. *Regulating the Poor: The Functions of Public Welfare.* New York: Pantheon Books.

———. 1977. *Poor Peoples' Movements: Why They Succeed, How They Fail.* New York: Pantheon Books.

———. 1985. *The New Class War: Reagan's Attack on the Welfare State and Its Consequences.* New York: Pantheon Books.

———. 1993. *Regulating the Poor: The Functions of Public Welfare.* Updated ed. New York: Vintage Books.

Podair, Jerald. 2011. "'One City, One Standard': The Struggle for Equality in Rudolph Giuliani's New York." In *Civil Rights in New York: From World War II to the Giuliani Era*, edited by Clarence Taylor, 204–18. New York: Fordham University Press.

Polakow, Valerie. 2007. *Who Cares for Our Children? The Child Care Crisis in the Other America.* New York: Teachers College Press.

Porter, Ann. 2003. *Gendered States: Women, Unemployment Insurance and the Political Economy of the Welfare State in Canada, 1945–1997.* Toronto: University of Toronto Press.

Powell, Roslyn, and Mia Cahill. 2000. *Nowhere to Turn: New York City's Failure to Inform Parents on Public Assistance about Their Child Care Rights.* New York: NOW Legal Defense and Education Fund.

———. 2001. *Still Nowhere to Turn: New York City's Continuing Failure to Inform Parents about Their Child Care Rights.* New York: NOW Legal Defense and Education Fund.

Prentice, Susan. 1989. "Workers, Mothers, Reds: Toronto's Postwar Daycare Fight." *Studies in Political Economy* 30:115–31.

Quadagno, Jill. 1994. *The Color of Welfare: How Racism Undermined the War on Poverty.* New York: Oxford University Press.

Rai, Shirin, M. and Georgina Waylen. 2014. *New Frontiers in Feminist Political Economy*. London: Routledge.

Reese, Ellen. 2005. *Backlash against Welfare Mothers Past and Present*. Berkeley: University of California Press.

———. 2010. "But Who Will Care for the Children? Organizing Child Care Providers in the Wake of Welfare Reform." In *Intimate Labors: Cultures, Technologies and the Politics of Care*, edited by Eileen Boris and Rhacel Salazar Parrenas, 231–48. Stanford: Stanford University Press.

———. 2011. *They Say Cutback, We Say Fightback! Welfare Activism in an Era of Retrenchment*. New York: Russell Sage Foundation.

Richardson, Lynda. 1993. "Nannygate for the Poor." *New York Times*, May 2, 1993.

Richie, Brooke, and Robin Epstein. 1997. "Day Carelessness." *City Limits*, August 1, 1997. http://www.citylimits.org/ 1997/08/01/day-carelessness/ 70.

Roberts, Adrienne. 2016. "Household Debt and the Financialization of Social Reproduction: Theorizing the UK Housing and Hunger Crises." *Research in Political Economy* 31:135–64.

Roberts, Dorothy. 1997. *Killing the Black Body: Race, Reproduction, and the Meaning of Liberty*. New York: Pantheon Books.

———. 2014. "Complicating the Triangle of Race, Class and State: The Insights of Black Feminists." *Ethnic and Racial Studies* 37, no. 10:1776–82.

Robinson, Sandra, and Ilana Berger. 2006. "Tighten Home Day Care Enforcement?" *New York Daily News* August 5, 2006.

Rose, Nancy E. 1990. "From the WPA to Workfare." *Journal of Progressive Human Services* 1, no. 2:17–42.

Sandstrom, Heather, Lindsay Giesen, and Ajay Chaudry. 2012. "How Contextual Constraints Affect Low-Income Working Parents' Child Care Choices." *Urban Institute Brief*, February 22, 2012.

Savas, E. S. 2002. "Competition and Choice in New York City Social Services." *Public Administration Review* 62, no. 1:82–91.

———. 2005. "Introduction to Welfare Reform under Mayor Giuliani." In *Managing Welfare Reform in New York City*, 3–17. Oxford, UK: Rowman and Littlefield.

Scharf, Rebecca L., and Barbara Carlson. 2004. "Lost in the Maze: Reforming New York City's Fragmented Child Care Subsidy System." *Scholarly Works* (UNLV School of Law), no. 610. http://scholars.law.unlv.edu/facpub/610.

Schram, Sanford F. 2018. "Neoliberalizing the Welfare State: Marketizing Social Policy/ Disciplining Clients." In *The SAGE Handbook of Neoliberalism*, edited by Damien Cahill, Melinda Cooper, Martijn Konings, and David Primrose, 308–22. London: SAGE Publications.

Sen, Rinku, and Gabriel Thompson. 2006. "The Welfare Nanny Diaries." *Colorlines*, September 2006. http://www.colorlines.com/articles/welfare-nanny-diaries.

Sexton, Joe. 1996. "Welfare Mothers and Informal Day Care: Is It up to Par?" *New York Times*, October 14, 1996.

www.ingramcontent.com/pod-product-compliance
Lightning Source LLC
Chambersburg PA
CBHW010139270326
41926CB00022B/4502